Prairie Volcano

Prairie Volcano

An Anthology of North Dakota Writing

Martha Meek and Jay Meek
editors

DACOTAH TERRITORY PRESS / ST. IVES PRESS

First Edition

ISBN 0-941127-15-X

Prairie Volcano has been co-published by Dacotah Territory Press, Moorhead, Minnesota, and St. Ives Press, Box 8367 University Station, Grand Forks, North Dakota 58202. To place book orders or for more information, write Plains Distribution Service, Inc., P.O. Box 931, Moorhead, MN 56561.

Editors: Martha Meek and Jay Meek
Consulting Editor: Mark Vinz
Production Editor: Mark Strand
Design: Michael Joachim
Cover Art: Jacquelyn McElroy

The editors would like to thank the following sponsors who have contributed to the publication of this book: The North Dakota Council on the Arts and the University of North Dakota, Office of the President and Office of Research and Program Development.

NORTH DAKOTA COUNCIL
ON THE ARTS

This activity is supported in part by a grant from the North Dakota Council on the Arts, an agency of the State of North Dakota.

Contents

Preface

Several years ago, I had the idea of showcasing recent work by North Dakota writers, those either born in our state or at one time resident here. Writing that profoundly attaches to North Dakota and its way of life has too seldom been considered as a whole, perhaps because of the widespread dispersion of our writers. Some, born here, stayed or moved on. Others, born elsewhere, immigrated to North Dakota, bringing a keen eye for the landscape. Still others, poets and fiction writers who studied among us a while, enriched other geographies with the craft and verbal imagination they began to nurture here. Our story is one of transience and settlement, of departures and homecomings, as recorded in the work of Richard Critchfield, who moved beyond his family home in Hunter, North Dakota, to examine village cultures throughout the world.

Surely, our home ground has its literary figures, native or resident, including Maxwell Anderson, Eric Sevareid, Era Bell Thompson, and the American Indian story-tellers who shaped their fictions on the northern plains. *Prairie Volcano* takes as its focus the work of fifty recent writers, to present some who are justly celebrated for their accomplishments and others who are new to the writer's craft. Many have studied at the University of North Dakota, one of the first universities in the country to offer classes in creative writing—as early as 1913—and still one of the relatively few schools nationally that has a doctoral program students may complete with a collection of poetry or fiction. Featuring new writers and established ones, *Prairie Volcano* means to suggest by the title it derives from

Jacquelyn McElroy's cover serigraph how powerfully the force of our imaginings rises from the drift plains and prairie marl.

The complex history of this book is a record of friendship. My colleagues and I began work on it by reading contributions submitted in our call for manuscripts. Initially, we looked just for poetry and fiction by writers who were still active, the exception being Thomas McGrath who at his death the previous year had left such a great presence; it is astonishing to recognize that his life coincided with three-quarters of North Dakota's first one hundred years of statehood. Now the book has broadened its range to include essays. Like a barn raising, the work suddenly came together this past year when, thanks to a grant from the North Dakota Council on the Arts, St. Ives Press joined with Dacotah Territory Press to produce a book that needed to see the light. That this anthology exists is a testimony to the energy of Mark Vinz, founder of Dacotah Territory Press, and to the determination of Martha Meek, on behalf of St. Ives Press. They brought *Prairie Volcano* into being.

There are others who helped see the book into print. I want to mention my colleagues in the creative writing program—John Little, Robert King, and William Borden—who served as members of the initial selection committee. Others have given their work and advice, and the editors thank Pam Callen, David Dwyer, Nancy Hanson, Ursula Hovet, Michael Joachim, Randy Lee, Robert Lewis, Ruth Marshall, Joe Richardson, Mark Strand, Thom Tammaro, Bill Truesdale, Betsy Vinz, and the monks of Blue Cloud Abbey. We are particularly grateful for the support provided by Vern Goodin and Patsy Thompson of the North Dakota Council on the Arts, University of North Dakota President Kendall Baker, former President Thomas Clifford, Dean of Arts and Sciences Bernard O'Kelly, and Kenneth Dawes, Director of the Office of Research and Program Development. The generous spirit of Norton Kinghorn stands behind what is best here; he championed the writers of our region. That spirit—communal, enduring, hard-won—charges the work of these writers, and it is to them our gratitude for this anthology especially belongs.

—Jay Meek

Writing from the Doughnut Hole

Though I've lived elsewhere for close to twenty years, I still think of myself as a North Dakotan and a son of the prairie, literally as well as figuratively. Both my parents are from North Dakota and both sets of grandparents homesteaded in North Dakota. I'd say my roots go deep, but with that wind roots have all they can do just to hang on.

             —Larry Watson

What seems to stay with me most deeply are the wind—and the cold at its coldest.

             —Roland Flint

*

North Dakota seems always to have been a space across which people moved: the original nomadic peoples; the immigrant settlers who came directly from Eastern Europe and as often as not walked across the continent to North Dakota; the trekkers heading farther West for gold; the farmers driven off by the long drought of the "dirty thirties." Now the children of settlers' children are steadily moving away, family farms are auctioned off, towns are dwindling, and we are left faced with Easterners' predictions that North Dakota will ultimately revert to its place in a vast Midwestern buffalo commons, and that it has already begun to do so.

This anthology is a gathering of recent poems, stories, and essays by writers who have lived or now live in North Dakota. North Dakota is an immigrant state; we didn't exclude writers who weren't born here. Nor did we snub them for leaving; leaving the state seems almost as Dakotan as staying. Why they leave is part of the story of what it means to live here. I don't want to oversimplify this story; the writing in this anthology certainly isn't urban, but neither is it provincial. There is a wonderful diversity in these pages that refuses to be circumscribed. For example, Elizabeth Hampsten has improbably made a part of Uruguay a part of North Dakota, as she describes the intricate balancing of her lives in the essay included here, "'Where Are You From?'" But, however difficult it may prove to characterize, writing in the state is surely richer for the comings and goings of its writers. I have been led in my thinking by what the writers themselves have said, and by the surprising extent of agreement that is evident among them. I have created for them this introductory colloquy, this choir, although they may not agree entirely with my conclusions. I wouldn't try to speak for them; they speak for themselves.[1]

*

There's a story that goes around in my family that my great-grandmother fresh from Russia, upon seeing her new homestead, covered her face and cried, "It's all earth and sky." She was fully aware of the gigantic task that lay ahead of her.
                                                                   –Debra Marquart

I remember the old women, in dark shawls and print dresses, working around their old clapboard houses, always working. Through my childhood they'd always seem to be outside, shaking rugs, or washing windows with gnarled rags and vinegar water, or hanging out laundry on sagging clotheslines, or bending stiffly from their waists to weed their carefully tended gardens.

The old men were always there too, wearing billed caps and vests, puttering around in the backyards, or struggling with storm windows, or sharpening knives at their pedal millstones, murmuring what I called then, to myself, "those old dead words." They'd talk about things I would misunderstand, like my grandfather, sighing about 'Die Schwarza Mehr'—the Black Sea—where I thought all those old dark words came from, sighing about how the weather in the old country was good enough for wine grapes, but nothing like that here, ay yah yei.

—"Family Stories," Ron Vossler

*

North Dakota proved resistant to permanent settlement, as it proved resistant to language. Half the people who came to Dakota Territory left again. According to the best motives of the American Dream, many of them said they came for the sake of their children, who were ironically among the first to suffer from the deprivations and hardships of pioneer life. Even very young children were expected to shoulder workloads that we might now see as hard for an adult to bear.

Schooling was treated as a break from the physical drudgery of farming, necessarily the main business of life. Subsistence farming left no time for literature, art, and writing. "School was for lazy people," a turn-of-the-century settler said.[2] Something of the same suspicion of education lingers even today. At the time I am writing, one North Dakotan has lobbeyed successfully for the enforcement of a long-ignored law requiring a loyalty oath of every teacher in the state, while other states are formally repealing similar laws.[3]

The lasting result of early suffering has been an uneasiness between generations, and among the adult children of settlers and their own children, an ill-sorted mix of resentment and pride in their heritage. These are people who too often still feel they must leave the state to pursue their artistic interests.

*

Very early I acquired a sense of having no identity in the world, of inhabiting by some cruel mistake, an outland, a lost and forgotten place upon the far horizon of my country.
—*Not So Wild A Dream*, Eric Sevareid

What the wide frightening expanses of North Dakota prairie did to me was remind me how extraordinarily small, insignificant, I am in the scheme of things. Being almost lost in a blizzard, as I twice was, made me very aware of mortality, and I think that the effect of the land on my writing has been that of making it (and me, of course) very much more serious about things than I had been before, and more fatalistic perhaps—and curiously enough, more ready to become philosophical about things, accept their passing . . . .
—Antony Oldknow

Any individual can walk out into the country and become quickly insignificant within the expanses of the horizons. In this sense, the prairie holds a kind of psychic danger, still near, which can make us identify with the earlier struggles on the land.
—Dale Jacobson

*

I am struck by a detail, by how much driving is done in these pages. Moving through the North Dakota vastness can seem like near-stasis. It is a dreamy space, like the sea, a contemplative space where people's thoughts wander. The detail points to a characteristic feature of Dakota writing: people tend to think in spatial terms, either from a long-time attunement to prairie life or from a sudden overwhelming recognition of exposure and vulnerability. Even the passage of time is often seen spatially in the North Dakota imagination, including the past time of nostalgia and the futurity implied by longing. Just as we speak of the here-and-now, in an immigrant state, *then* often means *there*—one's childhood belonged to Russia, for instance; and the future lies elsewhere.

*

I had every intention of leaving farming behind me, but whenever I sat down to write, I would discover that farming was a language, my native tongue; and much of what I had to say would have to be said through the broken English and imagery of farming.

—Ron Block

Few Negroes had ever lived in Mandan, never more than two or three at a time. Most of its seven thousand people were Russian-German, living in Dutch and Russian hollows, bits of the Old Country, complete in their quaintness, transplanted deep between the sharp hills at the north end of town. Scrubbed wooden benches leaned against light-blue and pale-green houses, earthenware jugs stood by the doors. English was seldom spoken.

—*American Daughter*, Era Bell Thompson

*

Time and again, the enormity of North Dakota dictates the terms according to which these writers must make sense of their lives. This collection presents a variety of the kinds and degrees of language provoked by the prairie. How should we speak against the force of the wind? My immediate response is that we should send only loud messages; perhaps it was inevitable that we would plant nuclear missiles, with their unmistakable burden of meaning.

There are two classic first reactions to this linguistically featureless terrain: some people are struck dumb and can't think of anything to say, while others can't stop talking. The prairie seems to require a counterforce: an explosion, an eruption of human energy and will, the passion that our title *Prairie Volcano* implies. When I arrived in North Dakota I thought I ought to pack a copy of *King Lear* along with the chocolate and candles in the winter survival kit for the car, in the event of a white-out. Now I'd take along Lois Phillips Hudson's impassioned novel about Depression-era wheat farming, *The Bones of Plenty*. Incidentally, she says that generations of farmers have sung aloud in the fields, out of a need to vocalize, to fill the air with human sound.[4]

Two specialized literary tendencies in life on the plains are tellingly duplicated in the early literature of a sparsely settled Australia: one, a polite and insistent gentility in writing and manners, and the other, a hearty folksiness as evident in the genre of "cowboy poetry." I wonder if these aren't each in their own way strategies to keep from being overawed by the land, by reducing the overwhelming scale of things here to specifically human, that is, to social proportions.

On the other hand, the prairie teaches some people how to use utter silence like a blunt weapon. In Ron Vossler's story, "Her Week of the Jew," the silences of Eva's husand amount to an absolute refusal to be dislodged from any position he may hold. Faced with the weight of such silences, Eva herself craves all the more the embellishment and flourish, the play of language that Mr. Mackovsky brings with him for one week every year. Perhaps we are all at times survivalists in our prairie fastness, our fund of conversation reduced to two clichés: "Cold enough for you?" and "If you don't like it here, why don't you go some place else?"

The literary style commonly thought of as Midwestern favors what we call "flat" vowels and a plain-ness of speech. It is not the King's English and not "proper" English suitable for the purposes of a literary establishment elsewhere. The idiom is "low" and "local"—homely, rather than elegant.[5] This "prairie vernacular" argues for a genuinely Midwestern literature reflecting the reality of life here. Read, for example, Mark Vinz's poem "North of North." But it is an occasional, and not a definitive, style for the writers in this anthology, one voice among a wide range of voices, and one language among many languages on the prairie, whose cadences and vocabulary and sayings (and history and sorrows) give our writing its characteristic timbre. *Uffda!*

*

Everything was in a straight line—the sun with its invisible ring of blazing million-mile petals, the tin flower of the windmill blooming with hot light, the point of the well pipe four hundred feet below the revolving blades, and the middle of the

*earth. He and his windmill were suspended between two
fires—the fire ninety-three million miles away in frigid space
and the fire at the core of the planet.*
—*The Bones of Plenty*, Lois Phillips Hudson

*I know where I am: not far from home;
not far from our glamourous,
extravagant star; lost in uncountable,
unaccountable light.*
—"The Middle of Nowhere," David Dwyer

*There is that feeling that always comes. To enter the center,
to go home.*
—"Peace Turtles," Lise McCloud

*

In North Dakota imagery, open spaces find their best like-
ness in greater space, greater vastness; we are easily moved to
contemplate the universe. Paradoxically, this state which seems
endless, is also envisioned as central. North Dakota lays claim to
being at the center of the North American continent, but the
privilege of this position is highly ambivalent. The ambivalence
shows itself in the spatial imagery of middleness, a constant in
Dakota writing and in America's psychic geography, generally.
This is the Midwest, Middle America, in sentimental parlance,
"the heartland," seen as a great repository of fundamental
American values that are both enshrined and ridiculed. The *center* is equated with the mythical, nostalgic *past* (once again we
see the temporal depicted in spatial terms); the coasts are the
cutting edge of style and thought. In the United States, to be
located in the center is to be marginalized. The country has a
kind of hole in the middle, like a doughnut. And far too often
people here acquiesce in the appalling assumption that the lives
of people living elsewhere in the country are intrinsically worth
more. We come to believe that literature "is something that has
happened in other times, in other places, in other words."[6]
Regrettably, as Mark Vinz has noted, "There's still that feeling in

most of us that regional means local, local means cut off or second class or 'not as good.'"[7]

*

I wrote "The Spurge War" when I was living in Tucson, Arizona, and homesick enough that I often entertained irrational fears of dying before seeing North Dakota again.
        —Peter Brandvold

My fictional characters come to me from North Dakota. The landscape is always in my heart. Most of my life I've been homesick for the plains—yet it is hard to live there, harder to ask anyone else to live there.
        —Heid Ellen Erdrich

*

Something is hard about life in North Dakota (a recognition everywhere in these pages): some indissoluble rock-hard core, some cairn of rocks in the field, some pill to be swallowed, some pearl that comes from relentless chafing, some pit or seed; in short, some fact you come up against. A few writers could not conceive of living in any other moral dimension, precisely because here is where you come up against fact. In others there is an uneasiness, a sense of being un-settled, which their writing attempts to negotiate. In "Memories of Unhousement," Clark Blaise describes his birthplace in a meticulously qualified sentence: "There is nothing obscure, really, about Fargo." Perhaps we hold onto the idea of freedom of choice, not wanting to feel claimed utterly by whatever is forbidding here. An old chestnut of a joke tells about a woman on her eighty-sixth birthday who is asked if she has spent her whole life in North Dakota, and she answers, "so far, but I'm thinking of moving."[8] I admit this may be funny only to Dakotans.

How do you plow inchoate space into plot, which is more moderate in extent, and on which may be impressed the pattern of intentional human action? This plot, this design, this map (this plat) is story, and for the Midwesterner, the quintessential story follows a pattern of escape and return. I read somewhere that L. Frank Baum was actually thinking about North Dakota in The *Wizard of Oz*. I'd like to think that his "Kansas" was North Dakota. Dorothy Gale moves in typical fashion from a longing for escape to an hospitable world of amusement, color, and variety, to a longing for return (that part of the story which may be the most fantastic, the most a matter of wishful thinking). In the course of her journey, Dorothy is compelled to examine what she means by "home"–a particularly Midwestern subject. Whatever may constitute "home," certainly the word when we use it refers to something central in a life, out of which all else flowers and derives, even when coming back may be possible only in the imagination and art.

*

What I do when I'm home–I drive farm roads, race the dogs, pick ditch flowers . . . .

–Heid Ellen Erdrich

It has taken me a long time to realize how unique is the place where I grew up, and how irrevocably I am a part of it. Writing "The Blizzard Rope" helped me articulate something I had felt for a long time: that the generations–their decisions, hopes, mistakes, dreams–are always with us, stretching out and touching us every day no matter how far away from the original homestead we may find ourselves.

–Debra Marquart

All that, those peasant ways of family, were just the remnants of an older way of life brought to the prairies; and as I grew, that world slowly changed–spun apart by the centrifugal forces of American life. Sometimes I feel a duty, an obligation, to chronicle at least part of that time, to try to make art from what I knew, so that the forgotten people I grew up among will have their time and place in the history of our country."

–Ron Vossler

*

The often elegaic writing in these pages registers the mounting losses—of traditions, farms, families. It is not a record of progress or the accomplishment of American dreams of prosperity and power. Ron Vossler says he goes home each year to "pay his respects" in "the windswept graveyards of McIntosh County": "Sometimes, unexpectedly, I'll happen on the grave of someone who should have loved me, or who I loved, or should have loved, but never had the chance—like that of my grandfather. It always comes to me unbidden, a rush of longing and love that carries me on it, into surprise that so much life, so many ties, can be bound up with one person. The Chinese have a saying for it: how when an old person dies it is like a library burning down."[9]

What gifts do these Dakota writers bring us? For many of them writing is an act of piety and grief. They want to get stories of an earlier time down on paper before the memory of those days and their hardships and Herculean efforts disappear entirely. They chronicle the changes overtaking the Dakotas, grappling with the painful sense of loss those changes bring. Many of these writers cherish the hard-won, homegrown pleasures of life on the plains. Thomas McGrath lyrically celebrates lettuce, onions, cabbage, corn, and the whole of the vegetable kingdom in the poem, "Praises," demonstrating how profoundly connected are the play of language and human desire:

> And let us praise all these
> As they please us: skin, flesh, flower, and the flowering
> Bones of their seeds: from which come orchards: bees:
>   honey:
> Flowers, love's language, love, heart's ease, poems, praise.

Does the work of these Dakota writers matter? When could writing matter more? Not for ingenious reasons; the issues here are fundamental. We have no need to compete with writing elsewhere, and every reason not to. We live on the plains under a constant threat of voicelessness, and we are the ones to feel how much is at stake. We test, we are tested by, some border between silence and voice that we have got to explore. I find myself wanting to give the last word also to Thomas McGrath, who so passionately saw the necesssity of finding a language adequate to the North Dakota landscape. It should be *our* last word, not the tourist ethnographies of travel writers, who merely gaze at what we have lived. To McGrath, writing was no frill, but a means for us all of human survival:

It is the poem provides the proper charm,
Spelling resistance and the living will,
To bring to dance a stony field of fact
And set against terror exile or despair
The rituals of our humanity.[10]

—Martha Meek

1. Unless otherwise noted, the quotations in the Introduction are taken from letters and other correspondence between the contributors and the editors.
2. Ben Walsh, "I Attended a Country School," 1980, University of North Dakota Libraries, OGL 589, qtd. in Elizabeth Hampsten, *Settlers' Children: Growing up on the Great Plains* (Norman: U of Oklahoma P, 1991) 41. I draw much of my characterization of North Dakota history from *Settlers' Children*. I am also indebted to Elwyn B. Robinson, *History of North Dakota* (Lincoln: U of Nebraska P, 1966).
3. Scott Jaschik, "Under Pressure, North Dakota State U. Begins Enforcing Law on Loyalty Oaths," *Chronicle of Higher Education* 27 July 1994: A24. See also Steve Schmidt, "N.D. Teachers: Pledge Your Loyalty to State," *Grand Forks Herald* 30 July 1994: 1A .
4. Lois Phillips Hudson, *The Bones of Plenty* (1962; St. Paul: Minnesota Historical Society, 1984) 113.
5. Dennis Cooley, *The Vernacular Muse: The Eye and Ear in Contemporary Literature* (Winnipeg: Turnstone, 1987) 182. Cooley focuses on Canadian poetry, but many prairie writers, both Canadian and American, find that, in balance, they have more in common than they have differences based on nationality.
6. Cooley 181.
7. Thom Tammaro, "Stirring the Deep: A Conversation with Mark Vinz," *Stirring the Deep: The Poetry of Mark Vinz*, ed. Thom Tammaro (Peoria, IL: Spoon River Poetry, 1989) 21.
8. Norton Kinghorn told me this joke years ago, as part of my prairie education.
9. Ron Vossler, "Family Stories," *North Dakota Horizons* Winter 1991: 10, 12.
10. Thomas McGrath, "Against the False Magicians," *Selected Poems: 1938-1988* (Port Townsend, WA: Copper Canyon Press, 1988) 65.

Prairie Volcano

Clark Blaise

Memories of Unhousement

I was born in Fargo, North Dakota, in 1940. Along with William Gass and Larry Woiwode. In that *Ragtime* spirit that haunts us all, I sometimes think of my mother pushing the pram, of Mrs. Woiwode pushing hers, of little Roger Maris, then six, dashing past us, bat on shoulder. Billy Gass, a bifocular teenager, squints a moment at these figures of life, then returns to the ice castle of his imagination, "The Pedersen Kid" crystallizing even then. *Beyond the Bedroom Wall* gurgles in his stroller. Babe Ruth's assassin takes a few mean cuts.

I am the only Canadian writer born in Fargo, North Dakota.

There is nothing obscure, really, about Fargo. In 1977, at a cocktail party in New Delhi, India, where my India-born wife, Bharati, was serving that year as a quasi-diplomat for a Canadian educational exchange, I found myself talking to an agreeable, white-haired American with a professorial manner, the U.S. agricultural attaché. I was merely a spouse, conscious of a peripheral role.

"I consider myself half a Canadian, really," he said.

"I'm more than half American myself," I replied. What it is that I am, fundamentally, is a matter of earnest agony to me. We shared a smile, wondering which of us would be the first to break. One-time Canadians in America have no problem; erstwhile Americans in Canada will always feel a little guilty. "I was born in North Dakota," I confessed. Then, covering my tracks, "My parents had just come down from Winnipeg."

"I was about to say the same thing. Where in North Dakota?"

"Fargo."

"Amazing."

He was the first North Dakotan I had ever met. "What year would that have been," he asked. "Forty, forty-one?"

"April 1940."

"I was just finishing my M.A. at North Dakota State that spring. My wife was an O.B. nurse."

Parallel lives were beginning to converge, as though a collision course plotted by children on separate planets had suddenly become inevitable. We said together, "St. John's Hospital?"

I added, "Dr. Hanna?"

He called his wife over. As she put her drink down and turned to join us, he said, "How would you like to meet the person who delivered you?"

Before the Interstate system obliterated the old America, you used to come across them at country crossroads: clusters of white arrows tipped in black, pointing in every direction. Somewhere on the plains you would see it, stop, and be thrilled: DENVER 885, it would say, or NEW ORLEANS 1045 or, better yet, LOS ANGELES 2000. Who decided on the city and the mileage, I'll never know. Perhaps they had taken over from the whitewashed rocks, the dabs of tar left by earlier waves of impatient travellers, when twenty or thirty miles a day was more than fair measure. Nowadays, the green mirror-studded billboards conspire to keep our minds on the effortlessly attainable, the inevitable. No more than two destinations, they seem to say; don't tease us with prospects greater than our immediate ambition.

We are deprived of that special thrill when our destination, our crazy, private destination, made its first appearance in one of those black-tipped clusters. No reason at all that on a road between Chicago and Madison, just outside Beloit, Wisconsin, WINNIPEG should miraculously appear. Yet in 1949 when I was nine and guiding my father on our longest trip home, it did. Nine hundred miles in a '47 Chevy with its split windshield, high fenders and curved chrome bars over the dashboard radio was a typical fifteen-hour long haul for my salesman-father.

How, I think now, he must have wanted to delay it. He, who

delayed nothing in his life, a man lacking all patience. For old times' sake, he said, we'd spend the night in Detroit Lakes, Minnesota. That's where they'd honeymooned. Up there in the headwaters of the Mississippi is where I was conceived.

We always returned to Winnipeg whenever my father ran out of work, or was run out of work, or town. We had left Fargo in 1941, Cincinnati in '43, Pittsburgh in '45 and–a week before–Leesburg, Florida. Every time we left, we headed back to Winnipeg, my mother's city.

My father was from the village of Lac Mégantic, a few mountain ridges north of Maine, directly south of Quebec City. Winnipeg must have been a torture to him. I remember him, slicing luncheon meats in an upstairs bedroom next to a leaking window in my grandmother's house, sipping forbidden beer and smoking Canadian cigarettes–their aroma so much nuttier than his American Tareytons–though Canadian corktips inflamed his lips.

He never spoke of his dislikes, he merely acted on them, without warning. He was probably not entirely sane.

My father possessed–or rather, it possessed him–a murderous temper. He had pounded out twenty victories in three weight divisions in two countries under various names that served him like flags of convenience, before getting knocked out–and quitting, he said, though my mother came to doubt it, years later–by Bat Battalino, an eventual champion. The kindest interpretation my mother could put on his behaviour in later life was brain damage: "All that pounding he took." To this day, I love boxing, and I realize that somewhere around the radios and under the porch lights of my childhood in two dozen cities, I absorbed the pointers of boxing. My father's friends, if it could be said he had friends and not just cronies, had often been boxers. The violence of boxing, of his language, of his friends, of American life in general, drove my mother indoors.

Boxing credentials were good for one thing in Montreal in the 1920s. The career path took him to Canada's most successful export industry, helping assure, through bribery and intimidation, the delivery of Montreal's finest whisky to Prohibition-dry New York.

The first return to Canada that I remember was 1945, following an assault charge against my father in Pittsburgh. We
crossed into Canada that midnight at Niagara Falls and were in
Winnipeg three days later. Canada was still at war, the same war
(I'm told) that had sent us to North Dakota six years earlier.
Canada, part of Britain's war effort, would be on the front lines,
everyone thought, as soon as the Luftwaffe finished mopping
up. Lindbergh assured us it wouldn't take long. German U-Boats
already controlled the Gulf of St. Lawrence. The French-owned
islands of St. Pierre and Miquelon, off the coast of the British
colony of Newfoundland, were rebelling against the Vichy
régime; no one knew how long that would last, a fog-bound
Casablanca. Once Britain fell, Newfoundland and Labrador
would of course be ceded to the Nazis, just like the Channel
Islands. The Frenchies in Quebec refused to fight an English
war anyway; Adrien Arcand and his Brownshirts were poised
for a coup whenever Hitler ordered it. All of which had left
Ontario, in 1939 and '40, feeling itself in the probable front line
of combat. Even the *bunds* of Buffalo and Detroit were stirring
up border hate. The Ottawa River would become America's
Marne. And so my parents had fled. I would be born in isolationist, accommodationist America. My father could be whatever he wanted to be, not just a dirty Frog in English Canada.

This is my first memory of Canada: the soldiers at Canadian
customs, their jaunty berets. The smell of a different tobacco in
the air. My Winnipeg uncle in his colonel's rough khaki, deep
lines and dark skin, bushy eyebrows and salt-and-pepper hair,
his thick moustache and his short, stocky body, reminding me
years later of a Sandhurst-trained Israeli. One summer morning
when I was five he had taken me and my cousins out on the
lawn—he in his full uniform, the rows of First World War medals
on his chest—and smoked glass for us. The scientists of the Free
World had gathered in Winnipeg in 1945 for a spectacular view
of a solar eclipse. I remember my twin cousins, limber girls of
eight, doing backward flips all around my grandmother's house.

My first long exposure to Canada took place five years later, following one of my father's failures in central Florida. We'd driven

up from Leesburg, those clustered signposts serving us well: ATLANTA 600, CHICAGO 1000. Yankee place-names frightened me; I was a southerner, I drawled inexcusably (I was soon to learn, in Winnipeg schools), I was as ignorant as a mudfish of history and mathematics. Yet travel excited me; in the bullet of a bus, the cab of a car, the world is concentrated, all perspectives converge. We tore around America, rolling double sixes on that old Monopoly board of two-lane blacktop. One day for Florida, another for the pine flats of Georgia. Then they came fast: Tennessee, Kentucky, Indiana, Illinois and, before the half-week was out, that sign in Beloit: WINNIPEG 945. We were in the green and watery states now, the Land o' Lakes and Sky Blue Waters in the lee of Canada—I expected moose, bear. We were in Fargo for an afternoon, and I wandered down the main street of my absurdly obscure hometown. We drove past the house we'd lived in that spring of 1940: Fifth Street S.E. My mother pointed out where the Hinckles had lived, the man who took all my baby pictures.

Many years later, when my first book of stories was published, I got a letter from a nursing home in Minneapolis. Mrs. Hinckle had read the review in the *Star*. There couldn't be two Clark Blaises, not born in Fargo of Canadian parents, she said. I had to be the sweetest little baby she'd ever seen, the one my mother had worried over, the one her late husband had adored.

How like my mother, I think now, to have found another woman, in Fargo, who would remember names, who would read books and reviews, even in a nursing home. My mother's friends; my father's friends.

Of all the distinctions I have invented in my life and come to believe in with the force of myth, the difference between Canada and the United States—so frail in reality, so inconsequential in the consciousness of America or the world or even most Canadians—is still my last, my most important illusion. It matters to me, or it mattered until very recently, that a border exists. That people so similar should be formed in such different ways. That because I inherited those differences, I should have something special to say on both sides of the border.

I was invaded by geography the way other self-conscious youngsters are *invaded* by God, by music, by poetry, or a butterfly's wing. Through my childhood and adolescence and well into my adulthood and the ragged fringes of middle age, the faith in a Canada being of a different order of history, experience and humanity granted me an identity. It was never easy to claim it, but I never doubted it was there and that I belonged to it. Canada was always the large, locked attic of my sensibility, something I would never *know*, but was obliged to invent; it cultivated a part of me that America never touched. The significant blob of otherness in my life has always been Canada; it sits like a helmet over the United States, but I seemed to be the only person who felt its weight.

North, North, North: that glorious direction, and the provincial bison shield of Manitoba, the narrow highway that cut through the wheat fields to the west and the French-speaking hamlets along the Red River to the east, their lone church steeples gleaming (to my mother's disgust) higher than the bluffs that hid the rest of the town, rising even taller than the wheat elevators that stretched westward, each of them announcing a calloused, sun-reddened Protestant or Ukrainian town. And then, the highway divided, trolley tracks appeared and we were in Winnipeg.

I think often of the compass points. Like the arrow clusters at cramped country crossroads, the cardinal directions still move me; I dream restlessly of the eternal *setting out*, steering on to a highway for what I know will be a long drive and reading that first, firm challenge to the continent. *East.* And I see fishing boats and a pounding Winslow Homer rocky surf and the great cities, and I think, *yes,* that's the direction for me. Culture, history, people, excitement, sophistication. But then, on my drives to the Pacific, I thrill to those days of unbroken signposts, the barren miles of low hills and bluffs and promotional museums of forgivable, fake-historical tackiness, and I think, *West, West,* let me ride to the ridge, let me be free. Well, this time it was *North:* this was just about as far north as anyone from Florida could think of going. This was the western end of the Canadian Shield; east of here and the town names turn French and the faces along the highway are unmistakably Indian. West of here, golden fields of the world's hardest wheat.

I know the South—*South*—too well. It's the only compass point that fails to conjure a dreamlike essence. When I think of the Florida I knew, I remember only walls of leggy pine with slash marks on their trunks, hung with resin buckets, and I remember the Coke machines in country gas stations where for a nickel I could lift a heavy metal lid (I can remember the first whiff of that cold, moist air; I remember the pleasure of trailing my finger in the dark, iced water), of spotting a bottle cap in one of the metal tracks and gliding it along to the spring catch my nickel had released. And I can remember draining those stubby little Coke bottles with their raised, roughened letters on the side, always checking the bottom to see where it had been bottled, how far it had come, though nearly all were good ol' bottles from Plant City and Orlando. Well, all I remember of *South* is sand and heat and thirst and skies the colour of sweaty undershirts. I remember the years of childhood, alternating threat with nightmare.

On Wolseley Avenue in Winnipeg, on the banks of the Assiniboine, my grandparents had their house. Three houses away, my aunt and uncle had an even larger home, with a garage full of canoes and kayaks and a basement full of hunting rifles and decoys and a special room for a billards table. Since my uncle was in those days a writer and commercial artist as well as president of the Wheat Pool and Ducks Unlimited—and was soon to become Winnipeg's best-known television personality—and my aunt was a broadcaster, they had studios and libraries on the second floor. The third floor held guest rooms and an attic full of bundled magazines going back to the beginnings of *National Geographic* and *Reader's Digest,* as well as the splashy American weeklies like *Life* and *Collier's* and *The Saturday Evening Post.* They kept the hunting and fishing magazine and everything Canadian, particularly everything relating to the prairies and especially the Assiniboia region of Manitoba. My uncle (still alive and now in his nineties) had been a

Homesteader, one of Manitoba's founders. Nothing important had ever been thrown out. The house was virtually a computer, although means of retrieval were still a little primitive.

That house, and their lives, represented something to me called Canada, that was more than merely attractive; it was compelling. In the various towns of my first ten years, we had always had lived in small apartments carved out of old servants' quarters, on the fringes of other people's families, and we always seemed to be sharing some vital function of other peoples' lives. Kitchens, bathrooms, entrances, hallways, washing facilities and later, when we moved back to the States in the early fifties, televisions. Whatever the reasons, Canada, by virtue of its cool, English houses and its politeness and its streetcars and its formalities and its formidable understanding of the world outside—as brought to us every day by the BBC noon news—was a more comprehensible and interesting place to live than America. Not that America was ever excluded. It's just that Canadians, like long-suffering spouses, knew they would be forced to know everything about America, while America knew nothing, cared nothing, for them.

My parents had moved back to Canada at a time when its differences from the United States were unforced but unequivocal. Canada was like a heavy novel that others found dull and difficult but that I found accessible from the beginning, thanks to my accidental placement inside an emblematically Canadian family. I visited my aunt and uncle every day and shot pool in the basement by myself or with my cousin. My parents and I were staying in the second-floor bedroom and study at my grandmother's. Between the houses and school, I became a Canadian.

Ron Block

My Egypt

There's a code of bird tracks in the mud along the Platte—
fish hooks, feathers, and an undulating line,
a snake that prints itself among the flakes of freckled shells.

Here, schools of flies attempt to read aloud
the parchment of a bloated fawn, and the smell
drives you away, across the flood plain

where a gapping footpath eats into a hill,
ravenous, cancerous, widening as the generations climb
to vandalize the concrete Indian, tilting at the top.

The hill is vanishing beneath its feet.
But here you can see the Thirty Mile Canal
cut a sharp ruled line across the crescent valley,

while the intestinal river bends back on itself,
turns against itself,
fans out in many veins to feed the black soil.

There are pioneer tombs carved into these hills,
an unmarked exodus.
You cannot see them.

But you can see the farmers, huddled around a church,
their graveyards draped in black,
the black plowed fields.

And if you wait long enough, at least until evening,
you will hear the locusts crawling out between
the pages of a thousand Bibles

and prophesy: *nebraska! nebraska!*
nebraska is a fat calf
waiting for the knife!

And as proof of this, the graves consent to bleed in the sunset.
The haunted air starts creeping from the packing plants.
The summer passes away. The rains do not come. . . .

It is then that you should pack your migrant's bundle
and go out of this Egypt, for after the locusts
chirp and trill themselves into a hungry trance—

and after seven thin cows have come to devour
the shrivelled husks of seven years of corn—
all that will remain of my Egypt

is this: the monuments of triangular augurs,
rising on scaffolds against the cloudless desert sky—
and the white and hollow bone-shanks of the grain elevators,

and the river, writhing and thrashing in its sleep,
until it flattens all that stands upright—
and the black, black alluvial soil,
that stays behind to feed upon these tombs.

The Apocalypse of Duluth

The city's receding from the shadow,
the chalk cliffs crumble, a sewer's rivulet
trickles down the slope.

The city climbs the hill to get away,
an immense black pool,
larger than the shadows of ships,

larger than the shadows of clouds—
as large as the shadow of a state as if
a state could stand up tall as Minnesota seems

with Norway pines, and hills that overlook the lake,
the loading docks for taconite
beaded with the blood-sweat of tiny railroad cars—

their shadows stretch to Canada.
Mysterious barrels bubble in the lake.
The spikes of churches. Houses with the lids blown off.

And everyone has given up as
furnaces click on in the ocean air.
A murder in Glensheen: a candelabra in the billiard room.

The city recedes like a withered lake as I
slide down the slopes on loose gravel,
following the rivulet.

And does a black bear mouth its cub
and dodge from me, frightened,
till she reaches the impasse of the inland sea?

and does the warped reflection
of a moon-lane-current offer a difficult
bridge across the shadow to another shore?

William Borden

Joining the People Tribe

It was a small building erected with cinder blocks, squatting like a mongrel abandoned for good reason at the curve of a road that would make its way eventually to the city five miles away. The gray building was nearly invisible, blending as it did into the summer dusk, only the Pabst sign and the neon BA alerting Jim to the building's character. He pulled up beside the battered red pickup, turned off the engine, and sat quietly a moment.

He wondered if he should drive on, find a bar a little more—well, respectable, a little less—uncertain. Yet this was, he reasoned, what amounted to his neighborhood bar, if you can call a scattering of rejuvenated farmhouses a neighborhood. Besides, at a respectable bar there was no one to talk to; respectable people wrapped themselves in their private agonies, and their personalities were as starched as the shirts they buttoned themselves into. Jim remembered traveling in Spain, in the second class coaches, where the peasants shared their bread and wine with him, and then, once, in the first class car, where everyone spoke English but not to him. Jim got out of the car and ambled around the pickup, the dust thick on the pickup's hood and a strange beaded talisman hanging from the rearview mirror. Jim loosened his tie and unbuttoned the top two buttons of his shirt.

It seemed to be dusk inside the bar as well as outside, and at first glance Jim thought he was alone—and as bereft as ever. Then he saw the dark shape slouched at the corner of the bar. It had its arms wrapped around a beer glass, and an old bandanna pulled the dark hair away from its face. Jim turned and started for the door as the bartender appeared. He asked Jim what he'd have, and he didn't sound as if he'd accept an apology or an excuse as an order. "Beer," Jim said quickly, figuring he could drink it and get away before anything untoward happened to him. Some liquid spilled from the glass as it slid toward him, and the bartender didn't wipe it up. Jim took a swallow and wiped his hand on his handkerchief.

The cold sparkle felt good in his throat. The shape at the corner emptied its glass. What the hell, Jim thought, and asked, "Buy you a drink?"

It took the figure a long time to look up. He looked Jim over. "I'm new in the area," Jim explained, unknotting his tie and sliding it, like a bad idea, from around his neck and stuffing it into the pocket of his suit coat, where he felt the thick, stiff papers. "Bought a house up the road. The old Johnson place. Know it?"

The man leaned on one elbow, his shoulder nudging his long loose hair, and looked steadily at Jim while his dark fingers turned the glass in little circles.

"New job, new house," Jim laughed. "New car. I guess I'm celebrating. What'll you have? Draft?"

The man wiped a strand of hair away from his eye. He didn't look unfriendly, exactly. He looked careful. Jim gestured at the bartender, an older man with gray hair and a large belly under his apron. The bartender reached for a glass. The man, not taking his eyes off Jim's suit, said quietly, "Chivas Regal." The bartender found another glass.

"Beg pardon?" Jim said, moving closer.

"On the rocks," the man said, pushing the old glass aside.

"You know your Scotch," Jim said, as quick as anyone with a bit of conversation. He could see the man better now, and his first suspicion was confirmed. He relaxed, because this man, he was sure, had a story to tell. His dark hair hung halfway down his back, and his face was chiseled in a familiar, yet foreign, style. He wore a blue work shirt, the sleeves buttoned around his wrists, and faded jeans, and boots. Jim said, "You're an Indian, aren't you? A Native American."

"Double," the man said, turning to the bartender.

"You people have been mistreated," Jim said firmly. "I get so angry. When I read those books—*Custer Died for Your Sins, Bury My Heart at Wounded Knee*—I want to cry."

The man drank his Scotch.

"But," Jim went on quickly, as if to take the man's attention away from his libation, "you have survived. You have kept your dignity." Jim was surprising himself with his garrulity. He was usually shy with strangers. But then, with his new job, new house, new state, maybe he should begin a new identity, as it were, commence a new conviviality. The bartender's hand was on the Chivas; his eyes were on Jim. Jim gave a nod and said he'd switch to Chivas, too.

"Have you gone on those marches? Washington, D.C.? Columbia River? Alcatraz?" The Chivas gurgled into the glasses. "I wanted to go, but I couldn't get away from work." The ice clinked against the thick cheap glass. "By God, I'd give you back the Black Hills!"

The Indian sniffed the Scotch, as if he were accustomed to following faint spoors.

"They belong to you!" Jim declared, raising his glass and drinking.

The Indian didn't drink. He said softly, "No."

"No?" Jim repeated.

"They don't belong to anybody."

Jim set the glass on the bar. "They belong to the Great Spirit," he said solemnly.

"You say 'Great Spirit,'" the Indian said calmly, "but you don't know what you're talking about."

"Well, we have different names," Jim said, "God, Creator . . . ."

"I never say 'Great Spirit.'"

"Of course you don't." Jim held his glass as if it were attached to a rope that would pull him up, above the fray, whenever he signaled.

"I say 'Great Mystery.'"

Jim looked at the Indian and nodded. The Indian drank the Chivas. The bartender left the bottle. The Indian filled their glasses. Jim asked, "Lots of problems with alcoholism on the reservation? I read that." The Indian filled his glass to the brim.

Jim babbled on, drinking, as if some stranger were manipulating his tongue. "It's not your fault! You're trying to forget two hundred years of genocide, oppression, agency schools—"

"I never forget."

"You bet you don't! You can't forget something like that! You've had your land stolen—Great Mystery's land stolen—your culture's been destroyed, you were forbidden to practice your religion, speak your language"—Jim sipped his Chivas—" a noble people annihilated!"

"I'm still here," the Indian said, ice cubes chiming like tiny jewels in a goblet.

"What tribe do you belong to?" Jim asked, sliding close. "Ute? Chippewa? Sioux? I love those names. Blackfoot. Apaches. Arapaho. Zuni. Hopi. Mohican. Ever read *The Last of the Mohicans?* I loved that book."

The Indian gave Jim a long slow look. Finally he said, "Those names don't mean nothin'."

"They're beautiful names!"

"They're white names. French, English, couldn't pronounce the Indian names. All those names mean the same thing, anyway."

"What do they mean?" Jim asked, topping off their glasses.

"They mean 'The People.' You ask any Indian what tribe he belongs to, he'll tell you, 'I belong to The People tribe."

"People tribe."

"That's right."

Jim stuck out his hand. "My name's Jim." The Indian took Jim's hand carefully, silently. After a moment, Jim asked, "What's yours?"

"My name's secret," the Indian said.

"Secret," Jim repeated.

"We go on a vision quest, Jim. We do a sweat, we come out, we're reborn. We go up on a mountain. Four days, four nights. No food. No water. Maybe it rains. Maybe it's cold. It don't matter. You stay. You and the Great Mystery. Maybe the Great Mystery will appear—as a deer, or an eagle, or an ant. Maybe he'll talk to you—in the wind or the cry of an owl. Maybe he'll give you a name. Your true name."

Jim looked at his hands cradling the cold glass. He said, "I wonder what my true name is."

"Sometimes you don't get the name you want."

"I want to go on a vision quest."

The Indian stared at his Chivas. Finally he looked sideways at Jim. He asked, "You got your insurance paid up?"

"What?"

"Sign your will? Put your affairs in order?"

Jim tried to smile. He took a swallow.

"A vision quest is no trip to the supermarket, Jim."

"Oh, I know that!" Jim took off his coat. It seemed suddenly hot in the bar.

"You may die."

Jim tried to see if the Indian was pulling his leg, but the Indian seemed dead serious. He went on, "People have gone on vision quests—never seen again."

"Really?"

"If you live, you may get your secret song."

A shiver, like a slow electric caterpiller, crawled down Jim's spine. He blurted, "I wish I was an Indian!"

The Indian studied his Chivas for a long time. Jim wondered if he'd said something wrong. He drank some more and refilled their glasses. The bottle was empty. The Indian spoke slowly. "It's not easy being an Indian."

"Oh, I know! I know! The suffering, the humiliation—"

A fresh bottle of Chivas stood at Jim's elbow.

"I don't mean that," the Indian said. "I mean you have responsibilities. You live on the edge. All the time. Right this second, Jim, I'm living on the edge." He poured the Chivas. Jim gripped the edge of the bar.

"On the edge of what?" Jim asked.

"Everything. On the edge between life and death. On the edge of the reservation. On the edge between white and Indian." He paused. "Between killing and not killing."

"Have you . . . ?" Jim couldn't complete the thought.

The Indian looked at the bottles behind the bar, doubled by the mirror. He said, "If you were an Indian, Jim, you'd have to be ready to kill."

"Who?"

"Your best friend, if you had to."

"Why?"

"Dignity, Jim."

"I don't understand."

"Of course you don't." The Indian swallowed the Chivas. "You're not an Indian."

Jim grabbed the Indian's arm. "Make me an Indian," he said. The Indian smiled.

"You guys make Presidents Indians!"

"Oh, Jim, we buy those war bonnets at J.C. Penney's. We don't make them real Indians."

Jim took his hand back. He stared at his drink.

"You want to be a real Indian?" Jim looked at him, no doubt in his eyes.

"Can you do that?" Jim asked.

"Sure."

"How?"

"You got to start over."

"But that's what I'm doing now," Jim said. "I just moved here. New house, new job . . . ."

"You got to start over again. Give everything away. Start fresh, like a baby."

"Everything?"

"You think the Great Mystery's going to listen to some half-hearted promises? You want a secret name, Jim, you got to give up something. We Indians do it all the time. We call it a Give-away. We give away everything we own. New house, new car, whatever."

"Who do you give it to?"

"Whoever wants it."

Jim shoved the bottle away. "I'd be like an Indian all right. I wouldn't have anything."

The Indian spoke quietly. "You got to make room for the important stuff. House, car—that stuff confuses you."

Jim took a drink. "I am confused," he admitted. The Indian didn't say anything. Jim went on. "I worked for that house. That car. Nobody gave it to me."

The Indian seemed unperturbed. "Not everybody can be an Indian," was all he said.

"I didn't take the Black Hills! I didn't give you smallpox!"

The Indian sipped daintily.

Jim grabbed his coat and took a step toward the door.

The Indian settled his elbows on the bar.

As if hurling a last brave challenge, Jim cried, "Where would I live? What would I drive?"

"I'd let you live in my house, Jim. Drive my car. You'd be an Indian, too."

Jim turned in a small painful circle in the middle of the dark floor.

"Don't feel bad. It's not easy being a People."

"You're crazy."

"You tried. That's something."

"You think I'm crazy."

"You're the one said he wanted to be an Indian."

"I'm not drunk," Jim said, clearing that up.

"Thanks for the Chivas," the Indian said.

Jim came back to the bar. He slapped the papers onto the wood. He slapped the car keys onto the papers. He said, "Now what?"

The Indian turned toward him, ignoring the offerings. He answered, "Now you're free."

"I don't feel free. I feel scared."

The Indian picked up the keys and he picked up the deed and he said, "That's the edge, Jim, that's the edge you're feeling. We live there all the time. You, too, now." He walked slowly to the door, his boots ringing on the bare floor, the keys jingling lightly in his hand, the deed tucked into his pocket where a wallet would be if he had one.

The bartender was waiting.

The Indian opened the door.

The new bottle of Chivas was gone.

Jim paid the bartender and left some extra. He asked, "You an Indian?" The bartender shook his head. "I'm an Indian."

The bartender pulled the money into his belly. He asked what tribe.

Jim gave the bar a pat. "People tribe," Jim said. "We don't have anything." He strolled out the door, knees shaking, breath shallow, as if he were heading for a dangerous mission he hadn't bargained for. He stumbled in the dark. Then the lights on Jim's car flared, and the car pulled onto the road. Jim walked up to the pickup with the beaded talisman hanging from the rearview mirror. He opened the door, dented and rusted. A key was in the ignition.

Peter Brandvold

The Spurge War

Lloyd Thompson surveyed the crops behind his yard, the half-grown wheat he wouldn't be harvesting this year. He knew it would be foolish to live out here another winter and risk the brittle cold when the furnace could quit, the pipes could freeze, and the roads could be blocked for days. Though he'd had a stroke, Lloyd wasn't as afraid for himself as for Marion, whose hip was giving out, and he didn't want to worry their children, all of whom had families and jobs of their own and enough to worry about.

He would have preferred his life to end like Joe Rasmussen's—while sleeping in the house where he'd raised his family. Or like Gordon King's, who had simply sat down against his barn wall during chores. But for Lloyd it was going to slip away slowly, leaving him only a shadow of what he had been. He wanted to take a last look at his country—a long, hard look—to take with him to Rugby, where he and Marion had found an apartment less than a mile from the hospital. They'd stayed there for the first time last night, and Lloyd had kept waking up thinking he heard the old lilac on the farm scraping the kitchen window. He hadn't planned on coming out here today, but he'd awakened early and decided to drive out and pack up the odds and ends of his tools instead of leaving the job to his kids.

Now his legs began to ache from the dew collecting on his trouser cuffs, so he turned and started back to the yard through the swaying shadows of the windbreak. The leaves, he noticed, were turning their deep summer green. He remembered when he and his dad had planted these trees, close to sixty years ago. Lloyd had been a boy with close-cropped hair, in worn coveralls and dirty boots. He'd followed his father with a wooden wheelbarrow loaded with honeysuckle, ash, and spruce saplings in damp soil. Lloyd could see that time as clearly as yesterday. He could see his young self as if the boy stood a few feet in front of him, but he could not think the boy's thoughts nor feel his feelings. That part was gone. It had vanished in what now seemed a day.

He was nearly back to the yard when a familiar shade of yellow in the brome and wheat grass caught his eye. He knew right away it was leafy spurge, a coarse, long-stemmed weed with dull yellow flowers and long, thin leaves. Sure enough, the windbreak was filled with it. Because of his stroke, Lloyd hadn't been able to spray with herbicide last spring. He'd always kept spurge out his yard by attacking it every year with Tordon, the only thing he'd found that killed it. The Pierce County Soil Conservation Service had declared spurge a noxious weed. It grew nearly everywhere and choked out virtually all other plants. Cattle and horses wouldn't eat it if it was the only thing left in a pasture. Sheep were dumb enough to eat it, but they'd devour everything else, too. Lloyd had seen abandoned farms dominated by it, growing from the main road up the driveway to the house's front step, an ornery parasite grossly indifferent to what had once been an orderly and efficient farm.

Nearly tripping, Lloyd stomped into the weeds, his jaws clamped together, and pulled several of the tough, milky stems. The pulp stained his hands. He knew that spurge's roots made it impossible to kill by only pulling, and the futility of his act only made him angrier. The goddamned weed had gotten a foothold on the farm while Lloyd had been laid up! Spurge had always seemed somehow intelligent, the way it waited for any sign of advantage. Then it suddenly appeared in a ditch, by the mailbox, across the road along the tractor trail, or, like now, in the windbreak around the farm. Sneaky devil. The weed reminded Lloyd of some people he knew. The Mennonite, Rolly Sleighbough, had been waiting for Lloyd to give up his land for years, and last spring at the auction he finally got his wish.

Earlier this morning, when Lloyd had pulled his pickup into the yard, he saw the Mennonite at the edge of the field, working on his stalled tractor, and Lloyd pretended not to see him. Now he could hear the faint, erratic whine of the jerry-rigged engine straining against the cultivator in what a year ago would have been Lloyd's corn behind the barn.

Lloyd stood up stiffly when he heard a car coming on the road, trailing twin plumes of dust. It honked as it approached, then turned into the farmyard. His daughter, Jean, waved from behind the wheel. She was helping Marion, who sat next to her, with the last of the moving—mostly plants, clothes, and a few thing from the kitchen.

Jean had backed her station wagon up to the porch when Lloyd arrived at the house, and she was spreading newspapers in the back of the car. Marion stood, hunched as if chilled, holding two potted plants on the steps. She was wearing a print dress with large yellow flowers, her hair pulled back in the same bun her mother had worn in old photographs. Her back was humped, pushing her shoulders down and her head forward. Through her brown hose Lloyd could see the large veins webbing up her legs, and it saddened him. He'd loved her for what seemed forever, a subtle, quiet love that had needed mentioning less as time passed. She would be dead soon, and so would he, and their love would be nothing, as if it had never existed at all.

Jean crawled out of the car and walked up to Lloyd. "Morning, Dad." She kissed his cheek.

"There's spurge in the yard." Since his stroke, he'd had to use short, simple sentences rolled out like unwieldly prune pits. He hated the curt, angry way they made him sound.

"Rolly will take care of it next spring," Marion told him.

"He'll spray the fields, drainage ditches. He won't keep it out of the yard," Lloyd said. "The yard doesn't mean anything to him."

Jean accepted the plants from Marion. "Be careful of the bottoms, they might be muddy," Marion said. When Jean had arranged the plants in the car, the women went inside for more.

"I don't want the d-damn stuff in the yard," Lloyd said to the porch door slapping shut.

Lloyd had always been proud of his trimmed hedges, his well-tended garden, and his carefully mown lawn. His plastic deer grazed forever at peace in this peaceful meadow. The windmill he'd made from the cowling of an old New Holland tractor eased back and forth in the breeze, a perch for the martins and jays. The yard had given him pleasure; its manageability was reassuring after the vast fields he'd worked from the distance of his tractor cab and would occasionally lose, as was always the risk, to hail, blight, early snows or late rains, drought. A sudden August wind could leave a season's worth of nearly ripe grain flat and torn on the ground. Beyond the straight, fenced borders of the yard, you just never knew.

And now with a feeling of vulnerability and hopelessness he looked across the fields and pastures. The land, ruled into furrows, stretched away until it met the huge sky or was interrupted by a windbreak etched on the horizon. Sagging fences, overgrown with dock and pokeweed, lined the pastures. Lloyd imagined the brome and wild oats standing up between the splintering wood paddles of the abandoned swather that was a speck in the distant section corner. Here and there, a two-story farmhouse, long ago cut off from the main road when its driveway went back to prairie, nestled from the weather in an ash or poplar break. If you drove by you'd see the house abandoned and falling into itself, a tire swinging from the frayed rope in the front yard, the dooryard choked with thistle and spurge, and birds winging through the broken windows. Soon the farm would be no more than a few piles of useless lumber and crumbling foundations at the heart of a thriving spurge field.

While the women worked in the house, Lloyd went through his tools in the old pumphouse he'd long ago converted into a workshop beside the barn. An electric grindstone stood against the wall and an insect-coated lightbulb hung from the rafters. All about the small, musty room were tools older than Lloyd—hoes, scythes, a mattock and a plow share, wrenches and wire-spreaders. The workbench was littered with woodworking tools, and in the rafters hung sickles and rakes and an old sled with rusted runners on which his boys had pulled his girls, brittle winter afternoons. Lloyd wasn't sure what to do with all these. One of his kids might want the sled for their own, but most of the tools were useless now, had been for years. But he couldn't just discard them; there seemed something repugnant and even dangerous in that.

He used the stepladder to bring everything down from the rafters, and by his third trip his bad leg felt as heavy and numb as if it had gone to sleep, and his breath grew shallow. What did he expect after lying around for a month? When he had the sled down and leaning against the wall, he sat on the nail keg and scrubbed the sweat from his forehead with his hanky. He regained his wind and went back to work, sorting everything into several groups, using a rag and gasoline on the tools he had no doubt about keeping. Around noon Jean walked out with a chicken sandwich and a thermos of cold lemonade. He was glad that she'd caught him during a breather, and that he'd taken the ladder down: she and her mother seemed to take personally his overdoing it. She told him that she and Marion were about to haul a load of clothes—did she want them to leave room for Lloyd? It was getting hot out here, she said. Maybe he'd be more comfortable in town. Lloyd started to explain that he wanted to finish the work he'd started and that he was feeling fine, but speaking around the horseshoe in his mouth only belittled him, and he resorted to a headshake. Jean left his sandwich and thermos on the grindstone.

In the lilacs behind the bar, shaded by a cottonwood, Lloyd sat on the ancient hayrake nearly buried in quack grass. He loosened his collar and rolled his sleeves up his forearms. He ate his sandwich with sips of lemonade. The lilacs were blooming, and their sweet, nectary aroma brought to him a charge of past summers. Like the year the foreign exchange student had stayed out here and worked in the fields with Lloyd's kids and told stories about Germany over the late suppers after the machinery had been shut down, the big moon in the kitchen window and the warm breeze pushing through the screen with the smell of wheat chaff. And the year the tornado tore the roof off the barn and picked the granary straight up and dropped it, then ripped a hundred-yard swath through the barley. Before it had hit, Lloyd had never felt the air so still, like a held breath, or seen the sky that sickly yellow-green. Summers of hot, dusty fields and grasshoppers bounding over the swather and a ring of sunburn around his neck. The cars of his teenagers crowding the lawn; his daughters' dates waiting on the porch in polished cowboy boots and a cloud of Aqua Velva; lightning-veined thunderheads growing on the horizon.

A mouse scuttled through the grass below the hayrake where Lloyd was finishing his sandwich, reminding him of the day a mouse ran up Ivan's leg. In a matter of seconds, Lloyd's oldest, the ladies' man, the Mr. Know-It-All, was stumbling around yelling in the weeds with his overalls down about his ankles and his white shorts glowing in the midday sun. Lloyd cackled deep in his throat and gave his head a shake, covering his mouth to hide his silliness from the Mennonite who was making his way toward this end of the field. Lloyd could see him turning back to watch the cultivator. When the Fordson accomplished this end of the field, the Mennonite saluted with a hand to the visor of his red Cenex cap, the tractor engine racing as he made the turn. Lloyd nodded.

When he finished his lemonade, he crawled down off the rake and started on a stroll to quell the gas bubbles burning his chest and rolling up his throat, like hot marbles. He walked along the tractor trail that hugged the fenced pasture east of the house, past the part of the field the Mennonite was working, down a slight grade at the bottom of which two cottonwoods stood on either side of the deep-rutted two-track, the leaves rattling and churning in the breeze. Years ago, on Sunday afternoons, neighbors had brought over softball bats and mitts and played with Lloyd and his kids in the pasture until the women called them to eat. After heaping plates of ham, baked beans, potato salad and a slice or two of German chocolate cake, they'd return to the pasture until they could no longer see the ball against the darkening sky.

Now Lloyd noticed something he wasn't surprised to find. Like children playing a careless game of hide-and-seek, spurge rose among the dock and brome grass. There were small patches of it wandering up close to the fence. Lloyd bit his lip. It wouldn't be long until the spurge spread into the barnyard, then into the lawn. It would split the porch steps and remain until the steps themselves were gone, then move in to take their place. Christalmighty.

Clumsy with a haste he was no longer suited for, his left foot twisted and dragging, he made his way back along the trail to the barn. Normally he would have used the large motorized sprayer mounted in his pickup box, but the sprayer had gone in the auction. He found his hand-pump on the barn wall, under an old, stiffened cattle blanket, and filled it with the Tordon he found in gallon jugs in the milkhouse, where he'd stored such things since selling his Holsteins to a government buy-out program several years ago. At the water spigot outside the barn he diluted the herbicide and primed the pump with a few slow pulls of his arm. Then he started on the spurge where he'd first spotted it and worked his way back toward the barnyard.

He gave each cluster a liberal dose, the poison fanning out from the spout and forming a rainbow over the weeds. The sun was heating up, and he felt good sweating. These last few years a perpetual winter had seemed to settle in his bones. His fingers and toes never really felt warm, and even in July, several times a day, he'd feel a chill crawl up his spine, like a tick or a box elder bug, making his whole body wince.

As he worked from cluster to cluster his mind wandered, and he felt his time slowing as the world's time moved ahead as always. He couldn't keep up. His skin and organs were withering and hardening, his blood slowing and clotting in his arteries, his bones turning so brittle that a swipe against his dresser mornings on his way out of bed left a charcoal bruise on his hip. He couldn't read without a magnifying glass, he couldn't hear the pastor's sermon unless he sat in front. Sometimes he had to stand over the toilet for fifteen minutes before he saw any action. Even his sense of taste had dulled so that he couldn't always tell the potatoes from the carrots.

But he didn't see himself as old. Old was Mrs. Halvorssen, Lloyd's mother-in-law, who had lived out here with Lloyd and Marion for the last ten years of her life. Her black shoes and hair like bleached cornsilk. Old was men sitting on café stools, buying each other coffee through an afternoon, oblivious to the world passing beyond the window other than to note the weather. It was men after church with broad, bony, age-stained hands clamped to canes, guided up the porch steps of a neighbor's house for coffee and rhubarb bread. They died in their sleep or in the bathroom, and their funerals were tedious affairs, with few tears.

Mornings before the alarm went off Lloyd still dreamed of not having his homework finished and being called on to say who wrote *Julius Caesar* in Mrs. Stanley's English class. He dreamed of his father's quick-stepping walk and admonishing eyebrows, and being late with chores. He dreamed of picking Juneberries hot mornings with Rosalee Burback when he was nine and so in love his ears rang. Deep down he was still that same boy. Little had changed—until he looked in the mirror or became winded from an evening walk to the railroad spur.

He sent another cloud of herbicide and water over a patch of spurge, coating the flowers with the dew-like beads. There you go. There. Thought I wouldn't notice, did ya? Well. He knew he couldn't get them all with only his hand sprayer, but only one part of his mind knew that, and the rest submitted to the comfort of trying. If only one of his sons would have taken over for him, but they'd all established themselves in lives that had nothing to do with farming, that were even an escape from it. They'd had enough of chores and fieldwork and long days cut off from outside faces, and Lloyd didn't blame them. He was bright enough to realize that the world his children knew was much smaller than the one he'd grown up in. In theirs so much was attainable; it left little to dreams or to hope, and he was sorry when he sometimes saw it in their faces. He wished he still had the power to call them all home.

He hadn't progressed much farther along the fence before his eyes filled with black motes, his arm and shoulder grew heavy and numb, his chest raw, and his leg stiffened from his hip to his toes, as if a pipe had been shoved up there. The prairie rose and fell like slow ocean swells. He dropped the sprayer and eased himself down against a fence post. No. Christ, no. Not now. He didn't want his wife and daughter finding him out here in the grass, a feast for the maggots and flies.

After a few moments had passed and he hadn't died, he realized he probably wouldn't yet. This was only nature giving him another jab to remind him who was in control. He sat and waited for the rawness to leave his chest and for strength to return to his legs so he could stand and get back to the yard before Marion and Jean returned. Jesus, they'd worry. They'd make a big fuss and probably haul him to the hospital in Rugby where, like last time, he'd lie half-naked on a cold table, staring at the fluorescent ceiling light. Nurses would squeak in and out on cork-soled shoes and prick him for blood samples. And finally, there'd really be nothing they could do.

He closed his eyes, felt the sun on his face. The distant purr of the Mennonite's tractor working gradually toward this end of the field lulled him. Then, though he hadn't known he'd slept, he was startled awake. The Mennonite was within fifty yards of Lloyd, the tractor droning into the distance again after a nearby pass. Thank Christ he hadn't seen Lloyd in the weeds, like a schoolboy playing a wounded soldier! The sun was lower, the pasture filled with green-gold light. Shadows flooded the barnyard. When he looked at the pasture again, it was filled with people, seventeen or eighteen of them playing softball. Lloyd's father was one. He stood on the pitcher's mound—an old feed sack—wearing his white Sunday shirt with the sleeves rolled up his brown, corded arms to his elbows. His hair, with only a trace of gray above the ears, lifted like a wing from his forehead as he lunged smoothly forward with his gentlest underhand pitch. Lloyd's sister, a small girl with fair hair, stood at home plate, smiling shyly at the ball. A boy called from third base, "Come on, Erin! Bring me home. Come on, Erin!" He'd taken his shirt off, and his chest was as white as flour while his forearms and neck and face were golden brown. His hair, sandy and sun-bleached, poked out from under his red baseball cap. He leaned away from the coffee tin he'd hammered flat for a base, ready to give everything he had to running home after his sister's unlikely hit. "Come on, Erin!"

Sitting against the fence post, Lloyd felt the pain give some ground. He used the post to ease himself up. His father, close to thirty years younger than Lloyd now, had pitched for both teams: he had a light touch for the frailer girls and less athletic boys, and a challenging wind-up for Uncle Burt, his wife's younger brother who would later die in France during the Second World War. The boy, in the outfield now, was waiting for someone to hit the ball to him—Uncle Burt, his cousin, Kent, or his older brother, Carl, who could lift two haybales at a time.

Lloyd felt time curving over him in the sky's lazy arc. It separated him from all the people playing softball on a warm Sunday afternoon close to sixty years ago, and it separated them from each other, though they wouldn't realize it until much later. At the crack of the bat, his nine-year-old self ran deep into the afternoon shadows, chasing down Uncle Burt's flier. His cap flew off and only his steely hair bobbed above the wheat grass. Slowly, glove raised, looking over his shoulder, he faded back into the past.

The pasture was empty. Lloyd turned away. Looking down he saw the spurge closing in. He left the sprayer where he'd dropped it. When he heard Jean's car pull into the yard, he released his grip on the post and stood there, steadying himself in the swirl of time. He wanted to run across the fields, like a boy. He wanted to hide. But there was nowhere to go. So he started home, to the doomed yard. The Mennonite made his final pass of the day and waved.

Madelyn Camrud

Those Other Worlds

Sometimes when I look at the moon I remember
coming home, summer Saturday nights. In the backseat
of the '41 Ford, I sat, having had my fill
of ice cream, maybe a movie—Fred MacMurray,
Claudette Colbert on a portable screen. Sometimes,
there was a magic show, women in mesh stockings,
a man with colored scarves that disappeared:
all of it in the town hall on Thompson's main street
where groceries were exchanged for cream and eggs.

The window of the car, like a crystal for gazing,
led to those universes, washed blue, where people
said real things, where they hugged as if they cared,
spoke loving words, and touched each other's faces.
In the moon, there were children who gave tears
like gifts, and told their mothers if they were scared.
Past the fields, vast as planets, there were
others who wondered about these things. Beyond the hum
of early insects in North Dakota, World War II,
I believed there were those, like myself, who wanted,
so badly, to reach farther, they almost met me halfway.

Just After Easter

Had it not been that you died
the way you died—if you'd not taken months,
shelling off flesh; if you'd instead
been struck by lightning, or fallen, crushed
by a tractor, things might have been different.
If you'd not sweat through a coma,
mouth open, throat rattling, hands darting
across the blanket, sometimes passing
underneath to your penis as if protecting
that last bit of manhood—Dad, if you'd not,
that last morning, gasped for breath
like a rooster pulled, drowning,
from the stock tank; if it hadn't been
quite as it was, I wouldn't have felt
as if I killed you. If mother, my sisters,
and I hadn't kept such religious vigil
at your bedside that last night,
standing, watching you fight death,
we wouldn't have seemed so much like vultures,
noses twitching from cancer stench.
And that last morning, when I held down
your leg, flesh draped over bone,
muscles pulling, then stopping
to stiffen—if only then, I had let go
and stepped back to cry, I wouldn't
have gone on to live your death these twelve years. Later,
when I grieved, I dreamed so clearly
of that morning: children climbing
through the window to the bedroom where you died,
like paper dolls of radiant color,
hand in hand, curling inside. Meanwhile,
bath towels hung on the clothesline:
cerulean blue, pink, yellow,
purple, a string of happiness from a childhood
I never knew. One by one, the children

tumbled through the window that June morning,
blatant as sin, as my denial that day
I'd passed you—dirty, in tattered jacket
and overalls, on the street—too ashamed
to speak. You never quite fit the picture
of the father I imagined. In the dream,
it was raining, towels flapping on the line.
I could almost see your face, tears
streaming in forgiveness as you flew
from that room, leaving us women—
the years of fear, simply standing there,
vacant, lifeless, a man no longer in the house.

Funeral: Holmes Church

Whenever I think of that drive, slow
down gravel roads, your body, drained
of blood, in the back of the hearse,
I never see you in white satin, the pleats
and puffs of that fabric, I see you, instead,
in the pasture, walking paths where cows
walked dripping milk, toward the barn.
Sometimes alone, sometimes like Jesus
on the way to Emmaeus, friends walk with you,
those who knew you as a brother, some you hired
to fill the space of a son. Long before
we get to church, before we see the steeple
cross, the even white boards, before we slide
into a pew, clutching handkerchiefs, before we sing
"What A Friend We Have In Jesus," you've gone off
whistling in overalls and jacket, splotched
with grease, the way you did all those Sundays
we went to church without you. Long before
we march in pairs behind the coffin's flowery lid,
you've gone ahead, without saying a word,
to walk the pasture—land squared-off
and lasting, honest as good friendship,
with a coulee running through like a psalm.

Barbara Crow

In This Room

my mother lies
on the iron bed.

The moon dips into the room.
It is late to come.

I sit in the chair by the bed
and watch my mother,

a curl of bone
between sheets.

The fan is on low.
It has such slow arms.

Its small winds play
with her hair. It's

fine now, her hair,
and thin. This wind

wants to love it.
I think this wind

wants to carry it away.

Visitation

After Mother's death,
my brother writes of his new home.
He can see sandhills from the front window,
hear the sea when the wind comes
from the east.

Birds gather daily out the back,
line up on the brick wall.
"I think they must want to be fed,"
he writes.
"The old chap who lived here
must have fed them."

"What should I do?"
he asks.

I write back,
"Feed them, for heaven's sake.
Don't you know who it is?
Can't you tell,
the way they start
early in the morning
and won't let up

till you go out
and let the sun
break on your cold grey face?"

Flight

Over the ocean, somewhere
between Hawaii and Fiji, it came to me

that my mother was utterly gone. I was flying
home for her funeral. Outside, clouds

dispersed. We're actually parting air,
I remember thinking. Far to my left,

there's the horizon, the very lip
of our finite universe. Always,

on this journey, the minute I see
that straight, clean line, I'm the first

voyager, the bell-ringer, the herald
of a truth: I'm nearly home,

the life I've taken in America
passing into obscurity, to be remembered

on occasion as a puzzle, or bit of one,
an engraving brought out for private

showing, but rarely missed,
even in sleep. I fly on to Aotearoa,

a plate of soft scrambled eggs and mangoes
on my lap. I'm breakfasting

in the Southern Hemisphere, and a Fijian
islander is gliding towards me,

extending his golden arm
like a sign, a burnished offering.

Christine Delea

The Rug Men Come to Town

During lunch with my husband in a Chinese restaurant
in the town where I grew up, a Gypsy comes in;
his partner stands outside guarding their carton of rugs.
From Persia, the Gypsy tells the Chinese woman
who owns the restaurant while I eavesdrop.
We both have trouble understanding him—his speech
is rapid and his accent, indistinguishable:
what a bad director might tell a bad actor
to sound like, "Make it European, but not specific."
My husband leaves to inspect the rugs, returns,
tells me they are of a good quality and, he thinks,
a good price, but the fellow outside
was as difficult to comprehend as the one inside,
who smiles nervously, like a scared student
about to give a speech in a class with a mean teacher.
I try to picture the Long Island of Macy's, A&S, Filene's
as a place of Gypsies selling rugs.
In my old hometown, with its ordinances
against fast-food joints, loud parties
and door-to-door sales, Gypsies are exotics,
their dress used for childhood Halloweens.
I remember my father telling me one day,
during the years when I might have dressed
as a Gypsy for trick-or-treat,
to some forgotten naive comment,
that some day he would show me where poor people lived,

right in our hometown. He never did,
but I found them anyway, when I spent
a few years running with the "wrong" crowd,
people whose parents used food stamps in the supermarket
where my mother bought expensive, imported ethnic foods,
people who were doing time while I studied in a private college.
And now there are Gypsies in town, selling
pretty rugs at good prices, but not having much luck
in the restaurant where I worked for spending
money during a few dull, plodding summers.
The Gypsy's smile worn out, the compassion in the Chinese
woman's eyes sincere but not a sale, he looks at us.
We shake out heads, he leaves to join his partner
and drag the carton in front of the health club next door.
The Chinese woman smiles at us and shrugs.
We are all a tribe on this island of the bad
and once-wealthy, looking for a nation to take
us in, to claim us and make us whole.

Tom Domek

After Chief Joseph

That my eyes
soak with the heartbeat
of earth. Green

like the phosphorescent wings
of a teal.
The green of cottonwood leaves

twisting like stars
in the wind. As green
as pony grass

soft in the meadow.
And at night,
when I close

to earth,
let my eyes soak
blue. The blue

of inevitable sadness
our children are born to.
Blue for the chosen hue

of spirit ghosts
dancing. As blue
as the great pure lungs

of the sky.
Throughout this life
I will shut my eyes,

then open them.
Let me dream
into shadows

wheresoever they fall,
feel the swirl
of circles submerging,

endlessly forming.
Life is sweet.
Let me never forget.

The Medicine Bow Mountains

They rise from the plains
with half the girth
of a promise

a mother kisses
to the eyes
of her infant son.

We exalt
at their profundity.
We should tell ourselves

that with the patience
of June snow
on a mountaintop

we will see
the westerlies
brushing cliffs

in whispers
and bighorn sheep
beveling up stone walls

like shadows
of clouds
gathering for storm

at timberline.
And if we pause
till awe

leaps from our eyes
we may even glimpse
the spirits

of Arapaho braves
Old West photographers
never could quite capture.

Holding

I pack my shotgun
into the hills.
From a yellow marsh,
Coyote appears.

When I stare
at his hide, our eyes
hold and they hold.
I point my muzzle

to the sky and fire,
but Coyote steps closer.
I toss stones at his
whiskers, but he smiles

back, black lips. I plead
with him softly, since
I'm hunting birds,
but his eyes roll,

and they roll. My toes
paw at the earth,
and his tongue hangs
in laughter. I let go

wild, full-moon laughter.
Coyote hoots, then spins
and leaps through my eyes.
All day I hunt for birds,

but I don't see a feather,
not a speck in the sky.
At dusk, Coyote crosses
my path, and he smiles

and yelps his song. His
ribs rise up then collapse
like a bony grasp. My nose
snarls with laughter. In

unspoken friendship
we trot from each
other, better
for laughter. Sometimes

I know I've forgotten
what it means to hold
to these lonely, wild
joys of laughter.

David Dwyer

The Higher Arithmetic

In heaven, I do not know that there are angels,
but I know there are numbers there, and light.
(Arithmetic and heaven are both uncountably
full of light.) Inaccessible cardinals, there,
will lord it over mere infinities;
the naturals will dance among the reals. . .

Apart from numbers, how little we know.

*There is no largest prime. The Halting Problem
is formally undecidable. Every subset
of a well-ordered set is well-ordered itself. And so on . . .*

Such things are true, even easy to prove.
Are there uncountably more, unknowably other
true things about the world?

I had to go away. A woman I love
(and this is true, too) put an icon
of an archangel into the glove-compartment
of my car. I haven't looked, but I know it is there,
as I know there is no largest prime.

Raphaël,

she said. *His numberless wings cloak all of us
poor travellers who do not know, but are not lost.
The angel,* she said, *of happy meeting, after all.*

The Middle of Nowhere

Storms on the sun, or between the suns,
out where the hydrogen atoms (some,
though they have not been there, say)
are born out of nothing at all . . .

And, moments ago, these swells of stripped
hydrogen atoms and disaffected
quarks that splash our electromagnetic
outer reefs, above Sioux County,
North Dakota, a moment ago,
they'd fled their star, passed us by
by half a million miles, not glancing
back. They never planned
to visit the provinces . . .

Storms on the sun, black if you dared
to look them in the eye, deceitfully
arrayed, just here and now, in lighter
watercolored ripples of watered silk as she
shrugged the robe off, oh,
it can't be twenty years? It can . . .

(I miss the sea, oh, and the barely countable
sands of the beach near where,
near when I was a child . . .

"The universe is nearly all
nothing at all," my mother told me,
"and most of the rest is hydrogen.
Still, it is all oddly attractive . . .")

Twenty miles or so—

I know where I am, whose stubble field of
sunflower bones I just now

stopped beside,
though it hardly matters. The car
shivers and snorts in the cold, its lights
clicked off. I shiver and pee in the black
ditch, wave functions
collapsing around me like waves.

I know where I am: not far from home;
not far from our glamourous, extravagant star; lost in uncountable,
unaccountable light.

Love and Poetry at Ground Zero

It's the journey that matters, not the destination.
—Montaigne

I

This must be middle-age:
                              I took George Meredith's great poem
about adultery to bed with me and read it
lovingly over, alone—my wife, my darling,
harbored safe in New York these last ten days or so,
among old friends and lovers.
                              Next morning,
while Amtrak was spiriting her away
through a dark tunnel beneath the Hudson, while agents
of the federal government were cooking
her breakfast,

                    Can I trust her
to these people? What choice? It's already too late, already
she is friendless, alone, in
New Jersey at their mercy.

                         next morning,
I read a bit of "Modern Love" again and called
East to an old lover.
                              We talked of youth,
of age, of middle-age; compared the triumphs
of our nieces—both of us childless still,
despite our dear and reckless past; compared
this sort of conversation with
the torturous logistics, all the fuss,
the terrible bother of adultery and found—both
of an age and "of a certain age"—found such talk,
some days at least, dearer than yet another
affair, though we did agree
that there's something to be said for both.

They have taken her into
Pennsylvania by now. A man in the pay
of the federal government, a middle-aged
black man with a kind face,
is pouring her another cup of coffee.

Next afternoon (once she had slipped
unhindered through Chicago), I packed a change of clothes,
an old book;

It is hard to trust these people.
What choice, though? They have said that, at nine
on the morning of the third day, they'll
deliver her up, unharmed, to me
near the Minot Air Force Base in North Dakota.
What choice do I have but to go there and see?

changed the sheets;
let our cat Goblin Market gorge
on the liver of some larger mammal, then
released her on her own recognizance; washed
ten days' dishes; got into our unexciting,
reliable, middle-aged Ford and drove
to Minot, across the enormous prairie, alone.

II

All across the enormous prairie, agents
of the federal government have built
a looking-glass world of silos upsidedown,
cavernous, deep as a mirror but not
(as mirrors are) peopled nor (as might seem
right) surrounded
with herds of looking-glass Brown
Swiss and Jerseys. Out of the light
there, monsters live.
Sometimes,
when you drive in their country alone,
you'll hear them talk;

Welcome (says one). *Welcome to*
my house. Come
freely. Go safely; and leave
something of the happiness you bring . . .

Always, they contradict
the quite official-looking signs, which say
we own the monsters' caves but may not enter them.
Indiscretion
costs them nothing, after all, and enormous

camps of their servants are near at hand; near enough,
they feel, should anyone misunderstand. A hundred miles
of prairie, after all, two hundred miles, is
nothing as they count distances.

One (in the voice of a little
child whom you hope to watch grow into
this enormous country, know very well
you may never see again), one mutters:

I can fly. I can fly. Truly, I can . . .

(So can they all, of course.)

You there,
you have a child, perhaps? Young children
find my depths, my twisting
corridors enchanting . . .

But, no, she can't bring
Kitty. No cats allowed. We are, you see,
so very fond of birds . . .

Hush, leave him be.
Be quiet. Let me sleep . . .

(They cannot sleep, of course.)

. . . and I bid you welcome
to my house. Come in; the night air
is chill, and you must need
to eat and rest . . .

(They do not choose to eat, just now.)

As you run through the night, the rest run on
in honeyed voices; they talk of secret places
in the earth they know where exquisite
fruits are stored and enormous combs
of honey boil with light
in the chill shadows . . .

A niece,
you say. How nice. How very nice. How
fond, how very fond we are of little girls . . .

I said over some verse
in my head, then aloud, from a more
self-confident age, and came down off the prairie
into the quiet prairie town. The land
moaned round with many voices . . .

Hush (a monster said),
hush, leave him be. Just leave them be. They come and go,
but they never go where we cannot find them—
hush—now do they? Hush.

III

Tomorrow, O lost
and rediscovered love, or never lost, my not-
quite-young, dear wanderer—we will be
safe. (I'm sure. How long, I do not know.) We'll kiss
and talk—my defrocked witch, my
pragmatist—of love and poetry, old friends, nieces and
cats, old lovers, ghosts and secret places . . .

Hush (the monsters say).

We'll slip nonchalantly into our middle-
aged Ford, in the middle of our lives and all, and drive—
my sweet, my Protestant—all morning into
afternoon, a scattering of birds and then
a silence enormous around us,
through the monsters' enormous kingdom, home.

Heid Ellen Erdrich

Translation

Enter the simple landscape
of snow on broken fields,
trust those lines it gives up;
two narrow trees, a dip in the land,
a farmhouse heaved into itself, abandoned.
We go to the doorway, no further—
beyond the threshold we would step into air.
The floor, collapsed as if a bomb dropped,
framed by walls hung with ghostly
impressions of pictures long gone,
tells of a great force. We imagine
a tornado, noisy as a pressure cooker
caught in the chimney, brought floor down.
No one home to open east windows,
front door, storm doors to the cellar.
No one let the air flow and equalize.
This is a place forever falling on itself,
a story we should recognize.
But we turn in that doorway, face the
blue glare, the horizon flat out like a lover
pressing close to field, rails, road.
We stare until the train tracks
trick our eyes, collide at the edge of sight.
We should go to them, lie side to side,
our ears to the rails, hear the low singing,
smell iron become a flat yet bitter taste.

And if we lie there until the train
makes an eye of light in the sky,
and if we stand or stumble
while the train spins the ground away,
if we watch until we are certain
there is no meeting of those tracks,
would we still think we might break
the law of a land with parallels so vast?
Our bodies, like sunrise, draw a glowing line
we cannot cross, yet we press close to try—
As if we are stories mere touch might translate.

The Red River of the North

Like all water it cares for its creatures.
They draw each drop they drink from it
and when they paw the ground or cut
a furrow in a field, river scent comes up.
They trust its unusual course, the path
lapping flat as a tongue to Canada.
In their veins there is a pull
direct as that flow: North,
forever, even through winter
frozen four-foot thick or
breaking in spring, brown,
surging ice chunks big as cars,
brimming in ditches, on roads,
seeping into fields, leaving June sloughs
thick with cattails greening then browning,
exploding in the dry July wind that whips
fields into thirty-foot spires of dust—
Drought drives the river underground,
exposes its bed: bottles and jars,
stranded fish sloughing their flesh,
leaving spines, wash boards and tires,
the river's bone and core.
People pick about for souvenirs or,
though the bullhead's flesh tastes muddy,
pull squirming netfuls from puddles.
And the snapping turtles, all plates and claws,
some big enough for a child to stand on,
their hundred-year-old faces
sunk in rings of wrinkles,
bask peacefully on strands between ponds
while beside the bridge abutment
young drunks park in their pickups.
They have come for the snappers
easy catches in a river so low.
They break branches, lurch toward
the turtles whose jaws lock,

clench the sticks and hold
and hold even as they are lifted,
even at the shock of the hatchet.
Shell trunks drop, trudge headless,
straight toward the water.
The young men laugh long laughs
throwing their own heads back.
They do not notice the sky go green
hung with hail teats to the west.
Herons, blue as smoke, rise,
seek higher ground. In the muck,
the soup meat is gathered up,
tossed in the bed of the truck.
The turtle bodies kick a reflex,
nails on metal scratch out a call.
The river answers in a flash of rain
swelling from a trickle to suck ankle deep,
whorling to the men's lips, pouring and
rushing in them, washing them inside
until they drink a first watery breath
in a world of heron and catfish—
This is the river swimming back
ignorant of banks and dikes and bridges
wanting only to rise and rise beyond
what binding or straightening inflicts
wanting to fill its creatures
with insistent murkiness, the cold urge
that pumps in every pulse: North
the way our blood goes in its sleep,
the way all things must go
in shells or scales or feathers.

Louise Erdrich

A Love Medicine

For Lise

Still it is raining lightly
in Wahpeton. The pickup trucks
sizzle beneath the blue neon
bug traps of the dairy bar.

Theresa goes out in green halter and chains
that glitter at her throat.
This dragonfly, my sister,
she belongs more than I
to this night of rising water.

The Red River swells to take the bridge.
She laughs and leaves her man in his Dodge.
He shoves off to search her out.
He wears a long rut in the fog.

And later, at the crest of the flood,
when the pilings are jarred from their sockets
and pitch into the current,
she steps against the firstwork of a man.
She goes down in wet grass
and his boot plants its grin
among the arches of her face.

Now she feels her way home in the dark.
The white-violet bulbs of the streetlamps
are seething with insects,
and the trees lean down aching and empty.
The river slaps at the dike works, insistent.

I find her curled up in the roots of a cottonwood.
I find her stretched out in the park, where all night
the animals are turning in their cages.
I find her in a burnt-over ditch, in a field
that is gagging on rain,
sheets of rain sweep up down
to the river held tight against the bridge.

We see that now the moon is leavened and the water,
as deep as it will go,
stops rising. Where we wait for the night to take us
the rain ceases. Sister, there is nothing
I would not do.

Indian Boarding School: The Runaways

Home's the place we head for in our sleep.
Boxcars stumbling north in dreams
don't wait for us. We catch them on the run.
The rails, old lacerations that we love,
shoot parallel across the face and break
just under Turtle Mountains. Riding scars
you can't get lost. Home is the place they cross.

The lame guard strikes a match and makes the dark
less tolerant. We watch through cracks in boards
as the land starts rolling, rolling till it hurts
to be here, cold in regulation clothes.
We know the sheriff's waiting at midrun
to take us back. His car is dumb and warm.
The highway doesn't rock, it only hums
like a wing of long insults. The worn-down welts
of ancient punishments lead back and forth.

All runaways wear dresses, long green ones,
the color you would think shame was. We scrub
the sidewalks down because it's shameful work.
Our brushes cut the stone in watered arcs
and in the soak frail outlines shiver clear
a moment, things us kids pressed on the dark
face before it hardened, pale, remembering
delicate old injuries, the spines of names and leaves.

Jeff Falla

Limitations

We don't have to test the limits
of anything. It just happens.
We don't need the world.
Worlds pass unnoticed

in the candle heat blackening the ceiling.
The limits of this room,
this town, this prairie
converge in the single containment

of your movements when you pass
a flaring match from one candle
to the next. We may remain
forever in the certain world

we've created in this room.
Everything here has names.
Nothing here has limitations.
Everything here contains everything

not contained beyond this room,
this town, this prairie.
And if we remain forever, here,
we test the limits of everything.

In the Ditch

Through the darkened room,
A crack of light
Around the unlatched door
Falls across your bed.

On an earlier evening
Your father's dark form would break
The light, the clicking

Of his pocket watch grow louder
As he entered your room.
Now it's only a memory

That scrapes your cheek
With unshaven kisses and passes
Through the darkness.
You stir under tight covers.

You turn to face the door
And the mattress pushes back.
You imagine it
Has orange stains and gaping rips
With foam rubber swelling out.

There is an urge
To pull off the sheets,
To expose it,
But then you see your father
Tossing junk from a pickup bed,

And there's the trailer, built
From the maple floor of a church,
Loaded with splintered boards
And rusty pipes, your mattress
On top holding it all down.

Everything is dumped into the ditch,
Your mattress left exposed
Like pale skin to the sun.

Next spring when you returned
The mattress was under water,
Rotted and saturated
Like the constant fear
Of what's outside the door.

World Imagineless

Our room is a dark ocean beyond imagination,
And we always believe what we can't figure out.
Over and over and over we try
Turning our love into a myth to believe in,
To save us from learning the destruction
Of knowing each other too well.
Meaningless is the label we've learned
For what's not understood, known.
We see ourselves

In dark corners as real,
Imagineless—and if I have to say it,
I'll say it (Gone are the ramparts!),
I'll say learning to know anything is an excuse
To destroy what isn't understood—
Burning piles of humanity like heaps of melting tires
No rain can extinguish. After a century of poison
You get to a point, boy. . .

I pray to you, our love, yours and mine, for salvation
From this withered world imagineless.
Give me a wilderness I can return to,
A wilderness where my voice will echo
And be heard by no one who doesn't hear
With imagination. Yes, destruction
Will not be our salvation but our baptism,
So Christ can descend from the heaven

He's been sent to, the heaven from which
He can be recalled at will.
We are responsible for our own destructions
Because we've doomed ourselves in language.
Oh, give me a wilderness,
For the wilderness echoes a mysterious tongue. . .

Forming the Language

Before we met I would lie in bed and dream
In a poet's language words
Ordered and arranged some hundred and seventy years ago
In a patterned quest for love and ideal beauty,
When such things mattered—and I saw myths
Sprayed upon trees and in the colors
Of a beautiful snake, in words written
By a boy sitting in a wooden chair under a tree,
And in words flowing from open veins,
Cooling the lightless fires of ages on ages—

Reeling from the dream I would rise,
Feeling the night's chill in my eyes. . .
Oh, to be up for a walk in the thick morning,
To forget the disappointment of this evening
When spirits failed to hear the reasons
I so eloquently spoke in candled darkness.
Now, something darker has my notes, words written
To give shape to sourceless sounds.
Something darker grips the pleasure I once found
In the enveloping warmth of love constant and secret.

The world is held in a dark embrace
Which could squeeze our hearts to purity—
Our hearts are held in that eternal squeeze
Twisting inside itself to infinity.
Something dark rises inside me and I feel sick
In solace, stalling for you to take my hand,
To seal this night, and finally meet me,
Stalling for you I've loved in secret
To shape the wordless finds I keep holding
In the endless dreams of this empty bed.

Roland Flint

Austere

"What did I know, what did I know. . . ?"

How she left kettles of water
On the kitchen stove for baths
Each Saturday night till hotter
Than needed (add cold), to wash,

In the corrugated tub,
The week's field dirt away,
Blown even into the crib
From a North Dakota sky.

How all of us take turns,
The young mother renewing
Clean heat for each till it runs
Out, as she's finishing hers.

I offer you her kettles, stove,
The kerosene-lamp light,
Her palm her soap her olive,
The tub, its velvety silt.

Varna Snow

I hadn't seen snow in summer
In the forty-three years it's been
Since, early that morning, in North Dakota,
It snowed for an hour on the Fourth of July.
It melted into the season's usual weather,
Into the day's parades, fireworks, and speeches,
So that by evening the snow, like the morning itself,
Was no more than a small boy's dream.
Gone away as that sounds, I can still see snow
Whitely silting the green fields of the farm.
Later, every summer, the tall cottonwoods
Would let fall their snow,
Softer than flakes, more finely formed,
Stuff that moves up and down
With the lightest breath of moving air,
A snow of dreaming, or the dream itself.
I haven't been back to my hometown
When the cottonwood releases snow
But in June I've come around the world to Varna
And trees here are snowing down
The same fleecy letting go
Of an early harvest in Bulgarian cottonwoods.
The women sweep it up each day,
As we shoveled December walks at home,
But still it makes such drifts
I gathered up three big handfuls
And stuffed the open knot of a tree with it—
I don't know why, some wooly evanescence
Returning snow to the hard tree of ourselves—
As if I were standing here in my own yard
Holding in my open hands this blessing of my journey,
A dry little foam of where I come from,
Where I am today, and where I'm headed in the snow.

Easy

While she starts the water and measures the pasta,
he sets the table and peels the garlic,
she cuts up broccoli, strips snow peas, readies fish,
he presses the garlic, fixes her a kir, him a gin,
she sautés the vegetables while he grates cheese,
fixes the candles, puts flowers on the table,
she puts pasta in the boiling water, fixes salad,
which he takes to the table with the cheese,
she mixes a salad dressing by hand, he opens the wine
and takes it to the table where everything is ready,
except for the pasta, so he lights the candles
and puts salad from the big walnut bowl into small ones.

Now she or he brings the pasta, greens and fish
mixed in, and they sit to talk, drink wine and eat.
Though October, they sit on a small screen porch
in the back of the house where they have lived
for twelve years of their twenty together,
the last six, the children gone, alone.
Once, during dinner, if they stop talking
and listen to the music, they will, without drama,
hold hands a moment, almost like a handshake
by now, most friendly, confirming the contract,
and more. She is a pretty woman of 51, who has
kept trim and fit. He is 56 and hasn't.

Later, they will clear the dishes and clean up,
and she will bring tea and fresh fruit to bed,
where they will watch a little television or not,
with herbal tea and the fruit. After that, if
they make love or not, they will talk a long time,
her work or his, the budget, the Middle East,
this child or that, how good dinner was, how
easy it is, the times like this, when it's simple.

First Poem

When I was eight or nine, Mr. Bina
Showed me how to saw a six-shooter
Out of plywood, which I did. And when
He looked it over, he said it was fine.

One morning it was gone, and when my
Siblings were cleared, mother said:
Honey, someone kindled the heater
With it, but he didn't understand.

In his Saturday woodcraft classes,
During the war, to tall John Bina
We were equally poets, who taught us
To make ducks, guns or dowels out of wood.

His high Czech face smiled seriously
When he explained: If I'm too old already
For war, I can still teach you about
The woods and saws, mm-hmm, that's good.

No—it wasn't a poem, I'm not sure
It was a pistol, but something
I believed was good. The war and
Woodwork classes ended when I was ten.

Then Clair Clemetson and Bobby Erickson
Came home from the Pacific, at last,
But many from Park River, like
John Kelner and Jimmy Colwell, didn't.

Jimmy's parents still came to the
Lyric theater, sat half-way back,
Holding hands—and you could hear
Ed's handsome laugh, sometimes.

Not the Kelners: John had been tough
Enough to survive the Bataan
Death March. But then something
Killed him—and killed their joy.

I didn't know the Binas as a couple,
Blanche and John, except as working
The garden between our houses, or in
Old country pleasure of their daughters.

Forty-five years later, all five, Irene,
Lorraine, Dorothy, Catherine, and JoAnne,
Were back in town and harmonized—
Full-voiced impromptu singing—at Irene's.

When they got ready to sing in Czech,
The second youngest, Catherine,
Nicknamed Mickey, said, O, I'll cry,
I'm crying already, and they laughed.

The daughters of Blanche and John stood
Singing them back to us, like poets,
No one needing to solo, or shine,
As the best ones rarely do. And it was good.

Strawberries like Raspberries

A few years ago in Bulgaria,
in Boyana, outside Sofia,
you had the best pear of your life,
a Bosc, and then another:
they had the highest pear taste,
the chewiest sweetness, an apple's
snap of October, the genius
or luck of Bulgarian horticulture,
which has also given the best
cherries, strawberries and peaches
of your life. The strawberries were
such a delicately sweet dark red,
that a friend called them, in Bulgarian,
"strawberries like raspberries," which
you misunderstood, taking that to be
a varietal name of *this* strawberry.
And the next day, shopping alone,
you puzzled and amused the grocer,
ordering in your baby Bulgarian,
yagodi kato malini, the
"strawberries-like-raspberries."

In one of your Bulgarian reading
lessons, in the communist textbook,
the country is called a "garden paradise,"
and so it seemed, always, on many visits.
But now you keep hearing and reading
about the brutal shortages of transition,
as if glasnost and apples can't
break from the same blossoms,
as if the national white cheese,
delicate as feta, from cows or goats,
as if the velvet yogurt, even milk,
even bread, even your favorite
grape brandy, are failing to find
their mouths: as the old systems

of supply and distribution, or
of politics and privilege, die
by their own dead weight or
from the freedom now to say so.

As if, for a while, at least,
the harvest will be only of fruit,
more bitter than sour cherries,
of what truly had been sown.
The party bosses (they called them
golemi kletchki, big sticks),
are dead or dying branches now,
who formerly drove to market,
or to Boyana, a pear to savor
forever, but not to discuss too
openly, with strangers, if it wasn't.

William Gass

Order of Insects

We certainly had no complaints about the house after all we had been through in the other place, but we hadn't lived there very long before I began to notice every morning the bodies of a large black bug spotted about the downstairs carpet; haphazardly, as earth worms must die on the street after a rain; looking when I first saw them like rolls of dark wool or pieces of mud from the children's shoes, or sometimes, if drapes were pulled, so like ink stains or deep burns they terrified me, for I had been intimidated by that thick rug very early and the first week had walked over it wishing my bare feet would swallow my shoes. The shells were usually broken. Legs and other parts I couldn't then identify would be scattered near like flakes of rust. Occasionally I would find them on their backs, their quilted undersides showing orange, while beside them were smudges of dark-brown powder that had to be vacuumed carefully. We believed our cat had killed them. She was frequently sick during the night then—a rare thing for her—and we could think of no other reason. Overturned like that they looked pathetic even dead.

I could not imagine where the bugs had come from. I am terribly meticulous myself. The house was clean, the cupboards tight and orderly, and we never saw one alive. The other place had been infested with those flat brown fuzzy roaches, all wires and speed, and we'd seen *them* all right, frightened by the kitchen light, sifting through the baseboards and the floor's cracks; and in the pantry I had nearly closed my fingers on one before it fled, tossing its shadow across the starch like an image of the startle in my hand.

Dead, overturned, their three pairs of legs would be delicately drawn up and folded shyly over their stomachs. When they walked I suppose their forelegs were thrust out and then bent to draw the body up. I still wonder if they jumped. More than once I've seen our cat hook one of her claws under a shell and toss it in the air, crouching while the insect fell, feigning leaps—but there was daylight; the bug was dead; she was not really interested any more; and she would walk immediately away. That image takes the place of jumping. Even if I actually saw those two back pairs of legs unhinge, as they would have to if one leaped, I think I'd find the result unreal and mechanical, a poor try measured by that sudden, high, head-over-heels flight from our cat's paw. I could look it up, I guess, but it's no study for a woman . . . bugs.

At first I reacted as I should, bending over, wondering what in the world; yet even before I recognized them I'd withdrawn my hand, shuddering. Fierce, ugly, armored things: they used their shadows to seem large. The machine sucked them up while I looked the other way. I remember the sudden thrill of horror I had hearing one rattle up the wand. I was relieved that they were dead, of course, for I could never have killed one, and if they had been popped, alive, into the dust bag of the cleaner, I believe I would have had nightmares again as I did the time my husband fought the red ants in our kitchen. All night I lay awake thinking of the ants alive in the belly of the machine, and when toward morning I finally slept I found myself in the dreadful elastic tunnel of the suction tube where ahead of me I heard them: a hundred bodies rustling in the dirt.

I never think of their species as alive but as comprised entirely by the dead ones on our carpet, all the new dead manufactured by the action of some mysterious spoor—perhaps that dust they sometimes lie in—carried in the air, solidified by night and shaped, from body into body, spontaneously, as maggots were before the age of science. I have a single book about insects, a little dated handbook in French which a good friend gave me as a joke—because of my garden, the quaintness of the plates, the fun of reading about worms in such an elegant tongue—and my bug has his picture there climbing the stem of an orchid. Beneath the picture is his name: *Periplaneta orientalis L. Ces répugnants insectes ne sont que trop communs dans les cuisines des vieilles habitations des villes, dans les magasins, entrepôts, boulangeries, brasseries, restaurants, dans la cale des navires, etc.,* the text begins. Nevertheless they are a new experience for me and I think that I am grateful for it now.

The picture didn't need to show me there were two, adult and nymph, for by that time I'd seen the bodies of both kinds. Nymph. My god the names we use. The one was dark, squat, ugly, sly. The other, slimmer, had hard sheath-like wings drawn over its back like another shell, and you could see delicate interwoven lines spun like fossil gauze across them. The nymph was a rich golden color deepening in its interstices to mahogany. Both had legs that looked under a glass like the canes of a rose, and the nymph's were sufficiently transparent in a good light you thought you saw its nerves merge and run like a jagged crack to each ultimate claw.

Tipped, their legs have fallen shut, and the more I look at them the less I believe my eyes. Corruption, in these bugs, is splendid. I've a collection now I keep in typewriter-ribbon tins, and though, in time, their bodies dry and the interior flesh decays, their features hold, as I suppose they held in life, an Egyptian determination, for their protective plates are strong and death must break bones to get in. Now that the heavy soul is gone, the case is light.

I suspect if we were as familiar with our bones as with our skin, we'd never bury dead but shrine them in their rooms, arranged as we might like to find them on a visit; and our enemies, if we could steal their bodies from the battle sites, would be museumed as they died, the steel still eloquent in their sides, their metal hats askew, the protective toes of their shoes unworn, and friend and enemy would be so wondrously historical that in a hundred years we'd find the jaws still hung for the same speech and all the parts we spent our life with tilted as they always were—rib cage, collar, skull—still repetitious, still defiant, angel light, still worthy of memorial and affection. After all, what does it mean to say that when our cat has bitten through the shell and put confusion in the pulp, the life goes out of them? Alas for us, I want to cry, our bones are secret, showing last, so we must love what perishes: the muscles and the waters and the fats.

Two prongs extend like daggers from the rear. I suppose I'll never know their function. That kind of knowledge doesn't take my interest. At first I had to screw my eyes down, and as I consider it now, the whole change, the recent alteration in my life, was the consequence of finally coming near to something. It was a self-mortifying act, I recall, a penalty I laid upon myself for the evil-tempered words I'd shouted at my children in the middle of the night. I felt instinctively the insects were infectious and their own disease, so when I knelt I held a handkerchief over the lower half of my face . . . saw only horror . . . turned, sick, masking my eyes . . . yet the worst of angers held me through the day: vague, searching, guilty, and ashamed.

After that I came near often; saw, for the first time, the gold nymph's difference; put between the mandibles a tinted nail I'd let grow long; observed the movement of the jaws, the stalks of the antennae, the skull-shaped skull, the lines banding the abdomen, and found an intensity in the posture of the shell, even when tipped, like that in the gaze of Gauguin's natives' eyes. The dark plates glisten. They are wonderfully shaped; even the buttons of the compound eyes show a geometrical precision which prevents my earlier horror. It isn't possible to feel disgust toward such an order. Nevertheless, I reminded myself, a roach . . . and you a woman.

I no longer own my own imagination. I suppose they came up the drains or out of the registers. It may have been the rug they wanted. Crickets, too, I understand, will feed on wool. I used to rest by my husband . . . stiffly . . . waiting for silence to settle in the house, his sleep to come, and then the drama of their passage would take hold of me, possess me so completely that when I finally slept I merely passed from one dream to another without the slightest loss of vividness or continuity. Never alive, they came with punctures; their bodies formed from little whorls of copperish dust which in the downstairs darkness I couldn't possibly have seen; and they were dead and upside down when they materialized, for it was in that moment that our cat, herself darkly invisible, leaped and brought her paws together on the true soul of the roach; a soul so static and intense, so immortally arranged, I felt, while I lay shell-like in our bed, turned inside out, driving my mind away, it was the same as the dark soul of the world itself—and it was this beautiful and terrifying feeling that took possession of me finally, stiffened me like a rod beside my husband, played caesar to my dreams.

The weather drove them up, I think . . . moisture in the tubes of the house. The first I came on looked put together in Japan; broken, one leg bent under like a metal cinch; unwound. It rang inside the hollow of the wand like metal too; brightly, like a stream of pins. The clatter made me shiver. Well I always see what I fear. Anything my eyes have is transformed into a threatening object: mud, or stains, or burns, or if not these, then toys in unmendable metal pieces. Not fears to be afraid of. The ordinary fears of daily life. Healthy fears. Womanly, wifely, motherly ones: the children may point at the wretch with the hunch and speak in a voice he will hear; the cat has fleas again, they will get in the sofa; one's face looks smeared, it's because of the heat; is the burner on under the beans? the washing machine's obscure disease may reoccur, it rumbles on rinse and rattles on wash; my god it's already eleven o'clock; which one of you has lost a galosh? So it was amid the worries of our ordinary life I bent, innocent and improperly armed, over the bug that had come undone. Let me think back on the shock. . . . My hand would have fled from a burn with the same speed; anyone's death or injury would have weakened me as well; and I could have gone cold for a number of reasons, because I felt in motion in me my own murderous disease, for instance; but none could have produced the revulsion that dim recognition did, a reaction of my whole nature that flew ahead of understanding and made me withdraw like a spider.

I said I was innocent. Well I was not. Innocent. My god the names we use. What do we live with that's alive we haven't tamed—people like me?—even our houseplants breathe by our permission. All along I had the fear of what it was—something ugly and poisonous, deadly and terrible—the simple insect, worse and wilder than fire—and I should rather put my arms in the heart of a flame than in the darkness of a moist and webby hole. But the eye never ceases to change. When I examine my collection now it isn't any longer roaches I observe but gracious order, wholeness, and divinity. . . . My handkerchief, that time, was useless. . . . O my husband, they are a terrible disease.

The dark soul of the world . . . a phrase I should laugh at. The roach shell sickened me. And my jaw has broken open. I lie still, listening, but there is nothing to hear. Our cat is quiet. They pass through life to immortality between her paws.

Am I grateful now my terror has another object? From time to time I think so, but I feel as though I'd been entrusted with a kind of eastern mystery, sacred to a dreadful god, and I am full of the sense of my unworthiness and the clay of my vessel. So strange. It is the sewing machine that has the fearful claw. I live in a scatter of blocks and children's voices. The chores are my clock, and time is every other moment interrupted. I had always thought that love knew nothing of order and that life itself was turmoil and confusion. Let us leap, let us shout! I have leaped, and to my shame, I have wrestled. But this bug that I hold in my hand and know to be dead is beautiful, and there is a fierce joy in its composition that beggars every other, for its joy is the joy of stone, and it lives in its tomb like a lion.

I don't know which is more surprising: to find such order in a roach, or such ideas in a woman.

I could not shake my point of view, infected as it was, and I took up their study with a manly passion. I sought out spiders and gave them sanctuary; played host to worms of every kind; was generous to katydids and lacewings, aphids, ants and various grubs; pampered several sorts of beetle; looked after crickets; sheltered bees; aimed my husband's chemicals away from the grasshoppers, mosquitoes, moths, and flies. I have devoted hours to watching caterpillars feed. You can see the leaves they've eaten passing through them; their bodies thin and swell until the useless pulp is squeezed in perfect rounds from their rectal end; for caterpillars are a simple section of intestine, a decorated stalk of yearning muscle, and their whole being is enlisted in the effort of digestion. *Le tube digestif des Insectes est situé dans le grand axe de la cavité générale du corps . . . de la bouche vers l'anus . . . Le pharynx . . . L'œsophage . . . Le jabot . . . Le ventricule chylifique . . . Le rectum et l'iléon . . .* Yet when they crawl their curves conform to graceful laws.

My children ought to be delighted with me as my husband is, I am so diligent, it seems, on their behalf, but they have taken fright and do not care to pry or to collect. My hobby's given me a pair of dreadful eyes, and sometimes I fancy they start from my head; yet I see, perhaps, no differently than Galileo saw when he found in the pendulum its fixed intent. Nonetheless my body resists such knowledge. It wearies of its edge. And I cannot forget, even while I watch our moonvine blossoms opening, the simple principle of the bug. It is a squat black cockroach after all, such a bug as frightens housewives, and it's only come to chew on rented wool and find its death absurdly in the teeth of the renter's cat.

Strange. Absurd. I am the wife of the house. This point of view I tremble in is the point of view of a god, and I feel certain, somehow, that could I give myself entirely to it, were I not continuing a woman, I could disarm my life, find peace and order everywhere; and I lie by my husband and I touch his arm and consider the temptation. But I am a woman. I am not worthy. Then I want to cry O husband, husband, I am ill, for I have seen what I have seen. What should he do at that, poor man, starting up in the night from his sleep to such nonsense, but comfort me blindly and murmur dream, small snail, only dream, bad dream, as I do to the children. I could go away like the wise cicada who abandons its shell to move to other mischief. I could leave and let my bones play cards and spank the children. . . . Peace. How can I think of such ludicrous things—beauty and peace, the dark soul of the world—for I am the wife of the house, concerned for the rug, tidy and punctual, surrounded by blocks.

Elizabeth Hampsten

"Where Are You From?"

Riding day after day on the ranch was all I wanted to do, and in my mind's eyes, I still am able to move through canyons and flat places as though I had a map. To the north the land sometimes opened into grassy valleys. After a rain, pentstemon and Indian paintbrush flowers came like drops of blood against the reddish earth. To the south were limestone hillsides with yellow roses and squawberry bushes with tart, bitter berries that Mother and I made into pies and jam. The Santa Fe railroad tracks made part of the southern boundary of the ranch. There was a railway section house named Corva, and near it sweat lodges used by the men who worked there. When a steam engine went past us once while we were mending a fence, my father said that might be the last one I'd see. There was dark and porous volcanic rock here, and clumps of tall pines, sometimes enclosing open parks. The Forest Service placed road markers wherever one dirt road crossed another, but mileage markers seldom added up. Every year I mourned the end of summer desperately, when I would have to go back to boarding school, comforted only by Mr. Bargeman's saying I was more useful than the cowboys they'd be hiring for roundup.

For me the years on the Double A, summers really, came at just the right time, and I was the right child for the experience, fascinated by it all and wanting to learn. Had I been male, I might have stayed and kept the ranch, I don't know. The temptation to marry a cowboy—the only way I could see of continuing there—was very great, but I must not have been quite as romantic as my father. (And I expect also I had sense enough to see that marrying a cowboy was not the same as being one, the wives I knew being even more confined to house and housework than my own mother.) As it was, I had had all the pleasures, the work, and the knowledge about ranching without the worry, surely a reason many children brought up on farms and ranches thrived and remember them so fondly, without having remained there.

While cattle prices always were low, the Double A did all right as a business, but once we children had left for school and college, I think the ranch seemed to my parents more an anxiety than a pleasure. The hot summer winds made everyone nervous; people hallucinated clouds, looking for rain. Mr. Bargeman left, victim again to the alcoholism that he could control only for a few years at a time. He had come home on horseback very late one night, left his horse saddled in the corral and walked sulkily to his house. I unsaddled and fed the horse, appalled, I remember, at what was happening, that ranch life was ending for us. The last summer there I came home to find that the Double A had been sold. I helped pack, and drove the pickup of furniture to Tucson, where my parents were moving. It had rained just before I reached the city. The desert was ablaze with flowers, and the air had that unimaginable freshness the desert takes on after rain. If nothing else, the ranch had given me a feel of land and landscape.

Indeed I realized at the Double A that people living in a place could form their identities in it, they could make themselves part of that place. I longed to participate in such alchemy, to belong, in some secret way, to the mountains and canyons and small towns of Northern Arizona. Some of Mr. Bargeman's relatives worked on the Santa Fe railroad, and when I'd hear them list section houses along the line, it was as though these residents were joined into the names. Such intimacy was exotic to me, seductive, but it did not take me long to realize I was not likely to achieve it. Nothing in my past had allowed such connections. The "Foreign Service life" did not permit very long residence anywhere; and in addition, I knew that while the Consular Service in Stuttgart had provided me with papers alleging I had been born "on American soil," it was no soil to stand upon. Yet those are merely happenstances, and even I could tell that belonging to a place had to be a deeper phenomenon. My mother would speak about Meadville, Pennsylvania, where she had been born and lived until she was eleven, with what sounded to me like a taking-for-granted proprietary attachment that partly identified her and that she would not lose. On a car trip to the East Coast in 1950, she and my father drove through Meadville. She wrote back that the town was much the same except for fewer trees in the front yard of the family's house and a gas station at the corner. It happened to be Baccalaureate Sunday, and the college faculty members were lined up in caps and gowns on the church lawn. It was "a special grace" to have seen it, she said.

My father, on the other hand, did not appear to me to think of himself as belonging anywhere in particular. He had grown up in Hartford, Connecticut, a town he always mocked, once pointing out to my mother an entire magazine page of Miss Rheingold contestants from Hartford and saying, "Now you see why I didn't marry a Hartford girl." We children called him by his name, Shiras (he was named for an ancestral Scottish judge), as though, I now wonder, he appeared hardly to have familial identity either—we would not have dreamed of calling him Dad or Father. (He complained once that "Shiras" did not show much respect, so for half a day we imitated stories in *St. Nicholas* magazines of Mother's we'd been reading and addressed him as "Governor," until he called it off.) Certainly there were places that drew him, particular ridges and valleys he'd ride out of his way for on the ranch, and he loved the city of Guadalajara, where he was assigned his first consular post, and where he returned in old age. But he did not appear to me to absorb his identity from any particular location.

Such a question of "belonging" to a locale I do not suppose would have occurred to me had my family not ever returned to the United States. In our first two or three years in this country, I could not have felt more a foreigner; it took me weeks to realize that a school "notebook" was nothing more complicated than a copybook, or *cuaderno* as we called it in second and third grade at the Crandon Institute in Montevideo. Montevideo must have been my Meadville, where everything I knew was orderly, in exquisite peace. The school I went to gave instruction half the day in Spanish, the other half in English. I could go up and down the aisles in the classroom and name every child: Felicia and Alicia, both with ringlets and each other's best friends; Jaime ("James" in English, I realized years later); red-haired Gloria and the rest. There were highly competitive jacks and rope-jumping on the playground, and roller-skating in formation to music in the basement gymnasium. The second grade provided the corps of angels for a school production of "Hansel and Gretel." Initially, and sensibly enough given my inability to carry a tune, the chorus did not include me; but when one of the angels took sick, I was put in her place. Those details are in Mother's letters to her parents; I remember only the bliss of wings and pink chiffon. One year I carried the American flag for a Fourth-of-July program, something that in Latin America can hardly now be the pure festival it was then. Our family left Montevideo in 1942. On the way to the port to board the night ship across the Rio de la Plata to Buenos Aires, we took Juanita home. Of all the people who had worked in our household, she was the one I felt closest to. We left her with her boxes in front of her house on the paving. While the taxi drove away through the narrow dark streets of Montevideo, I could see out the back window that she was waving. I felt sad in a new way for these endings. I would not see Juanita again, nor a way of life that had been so entirely satisfying to me.

To my delight, almost fifty years after that departure I am again in Uruguay, this time by myself, on leave from university teaching. I live in the summer house of the family of acquaintances, in a seacoast town, an hour and a half by bus from Montevideo. I arrived in midwinter. The village is on sand bluffs above miles of beaches, dunes, pine and eucalyptus trees, and small tidy houses nearly all empty this time of year. Besides shopkeepers, I seem almost the only inhabitant; a few summer people come on weekends to putter in their yards, their children turned loose on bicycles. The house I am borrowing is constructed against the heat of summer, with concrete walls, tile floors, lots of windows and a wide veranda that ensures the sun does not reach into them. By what I'm used to, this is hardly winter, and I enjoy devising schemes against the noticeable chill.

The only English I read is what I write myself (along with letters from friends, to be sure), or hear from the BBC Worldwide Service on the shortwave radio. It is an extraordinary experience, this respite one usually only dreams of. It comes after twenty-some years of living in the same house, in Grand Forks, and teaching in the same English department, at the University of North Dakota, longer than I have ever lived in any one place. Five children have grown and left home, although thirty years of marriage to my husband Richard have not matched this semblance of permanence. Returned from a year's teaching in Beijing, China, he had become so engrossed in that culture, I am supposing, that he could not continue supporting our two lives together. And so I find myself by myself, not always quite sure how to behave without a companionship that for me for so long had seemed firm and very rich. Right now, it suits me well to be a stranger, puzzling my way among a society that looks fixed and of long habit, with the stranger's priviledge of exploring other people's haunts, and permission to be inept. North Dakota, lost at the top of the map, is a state that no one even wants to drive through if they can help it. Nevertheless, I prize living there. I have built friendships and enough familiarity with the state that I look forward to returning. Yet for now, it is a relief to be obviously from away; even living in someone else's house makes me feel at home.

The first time I left Uruguay, I was right to think that my own connections to the world would not again be as benign. Our family next lived in a Washington, D.C., suburb while my father worked at the State Department. As the new kid in school, I was asked, as children always ask, where was I from? I tried "Uruguay," but no one knew where that was, so I said I was born in Germany, which got me sent home for a note, the school authorities anxious about German spies. I settled on claiming New Hampshire, in deference to my grandmother's having had me and my sister and brother at her farm there for the summer. That satisfied inquiries on the playground, but the question keeps coming, until it has occurred to me that "Where are you from?" is a judgment to the effect that one is not "from" wherever the conversation is taking place. When I travel about North Dakota, someone is bound to ask where am I from, and they don't mean Grand Forks; outsiders are assumed to be on their way to somewhere else. To elect to live in North Dakota, and to make an effort to stay there, appears to the locals as somewhat unusual.

Thus to be "from" somewhere I have supposed must be a gift, like the ability to carry a tune, that comes irrespective of class, educational experience, or whether one moves often, or travels. It is not particularly connected to knowing the history, the topography, or the origin of place names, but comes, it is my guess, with a kinetic sense of space. In North Dakota people identify not the town they live in or near, but name the county. In Uruguay people locate a school, a town, or their bus stop at the kilometer marker on the highway radiating from Montevideo, where at the capitol building begins kilometer 0. To such a method of thinking, other kinds of place-name information must seem arcane. In North Dakota, I have yet to find anyone among classrooms of students or audiences in other towns I might be talking to who knows the origin of the name of the town of Carpio. But even as people smile while I tell them (according to a WPA state guide, the first post office was in a railway car, so one went to the Car P.O.), they know that they are the ones "from" North Dakota, and I am not. Speech certainly is one of the markings of the stranger, the person who does not sound quite right; speech can be the passport to a very particular identification. Richard, who feels his origins in Southern Ilinois much as Mother did hers in Meadville, uses the phrase "in my dialect" to name variations he grew up with. In that sense, I cannot claim a dialect.

But certain regions attract me strongly, others I resist living in. The West draws me: the ranch in Northern Arizona, and Flagstaff where I went to college; Montana and Washington that gave me graduate school; and North Dakota where I feel I thrive now. To the East and Midwest I sense little connection. The

New England landscape is beautiful, but my grandmother was too stern and dour for me to want to linger. The Hudson River Valley, where the boarding school was located, in the 1940s was tree-filled, but I desperately resisted being at that school. And the agricultural Midwest, the much-sung heartland of America, where Richard had his first teaching job at Ohio State, sunk me into faculty-wifery. I felt alien to those parts.

This attraction toward or alienation from places is certainly colored not only by topography and landscape, but by the people or events associated with a place. One's "sense of place," I would assume, is inevitably confounded or enriched or at least complicated by whatever social situations or elements of personal affection happen to go with it. For me, the Mississippi River makes none too removed a boundary from territories I do not really want to inhabit again if I can help it. That prejudice I know I owe to a disquieting attachment to my grandmother who lived in Hartford, Connecticut, and Concord, New Hampshire.

Grandmother Morris was rich as she was strict; she was generous, and she wanted to be kind. Every Christmas, in addition to the books, she sent a box of clothes; in it, my best dress for the coming year, smocked, of soft wools or flowered cotton prints. Cousin Ronny, at about age ten, one later Christmas when I was visiting her, put just right her benevolent and stern materialism. His father was trying to get him bundled up to go home. Ronny stood on the top step between the dining room and parlor, looking over the ravages of tissue paper, and said, "Well, Grandmother, it certainly has been profitable." She welcomed us to her house in Hartford when my parents made their sporadic holiday leaves to the United States from distant consular posts. I remember a party she gave—I must have been about five and Charly and Felicia stairsteps beneath me—that still holds one of the exquisitely tactile moments of my life. The three of us discovered the silky black velvet, and very large, behind of one of the guests. Close together in a row we stroked that vast and soft posterior. How Grandmother carried off the rest of the evening after spotting us, I cannot think.

Facts, in this part of the family, are hard to come by. One fact nobody knew was Grandmother's age. She would not tell, and not even her children—my father, his younger brother (our Uncle Judson), and their sister (Aunt Grace)—knew how old she was. Oddly, I was the one to find out. In 1950, a census year, I happened to be with Grandmother in Hartford during a holiday from college when the census forms arrived. Grandmother was in bed with sciatica, which troubled her severely, and she told me to fill out part of the forms. An item asked for numbers of rooms in the house. There was a lovely circular staircase, and rounded hallways at either end; bedrooms had dressing rooms; there were pantries and maids' rooms. I called a "room" anything with four walls, a door and a window, and counted seventeen. Grandmother was furious. This was a small house, taxes would ruin her, how could I be so stupid? When she folded the forms and sent me to mail them, because they were not in an envelope, I could read the top lines by forcing the bundle into a tube. That was how I learned that in 1950 Grandmother was seventy-seven years old.

The least mysterious fact about Grandmother Morris was her being rich. The wealth was largely of her own making, and had begun with a small hardware manufacturing plant in Hartford that her husband left her when he died. She invested money cannily, into the Ford Motor Company when few thought that automobiles had a future, and into the Xerox Corporation at a similarly dubious time in its beginnings. She spent her mornings on the telephone at a small table in the upstairs hallway in conversation with her broker, Charles Cooley of the Connecticut Bank and Trust, names I still remember.

During the three summers of our family's years in the East before the move to Arizona, Charly, Fifi, our cousins Jay and Ronny, and I stayed at Dingleton, Grandmother's estate in New Hampshire. These summers elevated Grandmother from a mere distant sender of packages to an emphatic presence in our lives. Dingleton had been a farm once, on a wooded hill almost directly across the Connecticut River from Windsor, Vermont. Even the drive from town was dominated by Grandmother's force: from the highway that follows the river, she would cut into the wooded side road, rushing her station wagon in high gear up the very steep gravel road and shifting without stalling just before the first hairpin turn. Before long the road opened onto a meadow bound by a log fence, where her horses grazed, the banks on the upper side of the road heavy with blackberries. A little farther, the land opened again, enough for a large house, and gardens, barn, and pastures. You can walk beyond the edge of the vast lawn behind the house, where grass is cut for hay, and down a short but darkly shaded path to a lookout among the trees for a view of the Connecticut River and the White Mountains of Vermont. In early summer, there are strawberries underfoot.

After its time as a farm, Dingleton had been bought by two women who took summer art lessons from the painter St. Gaudens, who lived on the next estate on the same steep hill. The women had designed Dingleton's Georgian house, its pillared veranda supporting grapevines, its large kitchen, pantry, dining room, hallway, parlor, and what was referred to as the billiard room. From there (the room now is lined with books), a corkscrew staircase, where children were not allowed, led to Aunt Grace's bedroom and then down a long hall past Grandmother's room and two guest rooms. The back stairs led to a series of little wood-paneled maids' rooms above the kitchen that were given over to us children during the Dingleton summers. A wide wooden staircase led from the center of the upstairs corridor down to the front hall, where stood the most distinctive memento of the St. Gaudens ladies, a female portrait bust carved into an oak post in the front hall. Polished bare breasts met one exactly at eye level—you could hardly avoid the object either coming down the stairs or approaching from the front door. The post was the subject of much ribaldry among us children, although we never heard a grown-up remark about it.

Dingleton harbored a multitude of livestock: eight or ten horses of highly bred dispositions; bantam chickens; two sheep; a herd of goats; pigeons; two Afghan hounds; several cocker spaniels; and stray barn cats. Except for occasional hired men, Grandmother and Aunt Grace took care of all these animals themselves. I adored Aunt Grace. She was in her twenties and only fourteen years older than I (and if anything, even more strict with us children than Grandmother). Grace rode in horse shows and taught, or tried to teach, us children to ride. There was a Shetland pony who rushed at clotheslines to rid us off her back, and a Morgan mare that regularly ran away with me, and when she returned to the stable in foams of sweat, it was up to me to walk her until she cooled off. I learned to milk goats. I cleaned out stalls, and herded goats to the vast back lawn turned to pasture, where I tied their ropes to stakes. The chickens were unrelievedly nasty. Two Russian wolfhounds were let out of their pen each evening, and if I had not found some excuse to be indoors, they invariably sought me out in bounding leaps and knocked me down.

How Grandmother and Aunt Grace managed such a conglomeration of animals, gardens, woods and fields, buildings and machinery, to say nothing of five children, still amazes me. Perhaps survival had to have depended on strict discipline. One afternoon while I was riding, the other children turned to hurling the bantam chickens over the chicken house fence to watch them fly. When discovered by Grace, they were chased with a buggy whip to the house, where Grandmother sent them to bed and fed them supper out of dog pans. Little wonder we were docile when returned to our parents. Mother wrote of one of these returns:

> The children have grown so—Bitsy [my nickname] $1^1/_2$ inches since she went away, and Charly and Fifi each an inch. They have improved greatly too under their grandmother's tutelage and insist on making their own beds every morning and are so helpful and so happy about helping. They seem to have enjoyed their summer, but they're happy to be at home again too. They all have the fortunate dispositions of enjoying the present and the place where they are, and I don't think they are ever homesick, either for home or for Windsor.

Grandmother's passion was for the animals. Years before, driving through an industrial New England town, she had seen in someone's window a chicken trapped inside a bottle. Her outrage did not stop with berating the owner. She joined the SPCA and ever after used her barn and stables as hostelries for sick and injuried horses and other livestock. At Dingleton, no animal was killed or left to die unattended, and some years the stables resembled an animals' retirement home. There was a moral edge to almost everything Grandmother did, and with us children it was as though we were so in need of improvement she did not know when to stop. She took us for treats at the drugstore soda-fountain, but sneered at ice-cream flavors that were not chocolate, because, she'd say, they had no "character." Her scorn for people who chose strawberry was withering. Whenever she said to me, sternly, "Remember who you are," I knew that what she meant was I'd done something to disgrace her sense of who *she* was, for I was in trouble most of the time. Even during our earliest visits, in the garden in Hartford I'd lose my way among the long paths between clipped hedges that I could not see over or quite reach the ends of. I'd fall out of the high four-poster bed I was put into, and every night knew I was bound to awaken on the floor.

During the Dingleton summers, she liked to take us for drives in the wood-paneled station wagon that we termed a "banana wagon." There would be stops at historical markers, and if at supper we children could not name which Revolutionary general had done what at which site, we forfeited dessert. We played games naming state capitals; we learned the names of countries and their capitals and principal minerals. Children should know facts and stay out of trouble, she thought, and saw to it that we did both. The library room had a complete set of *Mother Westwind* books, and a "girls' series" set during the American Revolution. I read many years of the *Reader's Digest* and romantic novels like *A Lantern in Her Hand.*

When I was a little older than during the summers at Dingleton, I stayed with Grandmother in Hartford during school holidays. She lived by herself then, as Grace had married, and while Grace had only moved to West Hartford and visited nearly every day, Grandmother felt alone. It may have been that by now she thought I was old enough to listen, and in the city house there were not all the chores with animals and gardens to keep track of. In any event, Grandmother liked to talk, and these were my best times with her. She might be sitting on a kitchen stool after washing up the dishes or sitting by the small side table in the dining room next to the windows after breakfast (always oatmeal porridge because it "stuck to your ribs"), and she'd tell me about her children. There was my Uncle Judson, who had run off to college at Stanford; she still held it against him that he had gone so far beyond the civilized pale of the Connecticut River.

Her disapproval of my father rested largely on his having married my mother. Nevertheless, Grandmother was proud of Shiras, but I doubt she let him know. She told of how at college at Harvard he was to sing in a comic performance (it may have been "The Hasty Pudding Show"), and, forgetting lines to a song, made up others on the spot that were funnier than the original. She brought herself to tears telling of the time she went to his graduation to discover he was receiving honors and had not mentioned the fact. "I thought you'd expect it," was all Shiras had said. She visited him and my mother at his Foreign Service post in Germany, where others told her how kind he was and how good at his work. She told me these stories, I felt, rebukingly, as though I did not live up to him. She made people feel—my father and me especially—that we would never be able to do well enough to suit her, but that her disapproval came mainly because she loved us more fiercely than any love we could return.

My last visit to Grandmother Morris was in 1963 (if my look at her census form was correct, she would have been ninety), when I was married and living in Columbus, Ohio. I took Sarah, the oldest of our then three children, along to show her off, but also for protection, I suspect. The visit did not go very well. Sarah, far from awed, ignored her great-grandmother and climbed on the furniture. Grandmother's angry conversation those days was directed against anyone who opposed Richard Nixon or had it in mind to run a freeway through her house (which as far as I know has not happened). She died not many months later, but her presence is not one I am likely to shake off.

There was a reception one year given by the Virginia Woolf Society at the Newberry Library in Chicago. I went partly as an escape from the Modern Languages Association meeting in the Palmer House, where like hundreds of others who teach in college English departments, I was to read a paper. I had never seen the Newberry, the famous scholar's haven. It was winter, and raining in early evening, and I remember the light and opulence when I stepped inside the building—the high ceilings, dark wood, heavy furniture. The reception was in an upstairs room. There, women in long tweed skirts with uneven hems, wearing shawls or hip-length cardigans, were nibbling raw vegetables. Strange imitations, they appeared, of photographs of Virginia Woolf. The scents of sherry and moist wool and furniture polish took me away from literature and back to my grandmother's house and her severe instruction about the history and confirmation of Queen Anne chairs—forbidding me to sit on them.

But there was another more tangible trace of her here. Leaving the library, I stepped into a side gallery to admire the woodwork—bookcases with glass doors, carved arm chairs. Above the framed doorway of polished oak that I had come through was a portrait of a young woman in a rose Empire-style dress. Astonishing to me, the brass plaque identified her as the Duchess of Oldenberg, the name "Oldenberg" long fraught for me with mystery and scandal. The mouth and chin of the face in the portrait were exactly like my sister's, and the upper part, large eye sockets and high forehead, could have been my own. The painting looked to me like a prankster's combination of Felicia and me, and indeed might be, if the story I'd heard was at all correct.

Grandmother's parents had come from Germany, I'd been told, where her father was gardener to the Duke of Oldenberg. The family had arrived in the United States with more children than they could manage. Two infant daughters were placed for adoption; one, my great-aunt Ceceel, went to a family in New

York, and my grandmother went to a family named Root in Hartford. It may well have been that the father of my grand-mother was not the gardener to the Duke of Oldenberg, but the Duke himself, and that the parentage was a motive for allowing the little girls to be adopted. I know no more than that, but standing in the Newberry Library, it pleased me to suppose that the Duchess of Oldenberg with the somewhat bemused expres-sion on her face might be a distant relation of mine.

An uncertain heritage this, whether royally connected or not. During each of my Hartford Christmases, there would come an afternoon when an elderly man appeared at the door carrying an enormous box of gladiolus. The flowers were for Grandmother, who would accept the box but not invite him in. He was her brother, she said once, and that was all. Grandmother was vain about her slim and narrow feet—a shoe salesman had said, she liked to tell, that she "didn't have feet, she had slivers." The feet of the bringer of gladiolus were very large, I could not help noticing, and the dark suit he wore was in the style of a European workman.

Grandmother had traveled to Tucson for my parents' wed-ding, and mentioned the Lockwood family always with respect, but she never visited us on the ranch. As I said, beyond the Connecticut River, her map was populated by monsters around its edges. But her niece, our Cousin Faith, did come during our fifth summer there. It was the occasion for Shiras making our first family excursion to the Grand Canyon, eighty miles away, which, he always assured us when anyone became impatient to see this natural wonder of the world, would still be there when we did go. Cousin Faith was the daughter of Grandmother's sis-ter Ceceel, whom I remember as having a sanguine, even ebul-lient disposition. Cousin Faith may be even more cheerful and energetic than her mother. She was then curator of French eigh-teenth-century silver at the Metropolitan Museum as well as an inveterate world traveler. I think she and my father felt more closely drawn to each other than to any other relatives, and there were numerous trips she and my parents made together. She was full of enthusiasm for the ranch—on the day the two of us took a ride to a stand of flowering century plants on the top of a limestone ridge, she made me feel the sight was as spectacular as anything she had come upon in other continents.

I do not know why Grandmother should have been so angry at the world in general, but it makes me sad. She had her sorrows—her husband's death when my father was in college, and she spoke still of the event as though it had been recent. Sciatica troubled her always, a pain hardly conducive to cheerfulness, but I should not think circumstances alone altogether account for her unhappiness. When my parents became fed up with a fit of my bad temper and would say, "You are just like your grandmother," I felt very badly, although I know there are respects in which I do resemble her. I look like her, I am built rather like her. Like her, I can be fairly fierce, or so friends tell me. So, while I consider myself far from a discontented person, I think I have an idea that what drove her rages came partly from the strongest aspects of her character. Despite her conservative, not to say reactionary, politics, I can share her exasperation when things are badly done, or wasted, or when land and animals are mistreated. Grandmother Morris was a brilliant manager—of money, of her strange estate—and whatever she turned to was done with forbidding competence, traits I certainly admire. She was a wonder at wrapping packages—paper folded into sharp corners, string so taut it snapped. It was dangerous to be the one to place a finger where she tied the knot, but I am in awe of the hazard she created.

It was not only that she taught me to make my bed and wash my socks, but that for all her and Aunt Grace's exactitudes, work became interesting and worth doing ("well," they would have said). I learned to milk, to ride, to curry a horse, to clean out horse and goat stalls; I learned the names of the parts of the horse and what various straps on saddles and bridles are called. Grandmother paid us ten cents an oatmeal box for picking wild blackberries, and then I joined her in the jam-making, a production I still go through, every summer, wherever I am with whatever fruit is at hand. I would say that, at a ten-to-twelve-year-old level during those Dingleton summers, I became moderately competent in a few skills. I began to see the advantage of knowing how to do things, and it even dawned on me, although more slowly and through the murk of boredom, that a grasp of information could be useful. My impression is that Grandmother thought the world a dark and lonely place, where few were likely to be one's companions, and if anything was to be accomplished, you had best be prepared to do it yourself. Without subscribing to the whole of her dour vision, I feel sympathetic to the substance of her critique, enough to value competence and self-sufficiency.

She disapproved of our family's move west, and was disappointed in her expectations of me. As for me, I was least afraid of her in those moments when she was least anxious, or least in pain, and we'd be cooking jam or weeding a garden plot together, or when she would get into her story-telling mood, and a geniality and humor escaped her. When I listened to Leslie Fiedler's lectures in Montana on Hawthorne's novels, I realized that Fiedler was presenting the Puritanism of New England as though it were to him some distant anthropological rite. I said to him once that those people and their ideas were still there, and I had a grandmother to prove it. She was entirely New England (whatever that means), and I know that she is in my bones.

I expect one's sense of place is deeply psychic; I doubt we are moved by or drawn to mountains, deserts, rivers, woodlands, coast lines, or amber waves of grain alone and in a vacuum, but imperceptibly respond to them in combination with whatever human circumstances connect us to them. Hardly anything can be more lovely than the New England landscape—the view from the almost secret lookout beyond the lawn at Dingleton could grace a Christmas card—yet the briefest visit east of the Hudson renews my conviction that that is where medieval monsters lie.

Jon Hassler

Anniversary

I am home from the drugstore with the Sunday paper and a dozen ball-point pens, all of them red. I leave the paper in the living room for Donna, and I am halfway up the stairs to my den when I suddenly realize that today is an anniversary. I return to the kitchen and pour two glasses of sherry. On this date ten years ago, my wife and I and eleven hundred others filed into the University of Minnesota football stadium and were given, with a full measure of blessings and addresses, our degrees. We both were twenty-two at the time. The principal speaker was a bishop who said that life was short.

Carrying the two wineglasses, I step out the back door into the sunshine. Robbie, eight, is golfing across the lawn with my putter, digging up grass as he goes along. Donna is on her knees in the garden, loosening the soil around the rosebushes.

"What? Ten years?" says Donna. "I can't believe it." She smiles and sits back on her heels and takes the glass in her large, dirty garden glove. As we toast a number of things, including my ten years as a high-school teacher, a warm June breeze stirs her red hair and uncovers at the temples a trace of gray. Life is short, said the bishop.

"We will go out to dinner," I announce. "After I finish my schoolwork, you and Robbie and I will go someplace for a festive dinner."

"Don't tell me you're planning to spend the day in the den," says Donna. "Sunday is no day for correcting papers."

"Final grades are due in the office tomorrow morning. My briefcase is full of the scraps of the school year. Odds and ends."

We toast odds and ends; then Donna picks a blossom from the Flaming Peace rosebush and hands it to me. It has a long, thorny stem. Robbie joins us and I give him a sip of sherry, which he spits on the grass.

"Make reservations for three at some fancy place," I tell Donna. "We're stepping out when my work is done."

Upstairs in my den, I set the bottle of sherry on the window sill and I hang the rose by its thorns in the burlap draperies. It is a small blossom, unfurling from a tomato-colored bud. My window overlooks the garden, and as I crank it open Donna calls up to me, "Promise you won't be up there for the rest of the day."

I have never known Donna to be jealous of another woman, but I have at times a great appetite for solitude, and she is jealous of this room in which I find it. Once while working on my thesis, I spent fourteen days and nights in here, emerging only for sandwiches and a bath or two, and she never got over it. She said life was passing me by. And one day last winter, designing a new syllabus, I came in here and worked for twenty-two straight hours, and she broke down and wept. She said her mother had warned her about men who were consumed by their work.

I settle into my deep leather chair and open my briefcase. It is full of quizzes, exams, themes, term papers and office mail—everything I was too busy to read when it first crossed my desk at school. Some of it goes back several months. I reach in and pulled out a paper at random. It is an essay by Becky Burke titled "My Father."

Becky writes with a backward slant and she misspells all but the simplest words. She says here that she loves her father. "He has old fashion ideas," she writes, "and he argues with the length of my skirts but he is patient and he has a sence of humer." She tells of how he used to take her every summer to a "rodio." But now her father is not well. He has been in the hospital for six weeks. Becky fears he will die.

I want to write something tender in the margin, but if I am to read everything in my briefcase this afternoon, I must be off to a quick start. With my red pen I write, "Proofread!" across the top of the paper, and I give her a *C*. By English Department standards a *C* is too generous for spelling like Becky's, but I cannot give a girl with a dying father a *D*.

A sudden cold wind springs through the window, billowing the draperies. Clouds cover the sun and the room darkens. Cranking the window shut, I see a flock of geese flying south—the wrong direction for June.

Next I read a letter from Dale Wood, president of the teachers' union. He wants me to serve for a year as union griever. Although I pay my dues, I am not much of a union man. I lost my enthusiasm years ago when the union went to court to defend a junior-high drama coach who undressed on stage. (Academic freedom, claimed the union; but the judge said nonsense and sent the drama coach somewhere for observation.) Yet Dale Wood has been a friend of mine for a long time. When we golf together he tells hilarious stories. In the margin of the letter I print, in red: "Okay, one year only."

My red ink does not glisten as it should. I try the other pens I bought this morning, but none is any fresher. I have been sold a dozen dry pens. In my desk I have learned to understand the power of red ink. Red is alarming, decisive. Red puts everything else in the background. When I hand back a student's paper my red ink leaps out at him, and everything he wrote in blue ink has turned insignificant, powerless, faint. Red has the same effect with letters and memos. When I print my response in red it looks, no matter how innocuous the words, like a shout. If I leave my mark in this world, it will be a red mark. Red has force. But today my lettering is pale. It seems to fade before my eyes.

The wind grows stronger. Donna calls to me from the bottom of the stairs. She says she is going to take Robbie to his driving lesson and they will return in an hour. For a moment I am puzzled. Robbie is eight; he does not drive. She must mean she is taking him to the driving range. She must be bored.

"It's awfully windy for driving golf balls," I call to her, but she is gone. I hear the car drive away.

Another letter. This one too is from Dale Wood. Is this his idea of a joke? He writes, "You have doubtless received a letter of official thanks from the union office, but let me add my personal note of gratitude for the way you handled your job as

griever these past several years. I know it's never an easy job. . ."
My pen is poised but I can think of nothing to print in the margin. Sometimes Dale tries too hard for a joke. There is nothing
harder to respond to than a poor joke. I set his letter aside.

Next in my brief case I find an ad from the publishers of my
American-literature text. It says that the new edition, soon to
appear, will contain nothing earlier than *Leaves of Grass*.
Walden will be replaced by a report from the National Ecology
Council, and *Huckleberry Finn* by an assortment of comic
strips. The book is to be called Superlit. I write "Supertrash"
across the ad and drop it into the wastebasket. I pour myself
another glass of sherry. It is the color of a rosebud, and smooth.

Donna calls up the stairs: "I am not feeling well." Her voice
is husky.

"Are you back already?" I ask.

"I believe I'll lie down."

"Fine, Donna. Lie down. Where is Robbie?"

"Rob is over at Angeline's. I'm sure I'll be all right if I lie
down."

"Angeline's? Who is Angeline?"

There is a trace of steam on the window. I wipe it off and
look down at the garden. The Flaming Peace petals are drifting
to the ground. Well, it has never been a hardy bush. To get it
started, Donna nursed it through four summers without blossoms, and to this day it is easily discouraged by a sudden cold
snap or a sharp wind.

I resume reading. This is Alvin Turvig's essay on "Memories."
Who is Alvin Turvig? I have never heard of Alvin Turvig. He
writes, "My earliest memory is of my family watching, on TV,
American troops invading Panama." I read no further. In red I
print, "Yours must be the shortest memory in Adams High
School," and I move on.

Here is a letter from Cletus Hamsun, who sells insurance in
St. Paul. Cletus is the only college classmate I still correspond
with. In this letter he seems to be straining, like Dale Wood, to
make a joke. He says that he is retiring from the insurance business. He says that he and his wife from now on will spend their
winters in El Paso. "Why don't you and Donna join us?" he

writes. As I said before, a poor joke leaves me with no reply. I put a red question mark in the margin.

I take a sip of sherry and feel hairs or threads on my lip. Holding the glass up to the light, I pick from the rim the strands of a cobweb. There are raindrops on the window. Outside, a robin with an ebony eye stands on an elm twig, glancing nervously about him at the leaves shaken by the rain. The leaves of the tree are yellow. Can my elm be dying?

Another paper, this one by Peter Turvig. Peter Turvig? Who are these Turvigs? He writes, "My uncle Alvin, who can remember all the way back to the early '70s, is home on vacation. Yesterday he taught me how to fix the brakes on my bike. He goes back to work next week. He is on the staff of the U.S. Embassy in the Republic of Antarctica." This is nonsense. This is fiction written by an imposter. In red I write, "Who are you?"

Rain streams down the window. Here is another letter from Cletus Hamsun. It was mailed in Texas. It has a black border, and it reads, "Sorry to hear about Donna. All the more reason for you to join us in El Paso."

Daylight is fading. I open a letter from someone named Angeline. The envelope is scented.

Dear Dad,

We are settled at last in a house of our own, with a guest room ready for you whenever you want to use it. I know how lonely you must be, all by yourself.

Rob has been given a nice raise, but I think he is working too hard. I tell him if he isn't careful, life will pass him by. He sends his love.

My strength drains suddenly away. With great effort I brush the perfumed letter off my lap, and it falls to the floor and lies among a scattering of dusty rose petals as the rain, turning to sleet, hits the window with a ping.

Gordon Henry, Jr.

from The Light People
Arthur Boozhoo on the Nature of Magic

I'm different, you may have noticed. I was raised far away in a city. My father went there under relocation to work for a utility company, electrical people. After a few years he died; he was falling, they say, and to save himself he reached up and grabbed at some wires and was electrocuted on the spot. I was ten. We moved around quite a bit after that. We lived with my aunties and uncles, but there were so many of us we caused hardship, so we didn't stay in one place long. About four years later, my mother met a man somewhere when she was out drinking with her sisters. They married, but the man didn't want anything to do with us, so they sent all the kids away to live with our grand-parents. By then I was seventeen, and I made up my mind to stay in the city.

While my brothers and sisters returned to the rez, I got work part-time in a candy factory, and I was doing pretty good for a while. In a few months I bought a car and I could drive all over. I drove to see my mother once at a place in San Francisco, but the visit didn't seem to mean much to her so I left. After a year or so I got letters from my grandparents here asking me to come back, but I had already decided to go to college part-time. After I wrote back to tell them about my plans, they wrote and told me I could go to school full-time with tribal funding, at a school closer to the reservation. Instead I applied and got financial aid to attend college at San Jose State the next fall. At first I wanted to study everything, but after two or three terms, a counselor told me I should consider one field. I chose drama. I felt I could act, and that if I chose many different roles maybe I'd find the one I was closest to and live it. While I was taking the drama course work, I got involved with a group of people who believed that everyone has a personal magic that they can ignore or use. We'd all meet once a week to discuss those mystical concepts and study magic. By the end of the year all but two people had dropped out of the group. So there was just me and one woman. At our last meeting she told me the only reason she stayed in the group was because she loved me. I didn't know what she meant, and I told her I thought she was a very magical person, but I didn't think I loved her. That was the last I saw of her.

But I was in love with magic. So I quit school and I went around the city seeking out magicians and gathering an assortment of tricks and teachings from each one. I also studied magic books, every one I could find. In time I knew enough to make a living from magic, with illusion and memory tricks. But I wasn't sure about things. I kept getting letters from my grandparents and my brothers and sisters. They all wanted me to return to this place, the place of my grandparents, my ancestors. One letter brought me back. My youngest sister was sick. Doctors found no cure, and she was next to death. I got in my car and drove for two days straight.

When I got to my grandparents' house they took me into the room where the girl was dying. The light was such that her head was a shadow growing up from the bed with the floral print of the sheets.

I spoke to her: "Do you know who I am? Can you see me?"

The shadow turned from the window and became a face. I knew then her eyes didn't register. I was unrecognizable, so I moved closer. Grandmother tried to pull me back.

"It's catching, trachoma," she said. "Young people all over the reservation are dying."

But the child's voice moved me forward to the edge of the bed.

"Do you know magic?" she said. "Show me some magic, brother."

"Can you see me?" I said.

"No," she said, "I can't see you, but I remember seeing you."
"Then I can't do magic."

My sister turned her head to the window; sunlight surged out over her face, soaking into her skin, lighting her clearly, as I now see her in my mind.

"I can only see light," she said.

Two days later she died. In a week I came onto the same sickness. I could feel my sight going, but it was like the going had nothing to do with what I saw or what lived outside me. My sight was going from the inside, almost backward, like the memory of the operation of the eyes left out particulars and details, like my head was shoveling the inner light I needed to see into a great mound of expanding and hungry shadows.

I asked my grandfather about magic. "We have none here," he said, "at least not the kind you know, of the hand and the eye and memory games. But there are healers among us, men and women of gifts and visions. Some are relatives of light people. Sometimes their gifts can bring people back. Quite a few people have told us not to believe in those gifts, but with all the sickness around us and no cures by the white doctors, some people have returned to these descendants of the original teachers and bringers of light."

Then the old man took me to Jake Seed and he healed me. When I was well I went to Seed again and asked if he could teach me the magic he had. He told me to come every day and he would decide if he could teach me. I went to his place every day for about four years. Then he put me through a ceremony. After days of preparation and explanation of the meaning of the ceremony, he took me way back into the woods behind his place. We walked up a hill. I dug a hole; he prayed over it and put tobacco down. I stepped down into the hole and waited. Once again he prayed. Then he put a ring of tobacco around me and buried me up to my neck.

Darkness swelled out of the earth swallowing shadows, leaving only the light of animals' eyes and distant stars to compose the sights I saw. I was not there long when animals came shining low to the ground. They moved up to my face, scratching the earth, scratching dirt into my eyes. After a while, minutes, hours, a thousand blue blinks of stars, a hundred rustlings in the trees, animals sat in a circle around me, outside the ring of tobacco, growling and moaning. Then I understood their language and felt fear for all of creation. My thoughts raced in the darkness to find the old man, but my body was still in the hole, nervous, shivering in the cold night dirt. There was no magic to match the feeling; no illusions could pull me from the ground. I waited for power and I sang like I always do when I'm nervous. The first song came out rough, a coarse melody, bent with fear, like a sapling resisting strong wind. The deeper I went into the song the more I felt the fear slacken into a strength of human sound mixing with air and elements. Soon the animals joined in, growling to long musical howls, introspective calls and silences. My own vocals hung on for a long time; note faded into note; song faded into song. There were words and there were not words; there were sounds and there were voices from the once fearful gut, grasping each musical moment. Then, when the songs grew longer, I knew no more of the source of the memorized and invented tones. The animals left. I felt their shadows slink back out of the circle and bolt away, skittering across dirt into the leaves, into the bush. In silence and solitude, I heard footsteps behind me; then laughter careened, in a strange dance. I finally caught sight, out of the corner of my eye, of a small person. At first, I thought he was a child, but as he drew closer I knew he was a little man. He had a small drum in his hand and he sang in laughter.

Red day coming
Red boy dreaming
Red day coming
over the back of clouds

Eye of the Eagle
Swift and Swallow
Red day coming Red boy sings

Then the little man stopped, turned his back to me, and he wheeled back around. He held his enormous penis in his hand and pissed on the ground in front of me, close enough that I could see steam rising from the earth and smell and feel the sprinkle of his spray as he snickered. When he finished he abused me with gruff, untranslatable language, and he kicked dirt into my face. He swung his drumstick and struck the back of my neck with a force that astonished me with pain and the little man's power. I felt the sting of the blow vibrate in violent waves down to my feet. I rocked and twisted in the hole. I screamed, wailing anger. I cried, "Go away." I called to the spirit of god for mercy. But the little man stayed. He clubbed my ears, he crapped in front of me and danced with joy at my pain and degradation. Then I gave up. "Go ahead," I said, "do what you want, I surrender." Right then, in the middle of a wild raucous dance, in the middle of his ridiculing laughter, he stopped and sang again, a song of sorrow.

> *sees the fading stars*
> *sees the northern lights*
> *sees the eyes of animals*
> *all in the face*
> *all in the face*
>
> *the face eats*
> *the face speaks*
> *boy and man*
> *the faces love*
>
> *the faces love the stars*
> *the faces love the ghost lights*
> *the animal faces*
> *the faces eat*
> *the boy and man*
> *speak and eat*
> *the faces they love*

With that the man trudged off toward a huge stone, and walked around and vanished behind it. There the sky was coming onto dawn, and light shone red over and through the eastern trees.

Seed came up then, carrying a basket and a piece of red material. He sat down on the ground a short distance in front of me, took out a tobacco pouch and rolled up a smoke. For a long time he said nothing. Then he got up, reached into his basket, and brought out a plate of food. I smelled the boiled potatoes, and my eyes rested on the boiled meat as he set the plate in front of me. Next to the plate he set down a glass of water. "Let the eyes drink for you. Let the eyes eat for you," he said. Then he picked up the plate and ate the food, bit by bit, in slow reflective mouthfuls. Once in a while he took a sip of water. Throughout the meal he never said a word. When he finished the meal, he took the red material and twisted a handful of tobacco up inside it. Then he tied the material to a tree, toward the east, about fifty feet away from where I was buried.

That day the sun burned the memory of thirst and hunger into me. I grew angry at the sun, at Seed, at myself. I tried to sing again but my throat didn't work in the heat, in dryness. Then I cried. I cried for the rest of the day until the sun went down. At night I tried to sleep, but the animals returned, encircling me and keeping me awake. Just before dawn I heard laughter. I thought of the little man again, but I couldn't see anyone or anything in any direction. At last the sun pushed out red light, and I saw out in the east, on the tree where the tobacco was tied, a woodpecker, one of those big ones, pileated. The bird was laughing, driving its beak into the tree in the dawn light. Light streamed out from each place the woodpecker struck, as if the tree held its own sun inside and the bird conducted the light of that sun out. Time and again the bird backed off, lifted away from the tree, and landed on another part of the tree to peck and strike another place from which light flowed out. One final time the bird did this. Then the bird reached into the tree with its beak and extracted the light in a long bending waving string that followed the course of its flight to where it circled me. Then the woodpecker flew down over the hill out of my sight, with the long string of golden light trailing behind it. From there I saw Seed approaching, and after he dug me out I left the hole and the hill.

By the next spring it was clear that Seed had accepted me as his helper. Through him I learned to assist with ceremonials. At the same time, I continued practicing the magic I learned in the city, among the people of the reservation and the people of nearby communities. I ran ads in local news publications, and I posted my card on bulletin boards outside grocery stores, outside the tribal offices, all over. I got a few jobs but the work wasn't steady, so I started working part-time as a janitor at the Original Man School.

Things were going well for me. I was learning and I had work; I was surviving. Then in the fall I did my magic act for a children's birthday party in a town outside the reservation, in Detroit Lakes. I performed my most difficult tricks with the most success I'd ever had. One was a mentalist memory trick through which I heard, and recited back with my eyes closed, the names and details of clothing of every person at the party. For the other most difficult trick I had the birthday child rip up a piece of his parent's most important correspondence and put the ripped pieces into a fishbowl full of water. Then I threw my magic coat over the bowl and sang.

Sleep, peels, angles of angels sing of sign,
sword of words, elm smells concrete, encore
on the corner, a northern ornithologist, jest
in case, sends a letter which ends in ways to
sway opinion to slice the union onion with a
sword of words, without tears

After that and the conventional magical smoke, the child retrieved the letter from the family mailbox and returned to show everyone that the ripped-up correspondence was whole and dry. Everyone was impressed; I was impressed; the children were impressed; the parents were impressed.

When I returned to the reservation to see Seed, to tell him about my success, a young woman met me at his door. She told me that she was Seed's daughter, Rose Meskwaa Geeshik, that the old man was sick. She had come to see him after a violent disturbing dream and found him sweating, fevered and weak. "He's been reciting names," she said. "Oskinaway, Minogeshig, Broken Tooth, Kubbemubbe, Shagonawshee, Bwanequay, Nawawzhee, Yellowhead, Abetung, Aishkonance—he repeats the names and shivers. I don't know what it means."

In the time I worked with Seed he never mentioned any living family or any children. She took me back to see the old man. I followed her to the back bedroom. Seed slept there, on the bed, wrapped in a star blanket. Sundown named the hour in the window of the room. The songs of faraway crows coruscated into the room in sundown angles. I spoke to him. "Seed," I said, "it's me, Boozhoo. How are you? Seed, wake up; I need to speak to you." For a long time there was no answer. Darkness worked into the room and only an occasional cigarette, the flare of a match, touched off any semblance of sight. After a time Rose asked me to pray with her for Seed. She called on grandfathers, the creator; she spoke of her love for the old man. Her eyes squeezed tight in the intensity of her thought.

> Creator bring him back to us
> he is far away now within the sight of ancestors
> their arms are open across the silver river
> there are giants and abysmal sorrows in the river
> Some of us will float over
> Some of us will find the water solid beneath our feet
> Some will step on the backs of the giants and slide away
> into an angry foam
> Some will sink straight down into a place
> where the river has no bottom
>
> O creator do not take the man
> Dear ancestors sing a song that tells it is not time
> turn him back to us with your song
> Let Seed return to earth

Let the skies drench him again
Let him know again the fragrances of the great mother earth
Let him draw his strength from the love that is here
in my heart.

Rose prayed on and on, crying off and on between the words, at times screaming out into the darkness of the room, with a voice and a hope powerful enough to wake the most distant sleeping star. Still Seed didn't move; his face showed no change. Rose prayed on and on. I wanted to stay awake to help her, but only fear ever kept me from sleeping and at that time I felt no fear: maybe it was Rose's voice, maybe it was the strength I'd seen in Seed in times past, but I felt no fear.

Somehow I have come to sit on a log. After thinking I am asleep, I understand I am awake when a yellow dog crosses in front of me. Voices inside the log tell me I must learn to fly. So I make a man out of tall grass and call him by my own name. Then I throw him into the air and a whirlwind of leaves and human voices carries the grass man away.

Rose woke me at dawn with a gentle hand on my shoulder. "Have some coffee," she said, offering me a yellow cup. "He'll be okay now."

I took the coffee cup from her. "Where's the old man?" I said.

"Sleeping still, but he's okay. I think the fever is gone. He woke up for a few minutes, but he needs rest. You go wash up; I'll fix some breakfast. Then you can go home and get some rest. Come back later; he said he wants to speak to you."

"No," I said. "I'll stay for a while; I can watch him while you get some rest. He's been good to me, I'll stay."

Then I got up and went to the washbowl. There was no water, so I walked outside and worked the pump until water flowed out into the white bowl. When I came back inside Rose had breakfast ready. The table was set with eggs and fried potatoes, fry bread, strawberry jam and honey. Rose poured another cup of coffee for me, and we both ate heartily. After breakfast I went out to the front porch to smoke. The sun had cleared the tallest trees of the reservation by then, and I could hear voices on the road to the church hall. As I lit a cigarette Rose came out and sat down beside me.

"Go inside," I said. "I'll watch the old man as soon as I'm done here."

She looked out into the trees as wisps of black hair licked the bones of her chin and grazed the flatness of her cheek. "I don't know if I can sleep," she said. "I keep hearing the voices out here, I keep thinking of my father, this whole place. You know, where we all come from."

Oshawa's Uncle's Story

This stone has been passed down in our family for a long time. I'm showing it to you now because your grandfather just gave it to me to keep. When you are older then you can hold the stone for your generation.

Your grandfather claims the stone has gifts. Some stones carry earth histories, stories, songs, prayers, so their stone faces hold memories of the existences of other eras; other beings of the earth, air, fire, and water live on, embedded in shapes, in esoteric formations of strata and substrata, in scopic design and microscopic elementals we can only imagine in our limited view of the exterior stone. Beyond the life inside, the stone was also used to kill. The first great weapons relied on stone to kill. So some stones transport memories of death. This is why I believe the Chimookamon uses stones to hold his name while his body rides in the earth in death. As you see, this stone in my hand has those two sides painted on it. Each side tells its story. A person can use the stone to remember, or turn it over and use it as a weapon. Remembering with the stone will keep you safe in creation, since remembrance opens you up to forms of creation. Thus your safety will reside in your willingness to understand the story of the stone and use the story in the stone to understand and create your own story as you remember the stories of our family, our people.

Now as I hold this stone, I feel particular pride in our people, and at this moment, this stone tells me we can't be killed. We can be hurt; we can be changed; we can be consumed by the desires and passions of ourselves and other people; and we can be buried. But as a people we can't be killed. I know because when I was growing up in the old village there was a family living across the road from us in one of those shacks of wood and tarpaper. The head of the family was an old man named Moses Four Bears. He lived in that house with his wife and four children. One winter when I was about sixteen, one of his sons came pounding on the door early in the morning. Both my father and mother were out at the time. Father, I think, had gone to trade some skins for some food at a nearby town. Mother was visiting around the village.

When I went to the door, Four Bears' son said, "Get your father. My father needs your help."

"He's gone," I said. "There's no one else home."

"You come, then," he said.

We crossed the road as an icy wind rose up out of north and west, turning the village white in twisted mists. Inside the shack, the two younger children huddled under blankets near the wood stove while the two eldest girls and old woman Four Bears attended to the old man, who lay stretched out on a sofa. They applied medicine, ground roots, and tobacco, and they dipped cloths in steaming water. The lower part of his leg was gone—the leg was a shortened stump, wrapped in cloth, seeping blood. The cut-off part of the leg sat across the room in a wooden box on a wooden chair.

The old woman spoke as I came into the room. "He drank too much," she said. "Willow"—she raised her head toward her oldest daughter—"found him in that ditch where the sweetgrass grows, around the bend from the liquor store. The foot was frozen, part of the leg too. He had diabetes anyway; if it hadn't froze, it probably would have gone bad. We gave him more alcohol and they cut it off at the clinic in Fineday. I don't know, maybe this will be the end of it. He told us to send for someone, to bury the leg for him."

At that the old man opened his eyes for the first time since I entered the room. "Cut off part of the legging of my dance outfit, from the outfit with the flower and vine work on the lower legging," Four Bears called between clenched teeth. "Put a good moccasin on the foot and then wrap that whole thing up and bring me tobacco."

Willow left the room through the doorway leading to the back of the house. The other older daughter, Esther, drifted over to the table nearby and picked up a wooden bowl from the table against the wall away from the stove. When all was done as said, the old woman brought the leg over and set it down on the floor in front of the couch where the old man lay. The old man rose up to a sitting position, grimacing between words and action. He spoke in the old way, clenching tobacco in his palm. A few tears rolled out with his words, not from pain but from loss and the sincerity of his words, which I comprehended, though I knew only a little bit of the language. When the words stopped he opened his palm and dropped the tobacco into the box, where it fell on the leg in a thin sprinkle. Then the girls wrapped the leg in bright floral-print trade cloth and nailed a lid onto the box.

Four Bears gave me tobacco. "Take the leg out and bury it. But go beyond the cemetery, close to the big river. Just before you get to the riverbank, find a big tree near the bank. Bury the leg there. Take Sonny with you," he signaled with a quick lift of his head and pushed out his lips, toward the boy who sat silently, watching near the wood stove. "When you're done come back here," he said as he lay back down.

The icy wind pulled the door out of my hand and slapped it violently against the house as we went outside. Sonny fought to close the door. I looked back from the road, squeezing the leg into my body with both arms, and saw the boy as a crouching shadow, trudging against the wind to follow me. We crossed the road, stopped back home, and picked out a shovel.

Most of the time the walk to the cemetery doesn't take long. Even when someone dies, the distance is a few miles at most. But the wind ate into the day and spit snow out of winter's whistling mouth in deep, obstructive drifts of cold ghosts, layering a struggle to make it to the burial place with further struggles to make it to nearly invisible landmarks—the one-room library shack of books donated by churches, the bell tower that rang into our Sunday mornings and resonated in our heads as the remembered place of an old priest's flying suicide, the cemetery with all the missing crosses and illegible stones.

By the time we made the cemetery, Sonny looked lost. The wind sang in fear in his eyes. He was too young to go further into the cannibal intensity of that storm, so I told him to turn around and go back home. "I'll bury the leg," I said, taking the shovel. "It's okay, go back."

Then I turned and headed toward the river. I found a tree there, just off the river bank, an expansive birch, an old one. I set the box out and started digging. Under the fallen snow the ground was ice. The shovel bit back in stinging vibrations in my hands as I struck the earth. I struck again and again, but the earth didn't give, and I felt my face and hands flying into the air in numbness. I listened to a voice inside.

Old man Four Bears should have known. You can't do this now. Return the leg to Four Bears. Go back yourself. Sonny will tell them about the cold, this wind. Go back to Four Bears. No, leave the leg; you can't bury this; go back now; find a place for the leg. You'll freeze here if you don't go back now.

I listened to the voice and whirled around looking for a good place on the earth to leave the leg. I saw another tree, big and strong, with barren branches toward the bottom of the bank where the snowed-under weather met the river. I went to the tree and tried to climb up the trunk with the leg under one arm, to another, higher part of the tree, to a place where I could wedge the leg in and lodge it until the storm subsided. Then I thought I could come back and bury it. I did that and headed back.

The whole world was white then. I looked for my tracks on the way back, but the storm covered everything. I had no direction. Places that were so familiar were gone, swallowed by the storm. I kept feeling for my face; I let the shovel fall from my hands, hearing the voice inside telling me which way to go. I stumbled over crosses in the cemetery. I came to the church, imagining the warmth inside, but the big doors were closed and I couldn't get in. I called out, but the wind and the walls of the church consumed my voice, so I went on. Somehow I came out in the back of the library. Again, I struggled to open a door. But snow and cold and wind locked the door. There was no one inside. So I went to the side of the building and punched the window with my numb hands. I struck the window again and again, again and again, until there was space for me to get inside the building.

I fell into the room, my hands bleeding from the broken glass. But even inside, the storm still whirled out. Frigid wind pounded in through the shattered window space, turning papers up on the librarian's desk. A few books fell from shelves with each new blast in the opening in the room. And the room was cold. The old wood stove sat open-mouthed, in one corner, empty, near the only reading table in the place. I thought of fire. I found matches on top of the stove and thought of fire again. I looked down beside the stove, but there was no wood. I covered the whole room seeking wood. I found nothing, so I started on the books. I randomly pulled pages from fallen books that lay strewn about the room. I crumpled the paper and filled the stove bottom. When the fire gained force, I threw in whole books. In time the stove gave off heat and I felt my face returning. It came completely back to me when I felt the pain of the deep cuts in my hand. Then I moved the librarian's desk across the room to a place beneath the broken window. I turned the reading table over on top of that to block the wind.

I made a place for myself then, right near the wood stove. I went down the wall from the books nearest the wood stove to the books on the shelves farthest away. I stacked up volumes of books there next to me and kept feeding the stove. Some of the books burned for a long time, and a few of those long-burning books together gave me time to break chairs for wood, and then I had time to sleep and read through the storm.

Lois Phillips Hudson

The Dispute over the Mountains

It is over a hundred degrees in the shade, down in the valley of the Trinity. Above the wide hot meadows of Hoopa, the sun of northern California burns all day through the same small hole in the sky. This sun is like a dream or a grief; it will never let you go.

But almost every summer day at four o'clock a breeze will come from the west. It is regular enough so that you come to believe in it. When the breeze comes, it is as though every black cherry, asleep and waiting to plunge with its seed to the dry grass and the thirsty ants, instead feels a new command, a tide waking it, like the tide that wakes and washes the dull parched mussel where it clings by its thin blue edge to its little line of rock.

In the mountains between Hoopa and the sea, the cars cling to the little line of the highway drawn back and forth around the cliffs. It is less than twenty-five miles from the Hoopa Valley to the Pacific Ocean, but over where the mussels are waking, over where the sun will go at last, the temperature is only fifty degrees. It is the cold of the sea moving up the valley of the Klamath, then up the Trinity, then up the creeks that feed the Trinity, that brings the breeze to the inland mountains.

If you are driving one of those cars on a mountainside, the breeze may come just in time to save you from what seems, when you think about it afterwards, to have been an attack of madness. The one ceaseless note of the grasshoppers strums against you, under you, over you.

You listen to your tires on the pavement, waiting for them to explode, like all those other tires lying in three-foot strips of tread at the sides of the road. You begin to think that you will have to get out of your car and let the heat take it—blast it off the road and over the cliff, like those other cars, at the bottoms of cliffs. And you, like the people from those other cars, will be left hanging somewhere on the mountainside, breathing the smell of the heat in the sage and manzanita and pepperwood.

But when the breeze comes, things shift back into scale. Human beings, if you happen to see them or one of their cars a thousand feet below, no longer seem to have fallen out of the world you believe yourself to inhabit. They are tiny, just as you are tiny to them, but after a few breaths of cooling air, you are able to tell yourself that the only things wrong with you are the heat, the grasshoppers, the mountains.

When the breeze comes from the Pacific, you think of how these mountains are like a last sea wall thrown up by the continent, as man, in imitation, builds walls and jetties of concrete slabs swung out by cranes and thrown into the ocean, where they crack and break and settle, pointing this way and that into the waves. This continental sea wall is made of random slabs four or five thousand feet high—slabs so precipitous they seem to hang out far over you when you stand below them. The first Trinity gold miners swore that when a mule lost a shoe on a cliff trail two hundred feet above the north bank of the river, the shoe would fall on the south bank.

If you happen to be driving through these mountains from the sun to the fog when conditions are right, you will see the sun and the sea engaged in silent contention over the possession of them, as any wall may be a place of contention. What you see ahead, as you come over the top of the next-to-the-last western ridge, is a violent coastline five thousand feet above the sea. The breakers from the ocean, transformed but not defeated by the sun, are rising in a mist that looks denser than snow, rising five thousand feet thick beneath a sapphire sky and pouring across this last ridge of the continent, flowing like sudden glaciers down these last cracks and notches, over the emerald forests. The white of these breakers is the white of an unimaginable force—a white like the white you may once have supposed the Milky Way to be made of. In silence the five-thousand-foot breakers attack, and in silence the sun shears off their great round backs so that there is always the precise line between the flowing white and the sapphire space.

But no matter how unchanging the line may seem, either the sun or the sea will surely be winning. If you drive this way often, you may think: The sea-fog will lose today. It will be clear over there by the time I get home, and we will walk out on a windy brilliant beach and cook our dinner there. There will be an offshore wind, the wind is turning, and the fog will go back out over the water; it will retreat.

But if the sea and its fog lose the war today, the people waiting for the breeze on the Hoopa Valley Reservation, as they have waited for many centuries before their land became a reservation—these people may be disappointed. If there is an offshore wind, the breeze may not come today. Often the outcome of the day's battle fails to please men on both sides of the wall. For example, about three months ago, toward the end of March, that time of year when the sun seems able to lift the fog only high enough to dump it again on the mountaintops and let it rush down to the creeks, to the Trinity, to the Klamath, and back to the sea, a Sunday thunderstorm broke the silence of the battle. The storm came, like the summer breeze, about four in the afternoon, and it caused on the coast one of those glorious, early-spring, late-clearing sunsets, with the clouds changing their colors and shapes, passing behind and above and below each other, so thin they cannot shut out the sun, but only make it so big you can watch the moves it usually makes in secret. Then, as you can see the minute hand of a giant clock moving, you can see the huge savage sun cutting itself into the sea like a circular saw burying itself in a log. This is a sight the ocean people cherish; they do not often see it.

Over on the Hoopa side, that same storm of the glorious sunset caused a long saw of light to flash through an old digger pine, thus freeing the top of it to fall like a spear through the roof of a car clinging to the line drawn back and forth above the canyons. Sometimes a mussel, because it is old, or because the sea or a gull or a man is especially hungry, will lose its hold on its line of rock; or a black cherry, such a little while after winning its fragrant springtime battle with the dying blossoms around it, will plunge with its seed to the earth.

In this final way the car fell from its ledge to the foot of the mountain, to the flooding bank of Willow Creek. There in that spot where it stopped, now far from the narrow summer channel, it returns itself to the earth, rusting in the sun, spilling wheels and doors into the rocks and thimbleberries.

Somebody driving by above it before the four o'clock breeze on a late June day, might tell himself, in order to ward off that necessity to jump, that seizure of heat madness: A kid did that. One of these kids in this affluent age, with this peculiar kind of humor they all seem to have now, and this delight in littering the beautiful earth—one of these kids jumped out of his car at this horrifying, dizzy place and he sent that car down this cliff.

A few hundred yards downstream from the car two human figures are sitting in the shade of a boulder that has also fallen from the top of the mountain during some storm. A thousand feet above them a driver struggling to keep himself in scale on the mountainside would tell himself that it is the boulder that is big, not that the people are too tiny to belong to his kind.

Those people are not at all mysterious, he says to himself. It is just that all people seem to be mysterious when you see them a thousand feet below you. It is highly doubtful that these people have discovered a new vein of gold in the mined-out diggings of Willow Creek; they do not have a camouflaged sluice down there, or a rocker hidden in a cave. They probably are not uranium prospectors. They are not following an ancient blood-soaked map. They probably have not even found a deep pool of trout they want to keep to themselves, in a spot where no game wardens are likely to turn up. Perhaps they are rock hounds scavenging in the cone-shaped piles spilled from the one-man shafts that now look more like the abandoned holes of animals than of men. Most probably they are just people waiting for the cool wind to come and give them the will to hike back to the car they have left five rugged miles down the creek.

And that is, indeed, precisely what the people are doing, as they sit in the shade of the boulder, not thinking of how it once fell down the mountain, how it tortured its helpless self and the helpless earth on its way down. Nor do they look up the creek behind them to the fallen old car. They are telling each other, Frank and Alice Raymond, that this is the last week they can possibly make the trip. Every Sunday it will be hotter. But this means that every Sunday the creek will have shrunk more, and every Sunday there will be a new chance to find the little boy who was riding in the car.

He would have to be somewhere between here and the spot five miles downstream where the creek passes the Rain Rock. At the Rain Rock it is especially noticeable, the way the stream shrinks every week. In a rainy winter like this last one, the Rain Rock will be only a wet black point in the rushing dark water, but by the end of summer it will be a tall dry boulder a hundred feet from the edge of the creek. Here the creek leaves its wide winter course and withdraws to a deep cut it has made under the opposite canyon wall, as though it still hates the rock it has tried to drown, and will go as far away from it as possible. Perhaps because the Rain Rock seems to bear these hard extremes with patience and courage, the people felt that it was the right place to pray for rain. It stands on the last level stretch before the stream falls sharply into the bottomlands of the Trinity, and Alice, who is a full-blooded Hoopa, can remember, better than she remembers almost anything else in her life, how she followed her old grandmother up the steep trail from the river to the rock. They would have the soap root they had dug and crushed, and they would get water from the creek and climb up and sit on the hot dry rock and rub the suds of the soap root all over it. Alice has been a Christian for nearly sixty years, but still she remembers the feeling of her palms sliding with the suds over the stone, while she rubbed and washed and caressed and learned the old prayers from her grandmother.

They had found Frank Junior in the wide eddy that backs up at the south side of the Rain Rock when the creek is in flood. Frank Junior was the only one of the five that didn't drink. The

State Patrol sent some people—men with a pickup truck full of dogs—to look for the family that had been in the car. Halfway down the swath the car had made through the manzanita bushes, they found Frank's wife, and finally, two days later, they found Frank Junior in the Rain Rock eddy. Frank was a big man; he was long and heavy compared to the three-year-old boy. Because he was heavy and long, the men said, he was shunted off in that eddy instead of going on down to the Trinity and then on down the Klamath to the sea. After the two-day search they decided that the little boy, being light and short, must have gone on with the flood. He and his father—they would both have taken that last lonely flip from the car when it fetched up against the log at the creek's edge, but the boy would have traveled much farther.

If he had really gone all the way with the flood, the boy would have been the only one of the family to get home from the sun to the fog. He would have come, in the depths, against the wall built by the old feud between the Klamath and the sea—the long bar that the Klamath glides behind until it rushes out from a hole in the barricade to meet the sea in a last roaring encounter. Far above this encounter, on a cliffside reservation, the mother of the boy's mother lives in a trailer house on a neat patch of vegetables hedged by the chaparral. This old grandmother is so high above the ocean that on many days she never sees it—only hears it down there in the fog, tearing at the wall and building the wall all at the same time.

It was this grandmother who made them start the search for the family. When they didn't get home Sunday night, she began to worry. She told one of her boys to take her to a telephone, but he told her to go to bed. "They are having a long Indian visit," he laughed. "No," she said. "Frank goes to work on Monday morning. Your sister got herself a man that can keep a job." But still nobody would take her to a telephone, so when morning came she walked down the cliff to the road and down the road to the gas station and called up the schoolhouse in Hoopa, where Frank and Alice were working, and asked them when the kids had left for home.

The State Patrol did not find the car till Tuesday night; there were so many places it could have fallen off the line drawn back and forth through the mountains. And then it was two days more before they found Frank Junior. After that nobody would look any more for the little boy. Still, Frank and Alice could not believe the child could have gone so far from his father and mother.

Frank and Alice cannot believe he is gone until they find him. They know this is a silly way to feel; after all, they have lost, in other ways, children they cannot find. Still, only the finding of this child will prove that he is truly lost. But every Sunday it is hotter; now the cherries are ripe; now almost all of the creek has gone down to the Trinity and half of the Trinity has gone down to the ocean. The salmon have spawned in the shallows and the fingerlings have hatched and migrated to the deep green holes under the cool rock walls. It is only the shadow of a baby salmon that you can see—not the fish, which is never more than a flash of the sun, but only his more enduring shadow, which seems, in the swarm of shadows, to be but a thicker darkness in the mottled sand. When rain falls into a mud puddle, the flashing drops are still there, somewhere, but their light is always disappearing. The flashes you see come always from the new drops, because the flashes you just saw are part of the mud puddle. In the same way the baby salmon is always becoming part of the shadows in the sand under water that seems as though it is as plain as air. Here is a sea creature, far away from the sea, that can hide himself in the rain coming down from the mountains.

Frank and Alice will not admit that the sea can win so easily. They are not used to yielding to the sea; they live on the sun's side of the mountains. How can these babies hide themselves so cleverly, these babies that belong to the sea? But it is because they hide so cleverly that we think we must catch them; we can't let them disappear in the water and the flashes of the sun. Frank and Alice have seen, in ten different deep holes today, as many baby salmon as there are ghosts of all the people who have ever died on the earth. They have checked all these deep holes at least twelve times, at least once every Sunday. They cannot leave the baby boy under the shadows of so many ghosts—under the shadows of all the sea creatures.

Frank is worried about Alice's arthritis and Alice is worried about Frank's heart. Every Sunday each of them tries to make the other stay home and rest. Now, while they sip water from the creek and wait for the breeze, Alice is saying what one or the other of them always says, while they sit by the boulder and wait for the breeze:

"Maybe we shouldn't have sold, Frank."

Frank gives the answer that the other always gives. "They'll come in anyway. Now or when we are gone."

He means the lumber companies; but he is thinking about his oldest grandson, who lives with him—this nineteen-year-old boy down in the valley house under the cherry trees. This boy will have the conditioner on full blast and by now he will have got through half a case of beer, this boy, if he has not started something stronger. This boy is the son of Frank's oldest son, who is dead of drink. For some reason this boy cannot bear what his grandparents do every Sunday. Every Sunday morning, while Alice is making the sandwiches and Frank is putting on the rubber boots that come up to his hips, this boy, this nineteen-year-old boy goes to the refrigerator and takes out a can of beer. He would not even get out of bed for two or three more hours, let alone be drinking, except that he cannot stand what Frank and Alice are doing. The last things he says, as they are leaving, will stay all day in their ears, along with the one note of the grasshoppers, the sound of the pavement far above them. "Why are you still doing this? Why don't you give up? What do you think you will find?"

It is for this oldest grandson and for the other grandchildren, for the youngest one who is lost, that Frank and Alice have sold the timber—so all the grandchildren can go to college. The traders will always come—the Spaniards, the French, the British, the Americans. Now the Americans want the timber allotments and so they will get them. It is better to sell now than to die and leave the children to fight over the money the government men will keep bringing around. This way, with the money in their own hands, perhaps Frank and Alice can persuade the grand-children to go to college.

Frank and Alice go on repeating explanations for their lives to each other, the way old people do. They explain to each other why they have sold the mountainside where the whole Hoopa tribe hid from the government between eighteen-sixty-one and eighteen-sixty-two. It is because of that terrible year, away from the river, away from the hidden winter supplies of seeds and dried berries, the baskets of acorns and smoked salmon—because of that starving year the Hoopas still possess the land where they have always lived. It is because the Hoopas would not give in to the second set of promises after the first set of promises were broken, because the Hoopas fought and hid, that now the Hoopas live in the same wide splendid valley where their people always lived. Not like the people who have moved up to the cliffside reservations because nobody else wants that land.

The Hoopas have been slow to sell their allotments, because of the memory of that year. Everybody in Hoopa remembers, for instance, that Frank would not be here if his great-grandmother had not saved his grandfather that year. It is almost a legend, the story of how Frank's great-grandmother saved his grandfather, who was born on the mountainside two days after the people went to hide there. The leader said that the baby would have to be killed because his crying would bring the soldiers. So the new mother hid herself from the hiders. Nobody knew how she lived that year, but nobody heard her baby cry.

She kept him clean with the fresh milkweed fuzz under his little bottom as he lay in the new basket she had woven for him as soon as she knew he was coming. And somehow she made milk for him from the roots and acorns she found on the frozen mountainside. That was what she lived for that year—to keep the baby from crying. But she could never let him out of the basket. Finally, after the year had passed, the government man came across the continent and decided that the Hoopas could keep the valley and the forests where they hunted deer and gathered acorns. Then when all the people came down again to the meadows beside the Trinity, she let the child out of his basket and he stood up and walked. It was a miracle, a symbol—that was what the people thought. It proved something, what Frank's grandfather did that day.

Long ago, before the white men came, in a famine year when the people were starving, when the deer were dying and when the deer that survived were too clever to be caught, but clever enough to find and eat up all the acorns—when a famine year came, the mothers who had new babies and no milk for them would have to take them far up the mountainside that Frank and Alice have sold and leave them there in their new baskets. The mothers would make safe fires and put the babies down beside them. The babies would feel dry with the new milkweed fuzz and warm from the fires, and by the time they would cry, everybody, even the mothers, would be too far away to hear them crying themselves to sleep.

The mothers did not speak of it to their husbands when they came down the mountain. But the fathers could imagine, as well as the mothers, the crying beside the fires. It was not easy for the fathers when there were no deer, no salmon, no seeds, no roots, no acorns—when the sun won too many battles and the salmon fingerlings never got back to the sea.

Now they wish they were back down in the lower valley, beneath the mountain they have sold. It is so hot. How will they get back down through those rough places they have hacked out and dug out themselves, in this private trail they have made up Willow Creek? The first time they came up, the willows did not have leaves, only a green nimbus made of the metamorphosis of numberless gray velvet buds. Now the willows are already tired and almost gray again, drooping their dusty leaves, waiting for the breeze.

Frank and Alice have never gone closer to the car that fell down the mountain than they are right now. Everybody said the boy would be in the creek. So Frank and Alice have always stayed downstream behind this boulder. The State Patrol, the men with the dogs, they looked around the car that Tuesday night, with the rain coming down as though the sun would never stop until it had sucked up the whole ocean and dumped it again into Willow Creek. You could have believed, that night, that the whole Pacific Ocean was made from Willow Creek. That night nobody would let Frank and Alice look at the car.

And by the next morning the search had widened. Frank and Alice were told to look downstream. But now, on this Sunday afternoon, everything is so hot and dry. There is only the one last place to look. The car looks too much like a joke, like all those other jokes nobody wants to understand. Why do these young boys think it is so funny to send the cars over the cliffs? Probably it really is funny, that first moment, to see the car standing first on end, then somersaulting into the manzanita bushes; to see the car making its bounces into space between its landings on stratas of the mountainside. But the car is not funny after it has finished its short trip into space. There it sits, down below you, like all the ventures before it into space.

Something about the voyage into space is amusing, because otherwise the boys would not do it. This nineteen-year-old grandson down in the air-conditioned house in Hoopa Valley— he sent his own old first car into the Trinity the day after Frank and Alice gave him the new car and the money to go to college. It seems to mean something after it has landed, but what? It was only something for boys to laugh and cheer over while it was falling out of the world, but now there it is. Nobody wants to look at it littering the beautiful earth. Now this is the way Frank Junior's car looks.

The breeze is coming up the creek. Always before, Frank and Alice have turned away from the car and toward the cool wind from the sea and gone home. But now they climb up Willow Creek, through the rocks and thimbleberries. The breeze behind them makes a coldness pass between the wetness of their ribs and the wetness down the insides of their arms. From the uphill side of the car Frank works at the front seat till he clears it from the jammed door. Alice tries to help but it is an awkward job. Frank's face is dark and strained; his breathing is four times faster than it should be. But finally the seat comes out and they tear up the floorboards. The little boy lies there under the car. He has not been crushed; his bones were not broken. The sun had not given him back to the sea after all.

Did he lie here and wait, like the babies beside their fires in the years when the sun won too many battles? Did the little boy lie here and know that no matter how small he was, still it was his turn to possess the mountainsides? Did he wait and cry himself to sleep like all those other babies, because of some dispute over the mountains?

As you crawl around the last hairpin turn and top the summit in a final blast of hot rubber, you feel the cold of the sea—that suddenly. Behind you the grasshoppers strum, the cherries drop. Below, the mussels lie open, devouring foam.

Jan Huesgen

On the Burden of Expectation

*"December 23, 1884. I hope this book is kept as is in
that the one who gets it will hold it in honor and when
I am dead occasionally say an our father for me."*

There is always the regret. In faded shades
of gray her story emerges, her pen randomly touches
a well, thick and dark, arbitrarily shaping
a story out of letters, as vulnerable
and as permanent as unsalvageable regret.

I came to know her then the way I knew myself,
living in a prairie town: by labels—
I, a German, a Catholic; she, a miser and a recluse:
words that spoke for us, told others how we lived
or prayed, or what we ate; single words
that had more power than our names themselves.

There were stories, like the man with the golden arm
or the woman who preserved hands in pickling jars,
then ate them, about that house where Sophie Budde lived.
I never saw her, only a silhouette
at the edge of a window at night, the streetlamp
pulling from the shadows a relief
of the dead woodbine that clung to her house,
like fingers at a rock wall,
or something doomed grabbing
at something that would not help.

Her suffering now seems not unlike others'
I have known or read about: I now know
she loved children, but never carried one
full term, and there was always that regret.
There is no posterity for a life, here traceable
only to a book, rebound after a house fire
in Korschenbroich, April 23, 1884: a burden
to a girl who lived the next eight months
on a blank page following that now-forgotten day
on which a burning book was saved, and a mother lost.

Sophie's house still looked stubborn
and immortal years later in the July heat,
but that did not intimidate us
bent on seeing the auction through:
talk of rosewood tables from Germany,
Limoges from France, and Dresden plates,
inherited, stirred the town to life—
we wanted to see all the pieces,
to have a final word or two. Myself,
I bought a box of books, second bid,
ten bucks, and in it was Sophie's diary.

Now I begin again, and I wonder how provident
my purchase was, although the burden of its pages
is not so much in the unexpected event,
as in the humility of displacement
when a life has been taken
for granted, then lost in some unplanned-for moment
when the future falls our way.

Life on the Prairie:
Those Who Follow

Here, on this sea, some other Magellan
might have discovered the earth's roundness,
but for centuries no one grappled
with the unfathomable life of it,

buried deeper yet in the race to have
what other men want: first, the other side
and gold. But few in the rush across
saw it here, where gold was black,

and a man could go equally mad
grabbing at straw in the wind.
I was born in water, on this plain;
I began to arrive in 1885

as one who follows, like Elcano,
the forgotten captain of a voyage
that mattered to history books
and men who play at finders-keepers

until all the sides are had.
Few now know Magellan as the one
never to finish the great voyage:
his death en route matters little,

because he is great who goes first,
and those who remain at sea
on courses mapped by schooners
that have only touched the surface,

must seek our meaning in the deep-
down-things, and in the going round
still sail for home, as we, like Elcano,
finish a voyage in someone else's name.

Living with What Belongs to Us

We are looking for a picture
of grandmother as a girl, when we find
her long braid, not blond,
but gold in a silk-lined box,
afraid if we lift the heavy plait
that its weight might suddenly unravel
what has carefully been placed
so many years before. We spread it
over the table, letting our hands feel
the thickness and strength
of the softness that hung from her then,
like aplomb of callowness.

We find her at twenty-three, already held
in high regard, this young woman
musician who came to the prairie
on a mid-winter day to be married:
she is wearing the lambswool coat
that still hung behind an upstairs door
when I was a child in my grandmother's house,
for she never got rid of those "things
hard come by." She leans her head
left into his shoulder, an intimated
gesture; her hair, blunt cut
at the neck, lies marcelled over her head.

I have never forgiven her
the forfeiture of a music career,
my own disappointment in her fairy-tale,
cut short, like the unexpected ending
with a moral we cannot figure out.
She made all of us dreamers
grow up with her fancies stuck away
in boxes and bags, like kept lovers
who give refuge to the otherness

in our lives, and help us find comfort
in the passion within us.

There's no need to hang onto it now,
we say, setting everything back in its place,
while the late winter sun steals
along the floor, then catches our backs,
turned, at the far side of the room,
where we sit with a part of a woman
we could not live without,
for we cannot be the ones
to dispose, too easily, of that
which has been given freely, of that
from which we derive meanings of our own.

Reflection of Me, My Sister

The untrained eye cannot anticipate
the point at which two arcs will meet;
childhood moments, like drafting dots, connect
and move off in some private direction.
Now we have redrawn our lives
so rigidly they seem not more
than strokes in space, and we siblings
only serve to illustrate the law,
two parallel lines will never meet.

In the mirror this morning I saw you
combing my hair; years ago you trimmed it,
that precious tress that hung,
crescent-shaped, across my back. Then,
we both stooped to sweep the pieces
from the floor.

Now my hair is short,
and something much more fragile
and far less valuable than this mirror
remains between us.
Yet we hang onto our differences like old women
with hands paralyzed to empty handbags:
they are only bad habits now,
and we have forgotten to look inside,
we have forgotten the reasons to look.
Now we are treated with forbearance
and at our age—

We live with too much
determination on two sides of a river,
like armies camped: we drink and wash
from the same bed, as we stand on the edge
in bitterness and fear; we are suspicious
of what lies before us

and who is at our back. I am not sure anymore
of the reflection I see at the river.
There is no bridge between us
and I do not know how
to make water bend light.

       Yet there is hope left
in the bending of our systems,
a rather affronting hope, that seems clearer
only this morning, as I am caught
in an unexpected point in time,
a point at which an almost forgotten curve
leans to that perfect, fleeting degree
in which we touch.

Dale Jacobson

Hitchhiker

Beneath the lightning the thunder.
Beneath the thunder
the long distance back.

The Alphabet Mongers

1.

Oh, for the pure art!—*while the people hunger—*
the class struggle disturbs aesthetics,
and if the war dead, the millions of bodies,
equal with enough time broken glass in the junk heap,
then history is only the passing of facts
to which we are lost, as we must then be
lost from each other. Clearly, words not spoken
for the family or friends of the victims . . .

And while heaven or earth, or both, rage—
or a worker is secretly disappeared,
in some vague country south—
the funereal poets see only wings dipping toward
the (always) melancholy descent, the power of gravity
that attracts all failings, as if the details of war,
which still belong to the wider details of everything
under the ubiquitous sky, equal the earth's indifference,
equal nothing but the tiny or brutal changes of season . . .

With the bones of birds they will arrange the letter "A"—
two wings leaned together with one metaphysical rung between:
an ornithic icon to announce the alphabet.
And the water-sand-and-wind-eaten-artifacts of civilizations
buried with their discontents and broken usages,
they will put back together, in their own image
like hierophants so distantly tender of the dead!—
taking no sides where all are leveled in the city flattened,
rulers and slaves alike in the democracy of ruins
where no one need choose up from down, west or east—
a caboche vide: studying the stilled musics:
the crumbled foundation, broken gods, shattered arches . . .

They come too late to know the ruins are
the orphaned remains left to the rain's miseries,
the lasting poverties that refuse without astonishment
to be anything but hurt . . . calling at the end of all syllables . . .
in the past still owned—or in the future whose door
is already locked in the name of rent—which no suffering will open.

2.

For us there are no academics beyond our hardships:
the hungry have no use for a philosophy of hunger.

We are those born from the four deep foundations
on which the universe spreads its wings.

We go to the factories wondering where our work goes,
where it ends—go wandering the streets unemployed,
transmigrants out of time, living on the sum of nothing,
studying the habits of shadows, the length of the streets,
the descending slant of the light while something marginal
like a dark animal glistening
                              rushes away,
an angry apparition out of our wasted years,
turns back into our deepest haunts of endurance
where stars are black lights beneath a stone sky.

At dawn another solitude infiltrates the universities
where the academics arrive to define meanings . . .
the absence of our lives murdered again in the libraries.
No one speaks of the homeless who are elsewhere,
a fourth of the nation's children learning hunger,
the unemployed who are elsewhere, the soup kitchens
     elsewhere—
of Benjamin Linder, murdered by his own government,
who is elsewhere, and the bodies of workers
dumped into the rivers, which carry them elsewhere . . .

3.

You scholars of the despairs who discover birds die!—
trading in their bones,
                  those fallen alphabets of the wind
that mean for us our country lost—someday may you enter
the real world of words—spoken—urgent—
those words of many voices raised together against
Aristotle's name for a slave, "a living tool."

But first you must learn to listen how
the living tools talk, the hammer living as a hammer
in the hand that makes the hammer speak,
building against the silence, like a scaffolding
out of the sea's catacombs, like a deep bell
calling to alliance all the earthly elements:
a hammer pronouncing like a chime
rebellion in the hand of the maker—
the energies old that cause the universe to ring!

We are those who never sought out suffering
but learned it was more than the bones could augur.

Jeff Jentz

Wiping the Eyes of a Horse

Such a cold grey hour to be awake!
And me, his stableboy again, laboring at my morning
   chores in the red barn:

Scooping oats into a coffee can stuck to a frozen
Strawbale, scraping away snowy webs of fly
Husks, chopping out the ice-mirrored stock tank—
Hanging twines around the gate.

While roofbeams creak and grieve in the blizzard,
Matthias swings the lantern closer
Spilling snow-motes, sketching us into a parable.
He says, "Tears and matter crust 'em up.
   A horse can't wipe its own eyes."

Wiping the dark eyes of the horse,
An Appaloosa mare,
With its withers trembling beside me . . .
I am astonished by the traceries of blue veins
Within swathes of skin
That cover the volcanic eyes!
These grow enormous, as if jarred open
Underwater in the half-light
Of the kerosene-smoky winter barn.

Tearing at my glove with my teeth,
I offer a bare hand, unafraid, to the other horses,
But they don't approach right away.
Like trout, they are enticed by a lure . . .
The oats pail, even empty,
Makes them swivel their long tan heads.

Matthias says, "Clear the mote from a horse's eyes,
    Scratch behind its ears
    And it'll eat right outa your hand."

Steamy wisps of musty wet straw
Rise from the floor of the March snowblind barn:

Morning brightens our dust-smeared windows.

Robert King

Walking at Dusk

In the distance, birds fidget in trees. The fences
practice the curve of the land over and over.

The river memorizes its smooth curve through town
leaning into the bank, falling away. Even

the horizon rehearses what will happen when
I get there. Everything has occurred before me.

Against the last half-light, birds lift
into the air, like a hand thrown suddenly open.

Antelopeville, Nebraska

Nearing Kimball, I can pretend I remember
when it was Antelopeville that surprising day
my grandmother walked to school with her friend
and the county's wildest boy hauled up a rig.
The girlfriend turned as if she had planned, loaded
her books into my grandmother's arms, and jumped
beside him, the buggy lurching out of town forever,
straight toward everything they didn't know.

Later she would drive with her own husband
on vacation toward invisible mountains,
the dirt stretch finding its path like water
slipping through the easiest curves of the land.
Crisscrossing minor roads, guessing direction
from nothing in particular, they lost themselves
in the way lives circle from house to house,
habit pressing its own bare trail in the grass.

Dead-ended in one more farmyard after dark,
staying the night, she lay in a stranger's bed
almost exactly like her own, wallpaper
patterned into familiar prairie roses,
the very home she strangely could not leave.

Kimball behind me, mountains still a rumor,
I watch the antelope, tawny as dry grass,
graze and drift in the nineteenth century.
Far away, the Platte winds the same thin story
over and around, almost meeting itself
and almost leaving, the sun pouring west all day.

The Names of Central City, Colorado

(1863)

We called it Central, barely a name at that.
It was Jimson's Diggings at first, or Sacramento,
near Missouri City. You find a lot of places called
for something else, Nevadaville's a mile or so
up creek. We named everything we found,
the Gregory Strike, the German Tunnel,
every mule, the creeks, the women
like Slanting Annie, Red Eye Sal,
but calling something doesn't make it stay.

I worked with Smith, whose girl, Mathilda,
died at a year. The next they called Mathilda
for six months, two names on the same white stone.
Smith told me once there was a map for stars
that told you what they were. I knew the Drinking Gourd,
but some nights when I'd stagger out of the Buckhorn
or the Mountain Belle and look up at the sky,
trying to find an archer or a woman on a throne,
they'd scatter off to bits of light again.

After a few years I left, moving the direction
I'd been going, like following a treasure map
I made up for myself. And I remember standing there,
looking at the tailings fanning down the hill,
all loose and yellow rubble, and the creek
already turned the color of the rock. It seemed
that even the hills would wash away, the houses melt.
Turned out I was wrong, the city stayed,
but not completely, call it whatever you want.

Fourth of July

Beyond the trees shadowing the farmyard
wheat seethes the color of the sun. The long day
shimmers across the fields, not a breath of breeze.
England is in a book we haven't read.
The land reaches too far to be called America.

Inside the shade we meet the young new wife,
the older ones, and talk about the winter,
quoting ourselves, ice melting around the beer
and watermelon in the cold, galvanized tubs.
Here is a wheatfield married to someone else.
Here is a divorce with two names. There
are the children, playing as if they belonged
to everyone, cousins named for the past.
The old ones sit almost beyond sight
in the dark parlor, chairs straight as their backs,
remembering a mother with red hair,
a husband who lost three farms in a lifetime.
One of them begins a story, it is an ocean,
it is before the ocean. The room is dreaming
the story, night in another country.
The voices tremble along old cobblestones.
Outside, the horseshoes clang like late church bells.

Behind the windbreaks to the west, the sun
boils down into a round red cloud and sinks.
Those of us left pull flimsy lawnchairs closer,
the song of our dim talk drifting the children
to sleep, games blurred into the rhyme of dreams.
Air is as warm as the blood. The summer family thickens.
The fields widen around us, dark as a huge room.

Erosion

Outside of town, the sharp ravine eats in,
wearing away at the borders. At night,
and spring, the muddy creek cuts at the bank,
edging it nearer our houses. The cottonwood
roots reach out in surprise, curled around stone.

We have seen it in the eyes of our wives,
the past clinging to their skin like perfume,
something seeping away close to the heart.
Arguing in bed, we toss words up into the darkness.
Driving in dusk, we feel the land
thinning as the shallow topsoil weathers.

We have thrown all we could against the slippage,
pushed into the curves of the ravine our junk
and scraps, broken chunks of town sidewalk,
even the cars we've wrecked, shells scaling with rust,

the bodies pointing accidentally downstream
as if they too would pull away, everything
we've done adrift and thickening toward an ocean
the women warned us of, night after night.

When Everything Shall Become Known

We walk through the fall woods,
watching them thin like pretense,
relieved to see beyond ourselves.

The silver breaking in the trees
is the lake, or the sky shining.
We have been covered in luxuriance

and promise to strip ourselves clean.
The willows yellow to brush.
In the open meadow, shadows of deer

cross like memories returning.
The leaves melt into earth
the color of old dresses

and we feel our secrets floating out
from the dry husks of weeds.
There was a reason for hiding something,

we believe, afraid
of discovering it, day by day.
Finally, the air is clear around us.

We forget the overflow
of summer, the other truths.
Now that the trees are bare

we believe the branches always
looked like winter. We were foolish
not to think the moon cold,

ourselves alone, the barren premise.
This is the world, we say.
Yes, this.

Louis L'Amour

The Sea, Off Vanua Levu

There is a beauty in this beyond believing,
    A strength that is stronger than the hands of men,
There is a glory in this that is greater than grieving
    That brings a stillness to my heart again;

There is a power in this beyond longing or laughter,
    A grandeur unmeasured by cloud or sky–
There is a sounding here, and an echo after–
    A sounding of surf and a sea-gull's cry;

There is an ending here, for the time, of emotion
    Of sorrow and sadness, of envy and fear;
All these are forgotten beside the wide ocean,
    That gray rolling splendor, cold and austere.

John Little

Whopper John Fish Tales

Catfish Charlie

Let me tell you a story. Every town that has catfish has a Catfish Charlie. That's what they call the best catfish angler in town. I knew the original Catfish Charlie.

He was the best fisherman in my part of the world. He caught bass and crappie, but he made his name with catfish. He fished the Strong River and the Pearl River and the Big Black and the Yazoo and the mighty Mississippi and he caught catfish in all of them.

He caught his biggest ones hand-grabbing. Maybe you've heard about hand-grabbing. During spawning season the female lays her eggs in the riverbank under an overhang and the male guards the eggs. The hand-grabber wades the bank barefooted until he feels a spot smoothed out by eggs. He sticks his hand in and the catfish bites it. He grabs it and hangs on. Or tries to.

They call it log fishing in my neck of the woods, because the cats use hollow logs and stumps for their nests. Now let me tell you something. It takes gumption to stick your hand up a hollow log and hope it's bitten by a forty-pound catfish. You're lucky if the log has a catfish in it or if it's empty. You're unlucky if what bites your hand goes by the name of water moccasin or alligator.

Now a catfish don't have much for teeth. He's got a ribbon of sandpaper. Industrial grade sandpaper. Some hand-grabbers cheat and wear gloves, but that's considered wimpy. Charlie never wore gloves. He had an advantage. He didn't have a left hand. Lost it in a World War II foxhole. Charlie had a hook for a left hand. Perfect for log fishing. Well, not quite perfect. He lost a few because the hook was barbless.

Then one spring the catfish were running and Charlie had an idea. Some people say that idea was his downfall. He went to the blacksmith and had a barb welded on his hook. Said he could file it off in two weeks when the run was over. And it worked. For a whole week Catfish Charlie had the best fishing of his life. Channel cat, blue cat, you name it, Charlie grabbed it. Or hooked it. And with that barb on his hook, he never lost a one.

Then Charlie drove over to the delta, where the big Mississippi River flatheads come up the Yazoo to spawn. Didn't come home that night. We found his red International pickup parked on the bank the next day, about ten miles south of Yazoo City. No sign of Charlie. They found his body floating in the Mississippi three days later, just below Vicksburg, married to a sixty-pound flathead.

Showing Off at the Ramp

Everybody that owns a boat has had an embarrassing moment at the boat ramp. Fishermen can get impatient when they're putting their boat in the water. So you don't want to tie the ramp up with any kind of mishap or stupidity.

I hope you won't think I'm bragging if I say that I've tied up more boat ramps than any fisherman alive. I've had ropes snarled in rollers. I've had ropes break. I've tied knots that came undone. And I've tied knots that couldn't be undone. I've had my boat sideways and crisscrossed and upside down on my trailer. I don't mean to toot my own horn, but you can't name a boat ramp from Mississippi to Manitoba that I haven't tied up. And let me tell you something. If you do something often enough, you get good at it. You name a boat-ramp fix, and I've been in it. And let me tell you something else. With the help of my friends, I've got out of every one of them. I've been cussed a little more than necessary sometimes, but I've got out of every fix I've got myself into. In fact, over the years, I've become so good at loading and unloading my boat, I sometimes do it just for fun.

Sometimes I don't even fish. Sometimes I dump my boat in just to show off at the ramp.

But last summer I found a new way to embarrass myself. I was fishing in Van Hook Arm, out at Sakakawea. I had my limit of fifteen walleyes and me and my boys were racing a storm and ten other boats to the ramp. There must have been fifty trailers there and a crowd of people when I came in. Showtime. Now let me paint this picture for you. I'm driving my white Cadillac convertible. Got five-hundred horses under the hood, got front-end drive—perfect boat-ramp vehicle. Got the top down and the rain starts falling. I back my trailer in without a waver, jump into my boat and drive it on the trailer against a cross wind, winch it and hitch it and pull it out of the water and down the road I go, slick as a whistle.

The whole thing didn't take a minute and a half. I'm driving off into the mist, feeling the admiring eyes of the crowd on my back. Fifteen walleye swimming in my live well, five-hundred horses purring under my hood, when I hear another engine behind me, breathing down my back. I look in my rearview mirror. Nothing back there but my boat and motor. My fifty-horse, four-piston Mercury outboard motor. And you guessed it. All fifty horses and four pistons are purring right along with those five hundred under the hood. Everything went so smooth at the ramp, I forgot to turn my boat engine off.

When the boat-ramp crowd caught up with me at the fish cleaning table, they wanted to know if my water pump was still pumping. It was. That probably won't be the last time I embarrass myself at the ramp. But I hope it's the last time I show off. Well, unless the wind is calm and the crowd really big.

World Record

Jim Henry Garner was famous in my neck of the woods for cussing and catching fish and naming his three sons Oree and Uree and Oly. Oree and Uree married women named Pauline and Oree's Pauline was a sister to my Mama, which made Oree my uncle.

Oree was a carpenter and famous for sending kids to the hardware store for striped paint and wood stretchers and left-handed hammers. Some of his pranks had educational value. I learned that salt was soluble in water after he told me I could catch a bass by sprinkling salt on its tail. That was my first chemistry lesson.

His humor also had a tolerance for pure meanness, like the time we were fishing for blue gill and he paddled up to a bush that held a wasp nest and jerked it out and flipped it into my lap and said, "Think fast." I can still hear his laughter as he helped me back into the boat.

But Oree was serious about his crappie fishing. The world record crappie comes from Enid Lake, Mississippi. It went better than five pounds and has been a world record for forty years. But Oree fished for eaters, not records. He ate one-pounders, two-pounders, three-pounders.

He showed me how to make my first slip bobber, with a rubber band and a button. When he crappie fished, he used cane poles, six of them. I accused him of trying to surround the fish. Mississippi has no limit on the number of lines. People here get excited about a double or a triple. In Mississippi, a dozen is possible. I was with Oree once when he had a school on. He handled the poles clockwise, swinging the crappie on board, dropping the pole, reaching for the next one. I took the fish off, put the minnows on, put the poles back in the holders. Oree got mad when I couldn't keep up. Oree could cuss pretty good himself.

I stopped by his house just after supper in 1985. He had been fishing in Barnett Reservoir.

"I got one that went twenty-four inches," he said. He seemed excited.

"Got what?" I asked.

"White perch," he said. That's Mississippi talk for crappie.

"Let's see it," I said.

"We ate it," he said.

I sat down. "Did you put a fish stretcher on it?" I asked. Oree looked hurt.

"Ask Pauline," he said.

Pauline nodded. Pauline taught me eighth-grade math. She never in her life saw a truth or a fish worth stretching.

I did some calculating. I had just caught a thirteen-inch crappie that weighed one pound, nine ounces. A twenty-four incher was surely a world record, easy.

"It was right tasty," Oree said, rubbing his stomach, which did look several pounds heavier. It should have. It held a world record.

Catching Bait

I went up to Ball Lake, Ontario, last week to do some walleye fishing. We paid two hundred eighty five bucks Canadian for the leeches and minnows, enough to last ten guys three days. My share was sixty bucks for me and my two sons, and it set me to thinking about fishing when I was their age. Catching the bait could sometimes be more exciting than catching the fish.

We didn't have a bait shop in Raleigh, Mississipppi. If you went fishing, you had to do your own grubbing. That might mean rolling a log over for a slug, or digging for angleworms, which was pretty boring stuff unless you were lucky enough to disturb a snake. Sneaking up on a crawler with a flashlight after a light rain is still pretty exciting, but I don't enjoy the mud as much as I used to.

Working a shoreline for frogs was pretty good for thrills. Chasing a jumping frog through cattails and lily pads was a close second to robbing wasp nests. If you were any good at all, you got soaking wet. Water moccasins were fond of frogs, too. And the thought of competing with a moccasin puts an edge on the chase.

Doodling for crayfish was more on the quiet side, but still fun. My cousin Homer Lee was the champ doodler. He'd spit on the stem of broom sage and doodle it down the crawdad hole for about five seconds and drag out a crawfish clamped to the stem. Then he got to throw it on you or wait till you were foolish enough not to be looking before he slipped the pinchers to your skin. The best part about crayfish was if you didn't catch any fish, you could always eat your bait.

But the Cadillac of all bait catching for kids was robbing a wasp nest. If you were lucky, you got to climb a tree, knock the nest off a limb, jump out of the tree, and run like hell, all of which were favorite childhood activities. If you were fast enough, you only got stung once or twice. The icing on that cake was that fish loved those wasp grubs. Give me a wasp nest and I'd give you a dishpan full of bluegill.

I remember once fishing with my Uncle Oree. We were in his twelve-foot boat in a twelve-acre lake. He paddled up to a bush and jerked a wasp nest out of it and threw it in my lap and said, "Think fast." He got stung himself but he said it was worth it seeing me jump out of the boat. Oree always had the best sense of humor.

Night Sky over Baghdad

I saw some footage of Desert Storm the other night. The night sky over Baghdad was alive with streaking planes and flak attacks and missiles. Rockets were indeed bursting in air. It reminded me of the time I was in a boat with Dave Sogard.

Dave owns a cabin on Balm Lake near Bemidji, Minnesota. About ten years ago I was foolish enough to get into a small boat with Dave and two other people. That made three fools and Dave in a fourteen-foot boat. We were about to find that sharing a boat with Dave and treble hooks was like being in a beehive with a chainsaw. Live bees and live saw.

We went around the bend from his cabin to Beaver Bay, a small shallow bay with two beaver huts and cattails and lily pads and a couple of loons. It looked like a bass bay designed by *Field & Stream*.

Four people in a fourteen-foot boat is two too many. We were about to find out that if one of them is named Dave, that's three too many. Since bass lures have big treble hooks that can't tell a bass lip from a human ear, we decided that one person should cast at a time. We would go in order. It was a sound, cautious approach, but it didn't include the Sogard factor.

Dave went first. I'll never forget it. He was slinging a Hula Popper, which has two treble hooks. Six big hooks. His windup was like Luis Tiant on the mound for the Boston Red Sox: it covered all points on the compass. It put a new meaning into the word *buzzbait*. His windup made a figure eight look like a straight line. By the time the Hula Popper hit water, the two loons had taken flight and the three fools were lying in the bottom of the boat wishing for foxholes.

When Dave wasn't in his windup, he was jerking his popper off a beaver hut or cattail or lily pad. The only thing more disconcerting than a treble hook buzzing your ear is the sight of one coming at you after being jerked off a lily pad. The only time we felt safe enough to cast was when he was working on a backlash. Being in a fourteen-foot boat with Dave Sogard was like being in a phone booth with a helicopter. It was a little like being in the night sky over Baghdad.

Stephen Shu-Ning Liu

On Ch'ing Ming Festival

Imagining this time of year, at the peak of spring,
in the high country of Fuling,
you see magpies graze in the cavities of sand stones,
you smell cow manure on the humps of earth,
you hear someone weep behind the aspens:
townfolks have come to the hillside carrying food
to their ancestors' spirits, burning paper money
and paper servants and adding new stones and trees
to the graves collapsed in last winter storms.

And down the valley of dark ferns you see a man,
quaintly dressed, bury his head in the moist furze,
shamelessly he sobs, crying out that his mother died
on her bones, he did not attend his father's funeral,
he has wandered dark side of the distant street,
and has no face to see the sun . . .
But could these day sleepers hear him below the grass?
Could they see him rise, wipe his eyes, shuffle down
the road and leave his unburned paper coins fluttering
whitely in the massive bushes, like butterflies?

Ravens at the Summer Palace

Dissipated feathers on roofs, why roll
your eyeballs at me? You can't turn me on,
I've no nostalgia for archaic kingdoms.

Why drag your sooty gowns over the tiles,
where pearls and diamonds no longer shine.
Your snobbish walks remind me of the strolls
of some chamberlains tottering after a royalist.
You look like those eunuchs. Disgusting.

What do you want, dark orbs on the wall? Why not
go south with your cousins, the noble egrets?
Too late for a nest. You can't find such silk belt
of the Ming Emperor on the hanging tree.
Your cries are cold as these stone steps
to the Dragon's Seat, through painted hallways.

Away with your chattering. Your eyes annoy me.
Time has changed: no cramps or melon seeds left
by a wanton prince. The sun abandons the marble boat,
the balustrade, where court women once giggled,
where your ancestors gathered and croaked.
Be gone, obsequious shadows in the year 1990.
Queens are dead. No kings sit on the throne.

My Father's Martial Art

When he came home Mother said he looked
like a monk and stank of green fungus.
At the fireside he told us about life
at the monastery: his rock pillow,
his cold bath, his steel-bar lifting
and his wood-chopping. He didn't see
a woman for three winters, on Mountain Emei.

"My Master was both light and heavy.
He skipped over treetops like a squirrel.
Once he stood on a chair, one foot tied
to a rope. We four pulled; we couldn't
move him a bit. His kick could split
a cedar's trunk."

I saw Father break into a pumpkin
with his fingers. I saw him drop a hawk
with bamboo arrows. He rose before dawn, filled
our backyard with a harsh sound hah, hah, hah:
there was his Black Dragon Sweep, his Crane Stand,
his Tiger Leap, his Cobra Coil . . .
Infrequently he taught me tricks and made me
fight the best of all the village boys.

From a busy street I brood over high cliffs
on Emei, where my father and his Master sit:
shadows spread across their faces as the smog
between us deepens into a funeral pyre.

But don't retreat into night, my father.
Come down from the cliffs. Come
with a single Black Dragon Sweep and hush
this oncoming traffic with your hah, hah, hah.

Richard Lyons

The Letter

On the fifteenth of this month
the moon was to be full,
but there have been clouds, clouds,
gray and hanging all week.
There is no moon.
The sun is only a rumor
each day of my seasonless working.
Today your letter arrived,
with traces of stain on the envelope.
It had been dropped in the snow.
You are not coming back.

My world is overcast.
Clouds, clouds hang on the trees,
stifling buds, dispiriting birds.
"What's wrong?" my husband says,
"You look tired."

"I am," I say, "of the winter,"
startled that he notices
how I look at all.
I turn to look through winter glass
at clouds hanging without outlines.
He stands at my back,
and I can't see his cloudy smile.
He doesn't see my cloudy eyes.

The letter was clean,
untouched by the snow.
The stamp was canceled with cold.
There is no moon.

Debra Marquart

Bronze These Shoes

                         Peter says
I should bronze these platform shoes
that I found in a box marked *keepers*
in my parents' basement. Tan suede
with stars appliqued all around, heels
like paperweights, these shoes

were on my feet the day I went to
my Great Uncle Fred's funeral
and somehow it all comes back to me
when I see them—Fred ranging around
his big messy house in his wheelchair
for he had lost a leg to diabetes, and his wife,

Great Aunt Ida with her one gold tooth
and her cateye glasses, who liked to cook
but never liked to do dishes, who had
too many promiscuous daughters,
who stood on the front porch
and waved a hankie when you came

to visit. I wore these shoes
to Fred's funeral, and on that day
I wore a burnt orange minidress
that was all thigh and no hip,
and a heavy streak of eyeliner
and my hair was long and straight
and parted exactly down the middle.

And people took photos of Fred,
I recall, looking cool in his casket.
And all the ladies wept and sweated
in their big flowered dresses. And me,
tromping around, tugging at the hem
of my mini. And Ida, dabbing her eyes
with her hankie. All of us commenting
on how hard it was to believe that Fred

was actually gone. And I think about
those things we leave behind in boxes,
and about Ida who fell flat and died
in a K-Mart ten years later, rushing,
I've always liked to imagine
for some really good blue light special.

The Blizzard Rope

I have not forgotten,
ten and still holding
the blizzard rope you tied
around my waist, winter
of sixty-six. You said,
you are home base,
and stepped out
into weather. Snow

like a house built
around us. Holsteins
holding their milk
in the hungry barn.
You had no choice.
The straight path
you walked every day
a mystery, in this weather.
I have not forgotten,
thirty-three and holding
the blizzard rope.

White-out, you step out.
Your fine hands
climbing weather,
your dark coat, lost
to the great white.
Your footsteps
filling now with
weather. The line
has grown icy.
The weather worsens.
I am home base.
Go where you will.

My Father Tells This Story about His Brother Frank and the Wick (Every Time I Ask Him for Money)

¶your grandpa marquart he was a tight sonofabitch, you know, every night he'd come to the bottom of the steps and yell up, frank, go to sleep, you're wasting my oil, because frank liked to read, he was always reading something. he wasn't much for farm work, but he liked school and reading and just wasting his time on books. ¶so grandpa thought he better put an end to all that laziness and sloth. frank was pretty much worthless when five o'clock chores rolled around. it was more work getting him out of bed than just doing the chores yourself. ¶so this went on for years, this, grandpa coming to the steps at night and yelling up, frank go to sleep, you're wasting my oil, and frank setting his book down, leaving it open to the last page he was reading and rolling the wick down into the lamp and dousing the flame. ¶so finally frank gets this town job and makes a little money, and the first thing he does is buys himself some oil right off, see, so he can read as late as he pleases. then when grandpa comes to the steps at night and yells up, frank, go to sleep, you're wasting my oil, frank gets out of bed and goes to the top of the steps and yells back down, this is my oil, I bought this oil with my own money, and I will burn this oil however I see fit. ¶but grandpa, he had a way, you know, of seeing how things broke down, how they divided up, because he yelled right back, without even thinking, he said, but what about the wick? that's what he said, what about the wick? ¶your grandfather, i'm telling you, now there was a tight man.

Lise McCloud

Peace Turtles

Roberta Ottertail is a Chippewa with a certain set to her jaw, a
handsome face—dark, planar, young and bare; too honest and
stubborn to be called "pretty." Her hair is the kind of black that
looks red against sunlight. She has stone black eyes, amused
and determined by turns. She's speeding down the highway in
a new Aerostar, weaving through the too-slow traffic, quick and
slippery. Roberta is one of those round sleek indefinable
Indians you sometimes see, a shape-shifter, no exact size.

She's tensed in a bubble of noise, flowing through space.
The Doors are pulsing through the multispeaker units and into
her blood, connecting like a charge between her foot and the
gas pedal, her hands and the steering wheel. The children in
back are clamoring and bobbing in the way that squares her
chin. They keep singing Hello, I Love You, though the hoppy,
funky tune hits a climax and goes.

Without looking, she reaches into a bulging plastic sack
beside her and tosses a handful of candy backwards at the noise.
The gleeful screeching sound rises up and subsides like a flock
of gulls. She passes a car and regains the righthand lane. She
passes the giant turtle made of car wheels and then the Indian
towns are behind her.

The road will be clear now, all the way to Minot, so she can
go 75, 80. Everyone will be at the state fair down there or at the
annual summer festival back on the reservation. They'll be celebrating the North Dakota centennial at Minot, the unspeakable

glory of making everything square as long as the grass shall grow and the rivers shall flow.

Roberta considers the meaning of plows and dams and treaty words, imagining the land as her great-grandfather used to see it in the stories he told. The fenced pastures go by, the rows of crops like a long card shuffle at the side window. Hay bales hulk across the new-mown fields, dark against the pale ground like grazing beasts.

Back home there'll be fiddling and jigging and singing and car bingo and canoe racing and horse racing, among other things, and today's special powwow event that Roberta regrets she has to miss. It was something she planned on for months. Then suddenly Merle had to go away to this "teacher-technology" workshop in Chicago, and today she has to pick him up.

The kids wanted to stop and climb the wheel turtle, but their protests have Dopplered off to just the usual level of annoyance.

"Keep quiet back there now, or you'll make me have an accident," says Roberta from time to time, tossing candy. She makes her voice calm and authoritative but she is vaguely angry. She prides herself on keeping her dignity even though she has a husband, and four kids like stair steps. She knows she shouldn't drive so fast but something is pressing down on her and she wants to run from under it.

The nameless thing started a week ago and built up day by day, a grey heavy dread that finally cornered her in the parking lot by the post office right after the parade this morning. She clenched her fists and screamed at it, and her face contorted with rage. And then Orville Hiyazanpi, the way he looked at her like she was a witch or evil spirit. It left a kind of gritty afterfeel on her that she wants to shake off.

She laughs out loud—a short, defiant sound, banishing Orville's shocked face from her mind. It's not fair that visiting dignitary from another tribe had to see her yelling at the kids. It's not the Indian way; but these kids were going haywire on her. She was just trying to get them to stay buckled in their seats for the trip instead of crawling and screeching all over the car.

"Do you want to die?" she was hollering at the children. "Do you want to end up all bloody, broken to pieces, dead?" Perhaps

Orville heard those words even through the hermetic seal, or saw her menacing expression through the capsule's tinted glass. He would have seen the four children—innocent, helpless, frightened, for once frozen still with horror.

Orville had advanced cautiously toward the vehicle, his eyes round and troubled and wary. She stopped him short with a wild glare and spun out of the parking lot, throwing dirt at him. Perhaps she should have reacted differently, rolled down the window and explained how they were about to blast off into another dimension. The thought of being made to feel guilty is what makes her mad now.

"Look! Look! Another big turtle!" the kids shriek at the next town. This is the world's largest turtle, an enormous shiny-bright steel and fiberglass sculpture of a painted turtle sitting astride a snowmobile. A tourist turtle. The kids make all kinds of noise, wanting to climb it. Roberta clips right through town.

She thinks of her professor from the University Extension Team railing against the injustice of it, this tourist land stolen from the Indian people, the lake crammed with cabins and threatened by sewage, the woods chopped to pieces, this perverse destructive reaction to beauty by non-Indians! And she thinks of the trash people throw around the lakes back home, the beer cans and liquor bottles.

They keep rolling down the road. Behind them the hills rise up like a big blue turtle swimming on a green grass ocean. Above the fruited plain and waves of grain, now that the tall grass is gone. Gone under, gone the way of the buffalo. Roberta wishes she could see it for real, the turtle island of old-people tales. She hears the high, clear voices of her first-grade classmates echoing in the old BIA school gym, singing "America the Beautiful." She shivers at the memory, at the air conditioner's cold breath.

Roberta feels an odd speeding dreaminess as they start on the long prairie decline. The children become quiet, gazing out the windows at the lull of fields, tranquilized by the motion of travel. In her mind a reel of film unwinds, this morning's parade in backward motion, the cars and floats and horses and costumed people throwing candy and the children rushing to get it, glad and greedy, and she smiles to herself. The nine-day Novena ends with the big St. Ann's Day procession and field mass. But church has never worked for Roberta.

Roberta plays a different tape of those Doors, wondering at the words, the weird druggy sounds. Her instructor from the University, who was interested in Indians and always trying to share her 1960s experiences, gave the tapes to Roberta last month. The instructor liked to talk about the environment and "traditional culture" and things and wanted to know why people on the reservation listened to country-western music and dressed like cowboys and all that.

Roberta doesn't know what the instructor needed to hear, but she knows for certain she is an Indian.

"Peace frogs! Peace frogs!" laughs Junior incredulously. "They're singing about peace frogs, that's what they're saying." Junior is six, going to first grade this fall.

"You're right. Crazy, man!" says Roberta, enjoying the newness of the car and other things. She has never driven this far away from the reservation before, only been a passenger to places. But next month she's going to the University, on that Indian scholarship. She's going to be an MD or JD, anything that matters. She's going to make car payments now, too. Roberta feels dry-mouthed panic for a second. She takes a Roo-Barb drop out of the sack and sucks on it, wincing at the taste.

"What's that, Mama?" asks Junior. "It looks like a horsey-head. Hey, there's more! They're all over!" He points to the contraptions whose mechanical gallop is surrealistic in the great flat stillness, a stationary and scattered herd that somehow undulates into the distance.

"That's an oil well, and it sucks up oil that comes from rotten old dinosaurs way under the ground," says Roberta. The children watch fascinated for several miles. The land unfolds into bean-rows, alfalfa clumps, silvery shelterbelts of Russian olive trees, the occasional duck slough, yellow-headed fields of sunflowers. In one of these, a Minuteman missile waits under the ground.

"What's that? Is it a nuke?" asks Junior. "You can tell because those periscopes are sticking up out of the sunflowers."

"They're not periscopes," says Roberta. But she's not sure when he asks what they are, then. They're just something you see here and there, along with other sticking-up things, and you know there's a missile silo.

"I dreamed the world blew up," says Junior. "I dreamed it a whole bunch of times."

Roberta is surprised to hear this, and glances back. He has a strange look on his face, kind of scared, indignant.

"I dreamed my dad's airplane blew up, too." Now he looks ready to cry. All week long, there's been a big airline crash on the news, and the kids are afraid their dad is never going to come home again. They saw him get on a plane just like the crashed one, just last week.

The two smaller kids start crying again. "Where's our dad, where's our dad," says Amanda. "Why don't we ever see him no more."

"Our dad's in a plane crash," says wide-eyed Georgie.

"Here, have some candy," says Roberta. "He's not."

The nuclear threat and the airline disaster are instantly forgotten by Junior, Amanda, and Georgie, and the baby, Josette, is sleeping soundly, but Roberta still senses the inexplicable cloud. The sun bears strongly down on the land. Quicksilver waves shimmer across the asphalt ahead of her, mirage.

The dead Door sings about a rider on the storm, a killer on the road whose brain is squirming like a toad. The sky turns into the music turns into sheetlight, thermospheric motion, the ripple of mood or perception: gradations of blue, and invisible rain. Diamonds that vanish in air. The children drop into sleep through this, the miles of recurrent hayfields and windbreaks. And the odd dreamy tension seems to grip Roberta tighter as she approaches her destination instead of lessening its hold.

Parallel with the air force base outside of town, Roberta gets jumpy. She's only used to driving the backroads. Then she's there, being swept into the intersection where the airport is, being pressed on all sides by cars full of people she doesn't know. Close overhead she hears an immense, swift roar and then the boom that shocks the car awake. The sounds rattle Roberta quite down to the core but she makes her turn into the airport. The baby is howling.

The parking lots are jam-packed and Roberta has to park in a ditch nearby. Right away other cars come in just behind her and stop. Roberta looks around, bewildered. What is going on? There are people parking out next to the freeway, getting out lawnchairs and binoculars, a steady stream of them.

She hurries the children into the airport and looks at the big clock. She's late. But where is everyone? The place is empty. She walks the children to the unloading area to look out the big glass window, and then they see it.

Balls of orange flame and black smoke rolling across the runway and mushrooming into the sky. A hell inferno where the plane should be, billowing out to sear their hearts.

The five of them break into a stunned wail, and all the grief of war and disaster in the world is in that sound. "No more dad!" cry the children, over and over. Men in asbestos suits are jumping out of vehicles that speed up to the scene. They spray long-nozzled hoses full of chemicals at the flames to no avail. Roberta grabs the kids and hauls them away.

There's still no one around except over at the ticket counter, a potato-faced whiteman with thin hair, glasses, two comfortable chins. He's acting just like everything's normal, fiddling with his computer. And the other people, out there on the high-way, watching as if it were some kind of entertainment.

Roberta drags the survivors up to the counter and says, "Mister, there's a big fire out there. What's going on." She's on automatic now, in overdrive. She will not cry in front of any strange, bad people who watch each other burn up for a sport.

The man looks at her and her children with an expression of distaste. "Centennial air show. Pyrotechnics. Simulated bomb-ings," is all he says. He looks down at his paperwork, dismiss-ing them.

Roberta is blank for a moment as the relief sinks in. "Shhh, shhh, the man says it's just pretend. Dad's all right." They don't all quit snuffling or clinging to her at once.

"Well, OK then," says Roberta. "Maybe you can tell me what happened to my husband. He was supposed to come in on the plane today, ten-fifteen minutes ago."

Now the man acts like something's funny, hilarious. "Oh my, we have a woman here who lost her husband, and the four kids along too, crying! Ha, Ha! There's no plane," he giggles. After enjoying that he says, "What's his name." He's pretty slow, just then figuring out that Roberta wants him to look it up in the computer.

"Cahquenobway," Roberta tells him, spelling it out loud. But the man is already punching it up on the computer. He acts all fumbly and suspicious and put out, as if she were asking something unusual or inconvenient of him.

The man looks smugly at her as if he was right all along. "There's no such person," he says. "We have no record of that name." Roberta stares at him, and he stares back, but only for a second, because he's a fat chickenshit. He ducks into the little room behind the counter and she hears him shuffling about. She waits. This can't be all there is to it. She put her husband on the plane here last week. She and the kids and Merle's friend Linus, who drove them down, saw him get on. He didn't just fly off into the twilight zone.

The man peeks out a couple of times, but he won't come back out. Another guy comes out of a door at the other end of the counter. Roberta goes up to him.

She says, "Excuse me. I think my husband gave me the wrong day that he was supposed to arrive. Would you please check and see if Merle Cahquenobway is scheduled to arrive tomorrow afternoon? Here's how you spell it." She take the desk pen from its holder and writes the name down directly on the countertop to make sure they pay attention this time. Merle's not from here. Everyone has trouble with his different name.

Roberta decided way back that her own last name was one thing that no one was going to take away from her. That name is her history.

"Sure, he'll be here tomorrow, same time," the second man tells her, quickly retrieving that information, wiping the name up with a Kleenex, casually puzzled at it and her.

"Thank you," says Roberta, thinking of mean things she might say and do to her husband now. He told her the wrong date to come when he telephoned, that meatball. Roberta walks back to where the fat whiteman is hiding in the little room. She stares hard at him. "What did you do that for!" she says.

"I thought it was spelled with a K," he whines imperiously. What's the use of figuring him out?

Roberta drags the children out the door. She means to get right back on the highway and head straight home. Somehow, she is sucked downwards with the flow of gawking drivers. All along the airport side of the road she can see dozens and dozens of aircraft lined up in the fields. There is a huge, ominous camouflage cargo-lifter plane with a tank sliding out of its belly. There are traffic police standing in the intersections, directing people into the show, out of the show, into town, out. Finally, at the top of the ravine going downtown, she gains a turn onto the frontage road and heads north again. On all the boulevards, there are crowds. The parking lots of all the businesses are full. On the narrow grass strips between the frontage roads and the freeway, people are sitting and gazing up into the sky at two stunt planes and the faint loops and rolls of colored smoke they leave in their wake.

The children want to go to Hardee's. They're hungry, desperate, consumed with the idea. Roberta slides into a parking spot just in front of a driver whose face turns venomous. Inside, the kids won't stay in the line with her. She loses her grip on Josette's hand, loses sight of her in the crowd and then sees her toddling out to the deadly parking lot. She goes and captures Josette, but the people glare at her for taking her original place back in line, for having children, for being an Indian. Finally she has the food and follows the kids into the play room they have found.

There is an amazing thing in there, a big fishnet cage full of colored balls that two little black children from the air force base are diving into. They dive again and again, whooping with delight, completely submerging themselves beneath the red and yellow plastic balls. There's a carousel, too.

"Oh . . . just cute," Roberta murmurs, and her children chew frantically, half from hunger and half from distracted anticipation, their eyes on the fun thing. The air force couple is sitting behind them. The wife is a whitewoman whose yellow hair has had a home perm today. That chemical and the greasy plastic scent of the restaurant make Roberta ill for a moment.

"Mama, why's that white man so black?" asks Georgie.

"Camouflage. He's GI Joe," says Roberta, staring straight ahead. She senses the black man grinning.

A man and a woman come and sit down in front of them, followed by a big dumb-looking kid who she can tell isn't the man's son. The man keeps looking at Roberta as if he finds her more interesting. He's handsome in a leathery sort of way, a ranchhand or roughneck. He twinkles his eyes at her from time to time, but she only stares opaquely in that direction. She feels sorry for the boy.

On the other side of the glass Roberta is sitting next to, a cold-faced farm couple are looking sidelong at them, unhappy about their existence. They're probably blaming the farm crisis on the Indians and fuming over the "free things" that Indian get in exchange for the land.

Roberta takes off the children's shoes and lets them go. She watches them play, soaking up their happiness. She feels the heavy sensation start to lift, even with all these people and smells and the horny cowboy staring at her. She feels the shock wearing off. She wishes she could dive into the plastic balls, too. She wonders what it would be like. She watches the kids on the merry-go-round that plays goofy cheerful music.

The dull boy's mother gets up to go to the bathroom while he flops like a big carp in the plastic balls. The man winks at Roberta and says, "Welcome to America."

She looks at him evenly. "I should say that to you," she replies. The man half nods and half grins and puts his cowboy hat on and tips it slightly. She smiles through him at her children on the carousel. The man's date gets back and they leave. Roberta just sits for a long time watching her children play. People come and go. The farm couple look at her as if she were loitering before they leave. When the children are good and ready Roberta puts their shoes back on.

Roberta thinks how they were satisfied with that experience, going to eat fast food and dive into plastic balls, just because it was something new, something they hear about on TV, something from the little square world of visible lightray transmission. She planned for this day to mean something, though.

A few miles out of town Roberta decides they won't go home, since it's too late for dancing. And so they meander the backroads, looking at things and places, and Roberta tells them the stories for these places and things, and Roberta remembers her parents and grandparents and great-grandparents and the time when she was a child.

Once they stop beside a line of Russian olive trees and eat candy until they're sick of it. Roberta translates what the meadowlarks are saying to one another, laughing at her own imitations of her halfbreed grandfather imitating birds. *"Oh Jib-Jibaloo, have you seen Chi-Mawree?" "Do-si-do, do-si-do, turn-er round and letter go."*

She tells another of his stories, about a long-ago boy whose father was a great warrior chief and hunter. Wanting the son to follow his example, he painted the boy red in front and blacked him all over with ashes and left him to fast and pray alone until he'd receive a vision to make him powerful. But the boy was not fierce or strong, in fact he didn't like to kill anything at all, he only liked to visit people and sing to them, so he turned into a bird and flew away into the sky.

"He told his dad, 'Don't be afraid; I am happy now. I can always be found near the lodges of People and I will be their friend, and they will give me food and never harm me.'"

"Robin! Robin! It's a robin bird!" the children laugh, just as Roberta did once.

Crossing the buffalo plains, she keeps on remembering, telling, passing it on. And then the big blue turtle is there, swimming on the great grass ocean.

There is that feeling that always comes. To enter the center, to go home. To the Turtle on top of Turtle. In spite of everything it's still there.

This time she turns at the big stack of tire rims and lets the kids out to climb. Then they head north, toward the International Peace Garden. Alongside the road the woods start, and the Indian houses, and the sloughs with the horses and cows browsing on the edges. Then it's a wide fragrant cut meadow valley, the rotund bales of new green hay strewn here and there, a red barn perched on the dense oak hillside. Then the white woods again.

Roberta has always thought of the Peace Garden as a place for squeaky-clean whitepeople, bible-camp kids and senior citizens in seersucker outfits who watch Lawrence Welk.

They enter the Peace Garden and loop through the U.S. and Canadian drives, not just once but four times an a long lazy figure eight, the sign of infinity, and Roberta rolls down the windows and drives very slowly so she can hear the whispering of the trees, the birch and quaking aspen, and breathe their oxygen. The breeze goes thrilling the heart-shaped leaves.

She tells her children, "Be as quiet as you can or you might miss something. Don't talk or you'll scare everything. Listen to the trees. Watch for a deer. A porkypine. A moose. Look at those trees. Listen to the leaves. They're talking leaves."

Roberta appreciates the hush that falls over the vehicle, the noiseless engine of the vehicle, the purifying breeze that flows through it, through the trembling, talking leaves.

"What are they saying, those leaves?" asks Amanda.

"Well," says Roberta. "I think they're saying, 'Peace be with you.' 'And also with you.'"

"Like church, huh," says Junior. He enjoys being some kind of authority of things. Roberta laughs at his serious expression.

They stop finally and park beside the demonstration garden. Roberta studies the flowers and reads their names: Petunia Polo Salmon. Petunia Sugar Madness. Geranium Rose Orbit. Marigold Janie Yellow. Marigold Inca Orange. Dalberg Daisy Golden Fleece. Goldilocks Rudbeckia. There is a type of genetically engineered Indian paintbrush in different glowing colors.

Two teacherly-looking old tourist ladies are talking over where the kids are. Says one, "Isn't that the most gorgeous thing you ever saw. Makes you think of *ribbons.*"

"Mama! These things look like brains!" calls Junior. "Celosia Dwarf Mix," says Roberta, reading the sign. "They look like brains, sure enough. Little plushy brain plants." Magenta, golden, orange, deep wine red.

"Yes, they do," says the other old nice lady, and smiles at Roberta. "Perhaps you have a doctor or a scientist there."

Now that might be all right. Roberta once had a grade-school teacher who liked to say, absurdly, "Any one of you in this classroom could be President."

They go across and look at the floral clock that's 18 feet across. "Man, that's a peace clock," says Junior, awed. He climbs onto the green mound and peeks under the sweeping hands, trying to glimpse the workings. Roberta sees that it's almost nine p.m. already. She watches the second hand move and imagines she feels the greyness subside, stroke by stroke.

They walk to the formal gardens. They go to the stone terrace just above the sunken gardens and waterfall pool. The kids gain the overlook first and scream excitedly. "Turtles! Turtles! Come see, Mama!"

Roberta comes up and sees that the waterfall pool is full of painted turtles, which never used to be here before. Now they're loafing about on rocks and logs that are held up by posts. The pool is clear and newly-painted a bright turquoise. It winks with silver and copper coins. In its center is a rainbow fountain.

The terrace pool, too, is bright and glittering, turtles hanging on the sides. It is rectangular and flanked by curving mirrors in beds of Petunia Sugar Madness, the purple ones with the dark centers like a thousand eyes, and the kind that has red and white stripes and a dizzy spinning look like the peppermint candy in the sack Junior carries.

Roberta looks east over the terrace pool, down the long panel of grass and flowers, between the two flags, toward the reservation, and contemplates certain things. She goes to the overlook and looks west, gazing down the cascade that flows from under her feet to mark the border between the two nations, and she sights through the tall peace towers at the chapel end. The carillon bell sounds.

"Twenty, twenty-one, twenty-two," counts Junior. "There's twenty-two of these. These are peace turtles."

"Peace turtles," Georgie repeats importantly, looking up at Roberta's face to confirm this.

"That's right. They're peace turtles. But what is that?" she says, trying to figure out the flower bed design nearest them on the second terrace. One year it was rainbow, easy to see, but this one puzzles her eyes. Further down, she can see other big flower pictures, one a butterfly, and then the two flags, the stars and stripes and the maple leaf.

"It's the North Dakota flag I think," says Junior after a minute of scrutiny. "Maybe you need glasses, Mama."

The flowerbed has "Peace Garden State" written across the top, and "North Dakota" across the bottom, both in Dusty Miller Silver Dust plants. Begonia Scarlet Rios say "1889-1989." A sheaf of wheat and a radiating sun are in various marigolds and Zinnia Yellow Marvels. Ageratum Royal Delft and Salvia Victoria make the blue sky and purple border, Candy Tufts the white clouds.

Roberta stands there for a while, making a mental beadwork pattern of the scene before her, beads for flowers, row by row. Then she makes individual leaves and blossoms into Ojibway floral design, imagining how each kind would look, beaded. Last she does the turtles—wild roses all over the back, an orange and black pattern for the bottom shell, green and yellow rows of seed beads striping up and down the legs.

A jet streaks up into the blush glow that has begun to seep into blue, and the jet trails sunset behind it. Hummingbirds flit. Bees buzz. Petunias send their stubborn perfume into the air. Roberta feels the ponderous existence of turtles. The children make happy sounds. They wonder why all the money is in the water, and if they can swim in the pools.

"These pools are just to look at. They're wishing pools. You make a wish, then you throw the money in, but you can't say what you wished for out loud. It has to be a secret or it doesn't work."

Junior considers this odd belief for a moment. "Throwing money makes a wish come true," he states, skeptical. "Give me some money and let me try it then."

"We don't have any," says Roberta. She turns her pockets inside out and holds up her empty hands. She watches a turtle slide off a log and down through the water like a stylized design, dark against the blue brilliance.

"Well, we have candy," Georgie pipes up. "We have *lots* of candy."

"Candy won't work," says Junior scornfully. But he looks up quickly at Roberta.

"It works just as good as money, I bet," she tells him. The children fish out Jolly Ranchers, Tootsie Frooties, Big Bees. The candy goes arcing into the blue pools on either side of her, one for each wish. She look around and sees that there are no other people in the garden, that they own this view.

Roberta Ottertail stands before the terrace pool, seeing the bright-colored wishes of children alight among shining eagles, beavers, caribou, presidents. If she had tobacco she could offer it to the water, for that is what the women do, keep the water. She thinks of her grandmother praying, how she'd cover the mirrors before a storm. She says something to herself, a prayer. She regards the long cool pool that reflects the sky like a mirror. It's clear and calm. And that is how she is now, too.

She steps backward, seeming thoughtful, humming an absent tune.

And then she goes flying out of her shoes and into the water, streaming out under the glassy surface like the thing that her name is, doing a barrel twist and a skyward inversion. Past the startled turtles, whooshing up into air at the far end, she takes in the rush of dizzy petunia and yelping laughter, and turns back under to glide across the water once more, holding these things in as long as she can, grinning bubbles.

Thomas McGrath

Invitation

Fargo-Moorhead, about 1980

Friends, I am old and poor.
The ones who lived in my house have gone out into the world.
My dogs are all dead and the bones of my horses
Whiten the hillsides.

All my books are forgotten.
My poems
Are asleep, though they dream in many languages.
The ones I love are carrying the Revolution
In far away places.

This little house has few comforts—but it is yours.
Come and see me here—
I've got plenty of time and love!

Something Is Dying Here

In a hundred places in North Dakota
Tame locomotives are sleeping
Inside the barricades of bourgeois flowers:
Zinnias, petunias, johnny-jump-ups—
Their once wild fur warming the public squares.

Something is dying here.
                    And perhaps I, too—
My brain already full of the cloudy lignite of eternity . . .

I invoke an image of my strength.
                    Nothing will come.
Oh—a homing lion perhaps
                    made entirely of tame bees;
Or the chalice of an old storage battery, loaded
With the rancid electricity of the nineteen thirties
Cloud harps iconographic blood
Rusting in the burnt church of my flesh . . .

But nothing goes forward:
The locomotive never strays out of the flower corral
The mustang is inventing barbwire the bulls
Have put rings in their noses . . .

The dead here
Will leave behind a ring of autobodies
Weather-eaten bones of cars where the stand-off failed—

Strangers: go tell among the Companions:
These dead weren't put down by Cheyennes or Red Chinese:
The poison of their own sweet country has brought them here.

Love in a Bus

Chicago, 1942

It was born in perhaps the Holland Tunnel,
And in New Jersey opened up its eyes,
Discovered its hands in Pennsylvania and
Later the night came.

The moon burned brighter than the dreams of lechers—
Still, they made love halfway to Pittsburgh,
Disturbing the passengers and sometimes themselves.
Her laughter gamboled in the bus like kittens:
He kissed with his cap on, maybe had no hair.
I kept remembering them even beyond Chicago
Where everyone discovered a personal direction.
She went to Omaha; he went south; and I,
Having nothing better, was thinking of chance—
Which has its mouth open in perpetual surprise—
And love. For even though she was a whore
And he a poor devil wearing built-up heels,
Still, love has light which like an early lamp
Or Hesperus, that star, to the simplest object
Lends a magnificent impersonal radiance,
Human, impermanent and permanently good.

Against the False Magicians

for Don Gordon

The poem must not charm us like a film:
See, in the war-torn city, that reckless, gallant
Handsome lieutenant turn to the wet-lipped blonde
(Our childhood fixation) for one sweet desperate kiss
In the broken room, in blue cinematic moonlight—
Bombers across that moon, and the bombs falling,
The last train leaving, the regiment departing—
And their lips lock, saluting themselves and death:
And then the screen goes dead and all go home . . .
Ritual of the false imagination.

The poem must not charm us like the fact:
A warship can sink a circus at forty miles,
And art, lover's lonely counterfeit, has small dominion
Over those nightmares that move in the actual sun-
    light.
The blonde will not be faithful, nor her lover ever return
Nor the note be found in the hollow tree of childhood—
This dazzle of the facts would have us weeping
The orphaned fantasies of easier days.

It is the charm which the potential has
That is the proper aura for the poem.
Though the ceremony fail, though each of your grey hairs
Help string a harp in the landlord's heaven,

And every battle, every augury,
Argue defeat, and if defeat itself
Bring all the darkness level with our eyes—
It is the poem provides the proper charm,
Spelling resistance and the living will,
To bring to dance a stony field of fact
And set against terror exile or despair
The rituals of our humanity.

Poem

The shadow of midnight lengthens across the world.
In the darkness only the lucky really are sure
That the sun comes up at the dawn and the birds sing
And the ones they love come back from the islands of
    sleep.

Voices of night, the metal voice on the wire,
The cry of a child, the voices hosting the air
That cry or laugh in the radio's neutral ear—
All these are unreal: They cannot make me believe:

They are only echoes thronging an empty room
Where we talked with others. Now they have all gone
And nothing exists beyond the circle of light
But remembered landscapes full of my own ghosts

And full of sorrow—full of myself. How far
Now to the farm, or to Nice, or the Ozark hills
Where first I was happy? How far to the promised
    place
Where every image creates an indifferent joy?

All that is unknown land. It is far, far
And lost in the dark, and I carry all my dead.
My murders upon me, I seek that improbable peace
After some other midnight, darker, harder to bear.

Praises

The vegetables please us with their modes and virtues.
                                        The demure heart
Of the lettuce inside its circular court, baroque ear
Of quiet under its rustling house of lace, pleases
Us.
    And the bold strength of the celery, its green Hispanic
¡Shout! its exclamatory confetti.
                            And the analogue that is Onion:
Ptolemaic astronomy and tearful allegory, the Platonic circles
Of His inexhaustible soul!
                    O and the straightforwardness
In the labyrinth of Cabbage, the infallible rectitude of Homegrown
    Mushroom
Under its cone of silence like a papal hat—
                                        All these
Please us.
            And the syllabus of the corn,
                            that wampum,
                                        its golden
Roads leading out of the wigwams of its silky and youthful smoke;
The nobility of the dill, cool in its silences and cathedrals;
Tomatoes five-alarm fires in their musky barrios, peas
Asleep in their cartridge clips,
                            beetsblood,
                                colonies of the imperial
Cauliflower, and the buddha-like seeds of the pepper
Turning their prayerwheels in the green gloom of their caves.
All these we praise: they please us all ways: these smallest virtues.
All these earth-given:
                    and the heaven-hung fruit also . . .

                                        As instance
Banana which continually makes angelic ears out of sour
Purses, or the winy abacus of the holy grape on its cross
Of alcohol, or the peach with its fur like a young girl's—
All these we praise: the winter in the flesh of the apple, and the sun
Domesticated under the orange's rind.
                              We praise
By the skin of our teeth, Persimmon, and Pawpaw's constant
Affair with gravity, and the proletariat of the pomegranate
Inside its leathery city.
                        And let us praise all these
As they please us: skin, flesh, flower, and the flowering
Bones of their seeds: from which come orchards: bees: honey:
Flowers, love's language, love, heart's ease, poems, praise.

John McKenzie

In the Water, Made out of Water

She'd woken up so early that Sunday morning that by five in the afternoon the day had taken on an unappealing elasticity; it seemed that it was capable of expanding to fit any event. Maybe it was another country that she'd stumbled onto. In this other country, she told herself, one is never, never seen outside one's parent's backyard until after dark. This made her feel sophisticated, but then a little foolish. People who lived with their parents, or with their mother and her practically live-in boyfriend, weren't very glamorous.

Sara kicked off her spongy sandals and walked over to the white cement edge of the pool. Her hair had almost dried from her last soaking, and the splashy footprints leading away to the deck had evaporated into faint c shapes under the hot, bright sun. Resigned, she fell quietly again into the blue water. An explosion of air bubbles climbed up her nostrils.

Looking up, past the curtain of water, the cedar deck Rob had built for them seemed to float above the rest of the yard, disconnected from it. Sara could see her book and her ice tea on the rail. After a lovely, electric moment underwater, she allowed herself to be pulled back up to the air. Then again, it just looked like a new deck, a standard addition around here, and an omen of prosperity. Their deck was like that. It almost made their household unexceptional. It had been put up by a pair of bald men Rob had hired, an expansive look on his face as he counted out twenties from his money clip.

She swam a lazy lap or two, unable to do better. This morning she'd first been woken by her mother's aerobics tape. At four a.m., the birds hadn't even begun to chirp. The sound of metallic drum beats was all that made it as far as Sara's bedroom. It was almost grim to think of her mother's flagging body trussed up in Spandex, being ordered into ridiculous positions by a voice on a tape. It wasn't dignified.

"Each morning I arise to the music of Kitaro. I get out of bed immediately and do my breathing exercises. There's really no better way to greet a new day, Sara," her mother had said. "If you'd like, I can lend you my manual and you can read it."

This conversation had taken place at the breakfast table one school day. All Sara'd wanted to do was get out to the bus on time. She had her final in biology to get to. She didn't want to listen to all this. "After meditating, I eat a half cup of yogurt, with wheat germ added, and progress to my aerobics."

Her mother's boyfriend Rob worked days, so when he and Sara left, her mother would have no one to talk to until evening. Sometimes, toward the end of the semester, it seemed that she was actually trying to make her late for her homeroom.

Since school had let out the week before, Sara had begun retreating to the pool for hours each day. In that blue, chlorinated water, she thought she'd lose the claustrophobic feeling she got from being around the house all the time. This would be solved if she got a part time job, plus she'd have more money to go out with her friends, but she didn't want to work at Burger King, which was about the only place in town that was interested in hiring kids her age. That was where Kerith and Julie worked, and where they were at the moment. Maybe her friends' behavior hid her own maturity from view. Sara waited by the pool, alone, for the solution.

She heard Rob's El Camino pulling up the driveway on the other side of the fence. There was the ratchet sound of the emergency brake, and then Rob called out, "Hey Sugar, what's up?" This was addressed to her. Rob always called her Sugar. He must have been able to see her through the slats in the fence.

She rolled over in the water so that she was positioned as if she was in an invisible recliner, moving her arms in slow circles to keep afloat. The gate opened, and Rob's shiny face poked through, his eyes hidden behind oversized mirrorshades. "You still waitin' for your man?"

"I don't have any man."

"So you're still waitin'."

She couldn't think of any smart reply, so she just tucked her arms around her breasts and watched Rob progress up to the deck, clawing the translucent rings of a sweaty six pack in each hand. With her arms in, Sara had moved to a vertical position, so she had to kick to stay afloat. Rob's hick accent only came out after a few beers, so it was clear that he was a little intoxicated. This wouldn't go over too well with her mother, if he was still drunk when she got back.

After she had realized that the drum beats weren't going to let her go to sleep, she'd lain in a sort of grouchy trance for a long time, wondering why her mother insisted on getting up before dawn just to do her aerobics. There was no reason why she couldn't wait until everyone was out of the house. I'd be too embarrassed not to, Sara thought.

Then she heard Rob's voice in the hall. It sounded as sleepy and grouchy as she felt, but somehow she didn't feel any solidarity. Some men's voices distressed her. Men imposed themselves on the world, just by talking.

He must have been standing in the doorway to the spare bedroom, where her mother did her exercises. She could pick out words now.

"Can't you get it through your head, Cathy?"

"I couldn't sleep, you know when I can't sleep I. . . "

"Go back to bed, it's the middle of the night."

"I will not allow myself to be ordered around in my own house." It sounded like her mother was speaking through her teeth. "If you can't accept my lifestyle, then I don't know."

"Lifestyle," Rob said. "I just want to get some sleep!"

Sara's body was tensing up under the sheets. She hated hearing their arguments like this. They didn't even know she existed when they got really into it. They'd yell at each other across the dinner table, spitting particles of food, and Sara would just have to finish quickly so she could go and get her Walkman.

Then their voices became whispers, not because they'd remembered the third person in the house, but probably because they were making up. Her mother's voice quavered.

The aerobics tape had stopped; now it was replaced by Kitaro. What were they murmuring about? She couldn't tell.

That room had the squeaky bed, unused for years, and soon they'd set up a pretty good rhythm on it. Oh no, Sara thought, not this. I don't want to hear this. She could just pick out Rob's grunts from Kitaro and the sound of the bedsprings. Where's my Walkman, she thought, damn, I left it on the deck.

Now Rob sat on Sara's chair, twisting one of the cans from the six pack and popping it open. He had no way of knowing what she was remembering just then. He put his sunglasses up on top of his head, pushing the sweaty hair out of his face. "Your mother inside?"

She floated, uncertain how to answer. "No, I think she left."

"Where is she?"

"She didn't say where she was going."

"So you know she left, you don't know where."

"No," she said, "I don't know."

He sucked from the can to Sara's silent count of five, then put it down on the railing. "Ain't that a bitch," he said.

Actually, she did know where her mother was. She was at lunch with Sara's father. They'd been planning it for a week. This morning, after Rob had left to check in with his AA group, Sara had helped her mother into one of her slinkier dresses, and coached her: "You'll do fine. Dad isn't going to be judging your every move."

"You don't know him like I do. He's very concerned about me," her mother said, pouting in the bathroom mirror, applying a red line just beyond her thin lips' perimeter, a deception that was less likely to fool her ex-husband than anyone else. He used to watch her do this, Sara thought.

As her mother had click-clacked over the cedar planks in the deck on her way out, she'd said, "And I don't think Rob will bother you, I'm sure he'll go get blasted with his buddies, but if he should come back early, tell him Sandi had another attack, I had to take her to the hospital."

Even as her mother said it, Sara knew that it wasn't an excuse that would hold water, and that she'd just have to punt. It was always something like this. Sara left to find the late utilities bill and pay it, Sara left to deal with whatever man from the company had been dispatched to their address.

"You ain't heard from your dad in a long time, right?"

"He never wants to speak to me."

"He calls up your mom, though."

"Sometimes he does."

Rob tilted the chair back on its back legs, holding the can to his groin with both hands. "I get the feeling he might be something of an asshole."

She began to breaststroke to the deep end of the pool. "I don't know what he is. People do what they have to." Even she didn't know what that was supposed to excuse. When she reached the far edge, she turned and looked morosely into the runoff valve recessed into the wall, plastic stopper bobbing crazily. She put her hand over the hole, felt the sucking pressure, heard the slow, dreamy gurgle of water coursing past.

"D'you think Cathy's out with him right now?"

She didn't reply. A can clinked onto the cement, then skittered. She turned, and saw that it was bobbing high on the water at the other end. "Rob!"

He'd already lurched out of his chair over to the six-packs, and was popping another. He stood for a second, looking out past her, past the fence. A dog barked hoarsely in the distance. The beer had somehow endowed him with a brief stateliness as he slowly paced the length of the deck. "He gave her a pool, I built her a deck. What could I do? There wasn't room for another pool."

"Rob?" She wasn't sure he was listening. "Rob? It doesn't matter who builds what for Mom, she doesn't care about any of that."

He brought his gaze back down to her. "Oh, yeah?"

"Yeah, really."

He ran his hands through his hair, and then across his face, mashing her features together. The black T-shirt he wore was briefly lifted up by this action, revealing a hairy, somewhat distended belly. When his hands came back down, he was looking off over the fence, his big arm muscles slackening again.

These people, she thought, what am I to do? She reached

over backwards and dove down, to the white pool bottom, where a green tiled starfish smiled inanely up at her. The pool's small secret. Sometimes, when Sara couldn't deal anymore, she just wanted to run from wherever she was and dive into the pool, to come down here to the bottom and let herself dissolve a little. She ran the tips of her fingers across the tiles, vaguely furry with unexpunged sediment. The water was milky, shadowy, thick. She could almost hold herself down. We are mostly water, she thought, remembering her biology. I am mostly water. I am in the water, and I am made out of water.

Anna Meek

Josephine Hopper

To Edward

You sketched your father with his hands
Clasped, and then redrew his hands in the corner
Of the picture to clasp them tighter. In photographs,
His dark chin and shoulders seem like the unopened box
That you, at ten, drew in your first sketch. Though now,
You've caught Garret Hopper more startled than the camera did;
His eyes are frightened and defensive like an animal's.
I've seen that same naked wildness
Down the long empty streets you've shown me;
Their intimate dialogues with a morning light
Make me feel I've somehow intruded.
You've caught me too, painting me from behind
While I painted Wyoming; and your solitary women,
Each chiseled face gazing distantly to a place
Not beyond their windows—they're all me,
And as they sit in their cold sheets of light,
I can't help think they're survivors. It's the way
You pitilessly confront them and their privacy with the outside,
City rooftops, cinderblock walls, or shapeless trees,
And also the couples bracing themselves against
The sharply edged distances between each other
And the landscape. "I don't know what my identity is,"
You told an interviewer, but you've known all along,
Painting it away into tidy corners, and shadows,
And sightless windows. You've trapped countryside
After countryside in blank silent houses; it's how you've painted me,
It's how you've painted you against me.

Heatwave on Boston Common, 1947

(after a photograph by Henri Cartier-Bresson)

The Common is strewn with overcome men;
If we had found brass buttons,
bullets, this could have been a battlefield.
All day the shadows receded
from the scorched and trampled grass,
drew back into the objects that were thirsty for them,
and the long, beached shapes that press
the earth are now heavy with what have
left them. They've fallen at intervals
of courteous collapse, the politesse
that litter has, a distance known
by umbrellas left behind at the movies.
A distant faceless body, glowing
haloed, out of focus, seems the shape
which sometimes forms in clouds,
an occurrence, not a man,
that drifts beyond our field
of vision.   Had they all dreamed
the war—the ones who lie here
casualties of consciousness—to wake
stiffened from their sleep? The old man
in the foreground, hunched by his fedora,
grasps his knees as if to rise and greet us.
Dark suits, shoe polish, nail clippers,
and bandstands, are the rations he's grown
to live by. Now, we see him
with the understanding of these,
and of what we have survived through our allotments,
sharing his bent, exhausted reverence
for the common treasures we've risked our lives for
as if they'd melt away.

Jay Meek

Skylight

I come to my office like a lapsed believer,
unexpectantly, yet willing to be lifted up.
What will it be like in winter, down here,
under snow? I start my morning coffee,

and lean against the wall where light falls
on my small petitions, my great dracaena.
On our top floor, we're all entrepreneurs,
whether auditor, or poet, or violin maker.

Who knows if one day we'll divide stock,
live through buy-outs, or live fortunately,
and simply value another good day's work?
But I know on mornings I unlock my door

I've come to the place where words happen,
words and light, which to me are miracles.
Weekends, at the heart of an American city,
I feel an absence that extends all around me,

far out across the prairie. I cannot tell you
how comforting it is to work at the bottom
of my room, at the base of its sheer walls,
with shadows rising slowly to the ceiling.

How many thousands of years have passed
since I would have been sitting under water,
sending out my stories from an old lakebed?
But things change. That's why on one wall

I've hung the picture of a steam locomotive
arriving under the ceiling of a Paris station.
Exactitude, the lettering on the poster says.
Many years ago these were sleeping rooms,

dark cubicles. Where are the snorers now,
wandering over the plains to the polar cap?
St. Ives is the name I've hung on my door.
Of all the people I meet, only I come here.

Badlands

Medora, North Dakota

After the Marquis de Mores was murdered in Africa,
his wife wouldn't go back to the town
he named for her. Touring, I've come to the home
they left New York to summer in—

the *chateau:* that's what the settlers called it,
when they opened it to boarders.
How fierce these badlands are with petrifactions,
red clinkers, bentonite clay,

layers of lignite that have burned for centuries.
General Sully said it looked like hell
with the fires gone out,
the spent coals of a hundred one-night reveilles.

In the chateau, heads of antelope hang like pots
on the summer kitchen wall,
just as they did when Teddy Roosevelt stopped by,
dapper, ready for the hunt,

packing on horseback into the penitential buttes,
shining like a garrison
over the town where the marquis once killed a man
for lighting up the moon.

Beauty is often hard on the edge of fraudulence—
what ambition was it brought strangers
to the center of nothing,
to build their world on such grounds?

I drive among the buttes, past a herd of bison,
their summer coats buff and deep brown
as they graze on sagebrush,
their great heads moving through the dry leaves.

Counting the Birds at Christmas

1.

Climbing earth mounds behind the animal hospital
where the vet burns the carcasses
of what can't be helped, I log in four pine siskins
after a day of rock doves and crows,

and later, walking the coulee near the switch yard,
I pass a stand of buffalo berry trees
where five robins, stragglers,
count on a few berries for the deep winter to come.

2.

Last spring at Knife River, I walked among craters
where the Hidatsa built earth lodges
near the village
Lewis and Clark stayed the winter,
dancing at Christmas, on their good medicine day.

On buffalo kills, the horses of the Mandan hunters
worked the herd through deep snow,
and after the women dressed out the carcasses,
whatever was left the wolves took,

all night following the herd over the winter prairie.
Everything alive moves through here
to go elsewhere, on the road to Bethlehem or St. Ives,
lives, numbering and being numbered.

3.

How can I account for the years I have failed myself,
the times I have not acted out of passion
but out of some control I imposed upon my passion,
as if I feared what I wanted from my life?

Some days I feel ashamed of myself, even at my age.
Walking alone, I hunch my shoulders together
as if I wore great white wings,
scapulars I might pull around myself for comfort.

On other days, I have pulled feathers from my skin,
the tarred white feathers of a goose,
sparrow feathers, gull feathers,
feathers I've won in punishment for my wandering.

4.

Last year, birding with a friend by the sewage lagoon,
we counted a flock of snow buntings
skimming the ice, and now when I hear the long wind
fill with voices of the *wacipi* singers,

I hear dancers at a powwow beginning the grand entry,
their bodies stooped and arms crooked out
as though they were raptors.
After them come the tall men who are fancy dancers,

young and athletic, and then the traditional women
with blankets over their arms,
then the grass dancers, the whirling shawl dancers,
and the jingle dress dancers—

the high prairie ringing with ankle bells
and the cries of singers: stragglers, early migrants,
a few more beautiful species
passing through until there is no place we are not,

filling the emptiness with our wonderful proceedings,
digging in, crossing over, rising up—
little ghosts that fly,
the white feathers of my breath leaving in the cold air.

John R. Milton

Jamestown

At night, beyond our prairie town, the train
Glides softly through absorbent grass, a chain
Of window-blinking cars stretched out alone
Upon the flat and rimless land. The bone
It passes, lying restlessly in the dust,
Shines gray while lighted by the moon, a trust
From trackless times, when wagons roughly rolled
Across the plains, and townsmen tried to hold
The wagons for the town. Some stayed, proclaimed
Identity within the grass. They tamed
The land, they thought. We wonder, now, at night.

The train glides in and out, in lonely flight.
The whistle-call hangs tentative and dim
Beneath the distant moon, then fades in whim;
A promise, briefly made, the land denies,
And people of the town hear only sighs
From wind-blown grasses in the private dark.

The train has gone, and hardly left its mark.
Once more we are alone. The prairie's edge
Lies close and tight against the town. No wedge
Of steel intrudes to break us from the past
Or force us into reckless molds, quick-cast.
Cut off from city progress and brown brick,
Our independence flames upon slow wick.

We lie within the all-surrounding grass,
And listen as the nighthawk soars to pass.
The landscape moves, and one hears whispers then:
Ancestral ghosts uprooted from their den
Speak on the wind of sacred past events;
The cottonwoods nod gravely by the fence.
No longer do we darkly lie alone;
Although the train has gone and the hawk has flown,
The town lives on, beside the whitening bone.

Harold Nelson

Rapunzel at the Castle

My prince stops cutting the venison
in midslice. It lies in folds,
red like his royal robes.
"The front gate is grating shut,"
I say. He nods, knuckles white on his knife.
We know the witch howls in her tower.
"Probably the page boy," he says.

I met my prince wandering in the wilderness
after the thorns had poked out his eyes.
He bumped off branches, jerked like a puppet.
I fell on him. My tears filled his eye sockets
and hardened into glass. He watches
me through these blue marbles now,
stares at my head, bald as the ballroom floor.

We hear the witch howl through her canines again,
through the ragged rim of glass left in my window
that my prince jumped through. My head burns.
She has spat on my braids, my nest in her thorns.
"When will you fetch my hair?" I ask.
My prince looks at the red venison
our huntsman has killed, his eyes blue marbles.

Kathleen Norris

Gatsby on the Plains:
The Small-Town Death Wish

"You can't repeat the past."
"Can't repeat the past?" he cried incredulously. "Why of
course you can!"
–F. Scott Fitzgerald, *The Great Gatsby* (1925)

In the spring of 1984 a woman in her early 30s said to me: "You don't understand this town because you're an outsider. You don't know what it was like here twenty years ago. That's what we want; that's what we have to get back to."

Beyond the shock of hearing a young woman say she wanted to recapture the earthly paradise the world had seemed at 12, I began thinking: 1964. The nation was reeling from the assssination of John F. Kennedy. Our involvement in Vietnam was greater than most Americans yet recognized, and escalated that year with the Tonkin Resolution and our sending planes into Laos. Congress passed the Civil Rights Act after a long and bitter struggle. But Southern blacks had to fight to be seated at the Democratic convention; and civil rights workers Schwerner, Goodman, and Cheney were murdered by white vigilantes in Mississippi. College girls like me, if we knew women's history at all, thought that the "woman suffrage movement" had ended because, once women won the vote, all its goals had been obtained.

But Paradise had existed in a little Dakota town where it seemed that the homesteader's dreams of progress were at last being realized. Commodity prices were good, and a federal construction project was boosting the local economy. New churches and a school were built. Population was up, but the boom was not so great that stability was threatened. You could still get baptized, married, and eulogized surrounded by your own. The outside world, and the change it represented, couldn't touch this place. As the woman went on talking, I began feeling real grief and anger. Grief, after all, is the pain of loss, and this woman was taking away both the hard lessons and the progress of twenty years. The road from Selma to Jesse Jackson's speech at the 1984 Democratic Convention. From women in terrible isolation, just beginning to doubt not their own sanity, but the sanity of the "feminine" role demanded of them; to a loosely organized but dynamic global feminism with many victories, in both changed laws and changed social attitudes. Even 1968, with its assassinations and tragic convention; or the Vietnam war, or Watergate. Had all this meant nothing? Would we really be better off to pretend none of it had happened? Or that it had all happened in another world, having no affect on ours?

I began to wonder where her magic boundaries were: the family unit? the town? the state line? I spent my childhood summers in this town, in my grandparents' house, and moved here twelve years ago. But in my friend's terms I was an outsider because I'd grown up elsewhere: and even more importantly, because in defining the town's problems, I naturally referred to the world outside it. The national economy, regional demographics. This habit of thought made me suspect, a serpent in her Eden. Maybe I'd spent too long exposed to the world outside to really value the town she wants to see as a Norman Rockwell portrait come to life. It's a triptych with neat white edges. Dad is at work, Mom is at home, and the rosy-cheeked kids are spending their allowance at the soda fountain on Main.

What she's forgetting is that the soda fountain is gone, along with the drug store it was a part of. It's one of several empty buildings on Main. Paradise wasn't self-sufficient after all, and the attitude that it ever was is part of the reason it's gone.

One of the most dangerous myths that small-town people can operate from (consciously or unconsciously) is the idea that while the world outside may change drastically, the town itself does not. Population may shrink, as it has in the town I'm describing, from 3,500 in 1964 to around 1,900 today. It may grow much older, ending up with a median age that's old even for the Dakotas. But when myth dictates that the town has not really changed, ways of adapting to new social and economic conditions are rejected: not vigorously, but with a strangely resolute inertia. In today's agricultural economy this myth translates into a death-wish, and values that once served to protect and preserve the town become threats to its survival.

I've seen this most clearly in the local Chamber of Commerce. The town has lost many businesses in the last twenty years, but the idea that an Industrial Development Committee should be formed seemed preposterous to many. Their attitude was: Why band together to give a new business some breaks? "We were never given any breaks" was a comment often heard. Some businessmen dropped their Chamber membership over what they saw as foolishness that could not benefit them, and called the others "doomsayers."

They were indulging in a willful ignorance of their own regional history. Ghost towns that once had newspapers, banks, and stores are as close as seven miles away, but the common perception is that the process that ruined them is over. This town is seen as if it had a pristine existence outside of history, exempt from the dynamics of economic and social change.

When the Industrial Development Committee did form, there was talk of bringing light industry in. But aspirations were scaled down almost immediately. Inertia set in, along with old patterns of local greed. (In the past a radio station, bottling plant, and meat-packing plant were kept out by dog-in-the-manger businessmen and investors who didn't want enterprises established by outsiders free from local control.) So the Committee's efforts went mainly to attracting small-scale businesses that aren't likely to survive unless real industries, major employers, are also brought in. A craft shop. A gunsmith. An upholsterer. A dry cleaner and a shoe repair shop to replace the ones we had lost. The Chamber picked the theme "Alive, Well, and Growing" for its annual banquet without any sense of irony, and many were comforted by the boosterism. There'd been too much negative talk lately about how the town was going downhill.

"Sense of community" is a term journalists like to use when writing about small towns. A lack of anonymity is supposed to provide it. When everyone knows everyone else, the theory goes, community is highly valued. This may be true in pioneer towns very early in their history, or towns in which an immediate catastrophe, such as a tornado, has struck. But I'm beginning to doubt that community has much day-to-day reality in my town and perhaps in other Dakota towns that have seen three or four generations pass. The businessmen who opted out of the Chamber of Commerce weren't acting from an innate sense of community. In fact, in their vision of Main Street each business was an isolationist country; they saw no common interest in a battle for the town's survival. It was every storefront for itself.

When we begin to look at who lives in extremely isolated small towns and why, it will help us see through the myth of community. It is a given that these towns cannot hold on to most of the "best and brightest" who grow up there. They move on, after college, to better job opportunities than are available locally. Of course some who come back to run a family business or ranch are as bright as those who opt to leave. But I've found that even these people have a difficult time maintaining a normal sense of the world "outside." They start out regarding the isolation as a hardship, one that is worth enduring for the benefits of raising a family in a small town. But the isolation begins to exact an unforeseen toll and makes them more provincial than they'd intended to be. They drop subscriptions to national magazines, and get so they wouldn't dream of visiting a big city unless they had relatives there. Their curiosity about the world diminishes.

And by the time a town is seventy-five or a hundred years old, it may be filled with those who have come to worship their isolation. These are often people who never left at all; or who fled back to the safety of the town after a try at college a few hundred miles from home; or who returned after college regarding the values of the broader, more pluralistic world they had enountered as something to protect themselves and their families from.

The habitual smallness of their frame of reference begins to shortcircuit the way people think about the outside world, and can radically diminish their aspirations and their ability to adapt to change. Even the young come to view the world as static. Local high school students asked to prepare a resume for a mock job application replied: "Why? We'll never live anyplace big enough to have to fill out a job application." When attitudes like these come to prevail in a town, family is still important, but community may not be. Because it can't look outward, the town begins to turn in on itself, and another kind of shortcircuiting occurs as a schismatic, ultimately self-defeating dynamic takes hold. Reactions I've observed to the current farm crisis will serve to illustrate this point.

Most economists regard this crisis as the worst for farmers since the 1920s and 1930s. In the fall of 1984 *The Wall Street Journal* ran an excellent series on the farm economy that covered agricultural lenders, implement dealers, and farmers who were going under, as well as those who had modernized their outlook and operations and were doing well. Reading about one such successful farmer made me realize how ill-equipped most farmers I knew here were for adjusting to modern agriculture.

Here is an Ohio farmer: "A globe on his desk is a reminder that he must think of world-wide supply and demand, of distant politics and climates. These global factors figure strongly in his marketing now that America faces greatly heightened competition for world grain trade. Successful farmers today must have international savvy. The Richard family does. Dinner table talk is as apt to dwell on Brazil's weather as Ohio's. [They] subscribe to the *Financial Times* of London. Their bathroom reading is a magazine called *International Economic Indicators.*"

I recalled a farm family I knew here. I was helping them paint some buildings on their place and wanted to get a newspaper to put down on the floor. Another friend from town said, laughing, "A newspaper! Where do you think you are?" We had to settle for some pages from an old Sears catalog. That family went broke and had to sell their farm; he's now working as a welder in town. And the insular thinking that helped put them under continues to reign: only six people have read the copies of Dan Morgan's *Merchants of Grain,* or Gilbert Fite's *American Farmers: The New Minority* that have been in the local public library for years. Other troubled farm families who could benefit from Fite's analysis of the process by which America's agricultural majority of 96% in 1790 became a minority of 30% by 1920 and a mere 1.7% today are choosing to believe in conspiracies instead. (More clearly than ever, I'm seeing that conspiracy theories are the refuge of those who've had their natural curiosity bred out of them.)

Still, one is more likely to find realistic economic and social attitudes on the farms and in very small towns (those with populations under 1,000) than in the larger towns. Some ranchers, the few from this area who attend state and regional stock-grower's meetings, do keep current on issues that affect them. In developing strategies to help them survive into the 1990s they have begun to adopt a "wait and see" attitude towards the larger towns around them. They know not all of them will make it.

The tiniest towns have made do with so little for so long that they count themselves lucky to have a post office, gas station, and general store; they have no illusion that they are necessary to the farm economy. But such illusions do flourish in towns like the one I'm describing, that are large enough to have a merchant class, and a real "society" to which farm people may or may not belong, depending on who and how successful their parents were, and whether or not they wear their manure-caked boots to town. Over the last year I have watched "town-defined" people react to the farm crisis with a volatile mixture of fear and denial, and an unfortunate tendency to blame the victim. Of course one of the things they are busy denying is the extent to which they are victims as well.

Several articles in the *Journal* concerned the devastating effects the farm crisis was having on the economic and social structure of small towns. A prediction was made that no town under 1,000 would survive as a viable economic trade center. But businessmen here wouldn't read the series. Xeroxed copies offered at Industrial Development Committee meetings were left on tables, unclaimed and unread. The attitude was that, whatever was being said, it was being said about Iowa or Nebraska and couldn't apply here.

When it became obvious that local farmers were indeed in trouble, and the country sheriff retired early because his life was threatened by an old childhood friend he'd had to serve foreclosure papers on, fears began to surface in town among businessmen worried for their livelihood and retired people worried about an eroding tax base. But no "sense of community" helped them face these fears honestly or directly. Instead, it seemed that the habit of insular thinking had become so deeply ingrained that many townspeople couldn't help but turn the farmers in trouble into a new class of "outsiders" that the town had to be protected from. The fact that these outsiders were now neighbors fifteen miles down the road, and no longer strangers in Detroit, Pittsburgh, or Los Angeles, only made people resent them more. Some even began talking as if the town didn't need those dumb old farmers anyway, as if it didn't really need its agricultural economic base. "They got themselves in this mess; let them get themselves out," was one remark I heard. I knew that the process of turning "insiders" into "outsiders" had finally happened when I heard of an encounter between two "insiders," one a longtime town resident, and the other the patriarch of one of the oldest ranch families in the area. The man had been working desperately, during what was supposed to be his retirement, in an unsuccessful attempt to keep his son from going bankrupt. "There is no farm crisis," he was told firmly, in a spotless living room only fifteen miles from his farm, but a world apart.

The *Wall Street Journal* articles had been easy to dismiss because they came from outside experts. A favorite local saying is "an expert is someone who's fifty miles from home." While this has a certain folksy charm, it also reveals a smug refusal to use expert witness even when it might be in your best interest to do so. And when even "insiders" have become the outside enemy, ministers and other professionals make natural targets. In a situation like the current farm crisis they can set themselves up by simply doing their job, organizing stress and suicide prevention workshops, and county support groups for farmers in bankruptcy. When this happened in my area, the professionals involved were resented by many for making forbidden connections between the town and the world "outside," placing the town within a larger economic structure and historical process. People complained that they were only making things worse with all their negative talk.

Professionals are usually outsiders in rural towns. And they often find that they've moved to a place in which professional standards have slipped over the years. Some of this is a welcome relaxation of urban standards, as simple as the bank president not having to wear a tie to work. But when there's been so much slippage that it amounts to a refusal to see any outside standards as valid; when people have become habituated to not only accepting the mediocre but praising it, the standards by which excellence is valued are seriously eroded.

The state auditor finds the same errors year after year in the city books but no one thinks to change the way records are kept. A teacher lets a student enter a speech contest without either of them checking the pronunciation of the many French words in his talk. A well-educated newcomer with considerable experience in finance and endowments is hired as a church secretary and fired a year later for trying to push her ideas on the finance committee, which wanted to invest only in passbook savings and certificates of deposit as it always had. One complaint made about her was that she "came to meetings too well-organized."

I have come to see that a town's ability or inability to use the talents, insights, and resources of outsiders is a key to its survival. As all small towns in the Dakotas become threatened by a tightening farm economy, I believe we will find that those towns and institutions that actively seek to use the information and advice of knowledgeable outsiders will be more likely to survive than those that do not. It should come as no surprise that one of the most notable characteristics of the town I'm describing is its inability to use outsiders to benefit itself. Over the years it has developed a pattern of isolating, abusing, and expelling anyone it can't at least pretend to assimilate.

In part this is because the town is large enough to have built up illusions of itself as a social and economic center that is vital to the farm economy, instead of the other way around. Outsiders can pose a real threat to the existing social and intellectual order. If their "newcomers' enthusiasm" doesn't wear off, if their standards don't fall to meet the town's, and especially if they keep on trying to share what they know, they have to be discouraged and put down.

Teachers, doctors, lawyers, and ministers, especially those who either have or seek exceptional credentials, tend to live in small, isolated towns for a short time before moving on to a place where they can earn more money and advance their careers. Local resentment over this mobility can be contained when the inferiority of the town to the world is tacitly acknowledged by both parties. But when outsiders really like the area, especially if they're so different in background and in lifestyle that townspeople can't pretend they are "really just like us," then a new and very disruptive dynamic enters the picture, and resentments flourish.

In this dynamic, outsiders can find that their genuine interest in the area is mistrusted. The low self-esteem of the townspeople takes the form of an exaggerated sense of their own importance. The distortion of values that results can be spectacular. One minister here was criticized (in an anonymous letter to her superiors at the state level) for doing volunteer work for The American Cancer Society. As a survivor of a particularly deadly form of cancer, she'd been honored by the Society and asked to take on some speaking engagements. She saw this as a valid form of ministry. But her critics couldn't imagine that her work might reflect well on their church; all they could see was that she was taking time away from them. By this standard, if being honored by the Cancer Society is bad, then winning a Nobel Peace Prize would be much worse.

Newcomers sometimes stir up feelings of inferiority without being aware of it. I remember one minister who came here with a Ph.D. in Biblical Studies from one of the best seminaries in the world. He was clearly over-qualified for the parish but seemed to like it here. A few years into his ministry he found that one of his parishioners, a teacher, had nursed a resentment ever since his first call on her. She felt he had talked down to her, something none of his people who had only grade or high school educations ever complained about. In fact, he had a remarkable ability not to let his intellectual interests interfere with his ability to talk with just about anyone.

"He asked us about our cattle," she complained. "Didn't he realize that I'm well-educated too?" She had a masters in speech communication from a state teachers' college. This degree had established her status as an intellectual in the town and was supposed to guarantee it always, even if all she read anymore was the latest James Michener novel.

She could not acknowledge that her degree in a relatively nonacademic subject was any different from the scholarly doctorate it had taken him a full ten years to earn. He was supposed to ask her about Michener novels, not cattle, and the two of them could sit down and have an intellectual conversation. It never occurred to her that any intelligent outsider might assume that cattle are important in the West River of Dakota, even to a teacher whose husband is a rancher. Apparently she didn't think of curiosity as one thing that defines an intellctual, and that she might learn from him about the Bible as he had tried to learn from her about cattle.

Instead, she joined forces with other threatened "insiders" who were determined to expel this irritating "outsider" from their community. A friend of hers, representing the search committee of the church that had hired the man, told him bitterly: "The only reason we gave you a call was because we were desperate." This remark was both comic and pathetic, and the minister must have felt as if he'd stepped, like Alice, through the looking glass. Her church could barely afford the minimum salary required by its denomination, and as an experienced pastor he could easily have earned twice the money elsewhere. (In fact, he had turned down the pastorate of a 2,000 member urban church in order to take the small town call.) But, as the French say, "No good deed goes unpunished."

What he was hearing reflected a perfection of the process by which a small town's values come to supersede and ultimately reverse those of the world outside. A community in which this process has occurred is a very fragile one, and it needs to see itself as idyllically good in contrast to the bad world outside. This kind of insider/outsider thinking has been well documented in history. It has schism built into it because the insiders must keep using expulsion as a means of maintaining the "good." It is common in a "witchcraft cosmology," as Mary Douglas explains in her book *Natural Symbols: Explorations in Cosmology*. She writes: "Expulsions are used as the method of control which enables the group to go on believing in the possibility of living united."

Lest the reader feel I exaggerate in comparing my small town with a group oriented towards a "witchcraft cosmology," let me relate one final story about the minister. It is well-known to historians and psychiatrists alike that those on a witch hunt begin to see their prey as something less than human, and project their own fears onto them. This man truly began to be seen as an "irritant" and not a person deserving of consideration by those who desired his expulsion. One woman said that he had "caused all her problems," but that everything would be all right again once he left.

The first time he was aware that a group in the congregation was hostile to him was when he was attacked unexpectedly at a meeting of his church council. No one had come to him before. Later, when he talked with the young man who'd done the attacking, he was offered this by way of explanation: "Well, we'd been planning it for about a month, and it seemed like a good time" (It was, in fact, a few days after the minister had been released from the hospital after a serious illness.) This explanation was in no way an apology. The insiders had simply exercised their right to move against the "bad" outsider, who so contrasted to the "good" they perceived in themselves that he no longer deserved to be treated as a human being.

Most outsiders who leave this town do so under a cloud: it's been true of ministers, teachers, doctors, and mental health professionals for many years. They are turned into a kind of witch-figure by a group that can't face its own internal differences. Douglas writes: "The witch doctrine is used as the idiom of control, since it pins blame for misfortune on troublemakers and deviants. The accusation is a righteous demand for conformity. In a community in which overt conflict cannot be contained, witchcraft fears are used to justify expulsion and fission. These are communities in which authority has very weak resources."

Authority often does have weak resources in a small town, and sometimes that "Aw shucks, it's just us chickens" kind of egalitarianism is a good thing. But it becomes false and destructive when a community refuses to recognize any outside authority or standards, and won't allow even the legitimate exercise of authority by the professionals it has hired to work and live in the town.

Another well-educated and experienced minister was resented when he visited women's Bible study meetings to offer comments and encourage discussion. Some of what he said contradicted the material printed in their study books. A teacher was told by a school administrator to stop teaching Shakespeare because "the kids don't need it." She got her revenge by teaching "Antigone" instead. A librarian found she couldn't get twenty people to sign up for a program sponsored by the state Humanities Council in which for a nominal fee people would receive three paperbacks and admission to lectures by visiting scholars. She had thought it might work: the series was on the Dakota heritage, and one of the books was Rølvaag's *Giants in the Earth*. She was told by the leader of one group she had approached: "We decided we already had enough books."

Small towns need a degree of insularity in order to preserve themselves. But insularity becomes self-defeating when people like the minister and the librarian grow weary of pretending not to know what they know, and either leave or simply withdraw by ceasing to offer themselves as resources whose knowledge could benefit the community. A point of diminishing returns is passed after years of tumultuous turnover in the town's institutions. And the resulting vacuum of authority begins to dictate how a newcomer will fare before he or she has even arrived in town. We're now looking for a new school superintendent, and I heard one long-time resident say, "I hope they don't get someone who wants to change everything."

Finally, mediocrity reigns and there is little continuity within local institutions. Ironically, it is the town's most cherished values that have helped bring about the devastation, and the town's own true history that is lost. A few years ago a school librarian had the only bound copies of the high school newspaper, dating from the 1920s, taken to the dump and burned. These volumes would have been gladly accepted by either the Public Library or the Historical Society, but chances are she did not know they existed. She was new in town—there's a big turnover in the school system—and whatever orientation to the town she'd received most likely did not include mention of them. We don't like to connect here.

We don't need to connect. And old newspapers might not let us hold on to the glorious past we've invented. What we need, as my friend suggested, is to turn back the clock to the way things were twenty years ago. The town was booming, and the world made sense. There were no mixed messages, nothing that couldn't be judged by the values we all shared. She may find, as Gatsby did, that disconnecting from change does not recapture the past. It loses the future.

G. Keith Gunderson

Letter: A Reply to "Gatsby on the Plains"

Kathleen,

There are a couple of things that make me unable to respond to your essay objectively. First, although my life is overlaid with the veneer of liberal education, underneath I am one of "them." Second, since I am one of "them," I find myself reading defensively at times.

The geography of the prairie heart, which is fueled by emotion rather than reason, is what you seem to have encountered. Prairie people are often reasonably aware of what goes on out in "the world," but they are acutely aware of what goes on in their own. Sometimes trends seem to pass us by (geography is a very difficult obstacle to overcome, if it can be overcome at all), but what happens to us in this time and place is part of every prairie heart.

Outsiders have always been welcome here. Outsiders have never been welcome here. That is the paradox of prairie existence. Prairie people are curious about lives lived in other times and places, but become defensive when their own lives in this place are left out of the larger picture. What goes on in Minneapolis, Chicago, and New York is nationally important; we all know that. But we deeply feel that what has gone on in our lives during our time in this obscure place is important too. We do not consider our prairie existence to be of no value at all. Outsiders are welcome here if they take us seriously. We are extremely sensitive to exploitation, and that sensitivity creates natural tension between insiders and outsiders. A wall gets built up from both sides.

Outsiders, especially professional outsiders, have made little attempt historically to integrate themselves into existing prairie societies. And insiders have been reluctant to admit who hasn't been around here a long, long time. Perhaps what you find happening in your town is the result of generations of this tension, a tension now compounded by economic stress and cultural decay. Prairie people who experience tension tend to retreat into their inner worlds, into the geography of the heart. This retreat can be positive if it brings that geography to critical consciousness and is used as a tool to inform everyday life. But it is negative if it remains uncritical and subconscious: then, instead of informing reality, it seeks to escape it instead.

This negative *Heimat** is perhaps the most self-destructive enterprise that prairie people can be caught up in, for at root it leads to decay, insensitivity, denial of reality, and eventually death. Our struggle is simple. Either we control the geography of our hearts, using it to inform and enrich everyday life, or it controls us.

Another fact of life out here that prairie people have become accustomed to is powerlessness. Perhaps it is geographic paranoia, but when decay begins to erode the communities and the societies we have grown up in and loved, we feel like powerless pawns of faceless outside interests. Perhaps in that situation we tend to see all outsiders as symbols of exploitation, and respond to the hurt we feel by hurting those who seem to be closest to those forces causing the pain.

It is a terrible trap, and solutions to it do not yet exist. Even I, so much a prairie insider, am viewed by some as a dangerous outsider because of my role as a minister. I represent exploitation, cities, railroads, and robber barons. I represent the church. Those who've attacked me don't trust me at all, and not without reason. Sometimes I have a hard time trusting myself and my own perceptions. I do not always see things clearly, and no matter how objective I try to be, I know that behind my "prairie

* German for native place, town, or land with strong positive connotations or attachment and feeling for it.

eyes" moves a sensitivity to expoitation and a suspicion of all outsiders so deep no one has ever been able to see the bottom. Even you. You "live" here, but you are not "from" here.

You never will be. The prairie society does not belong to those who have the opportunity to come and go. It only belongs to those who are forced to stay. I am outsider as well as insider because horizontal mobility is possible for me in my position. I don't have to stay with the people in this little town and be torn by their sorrows and elevated by their simple joys. I can pack up and leave anytime I want to. And I probably will, like every pastor who has been here before me.

But the prairie people stay. They're deeply rooted in this place and its heritage, and are scared to death of ever having to leave. "Where would we go? What would we do?" *Heimat* becomes a retreat, an escape, when these questions are asked. All outsiders are shut out. And when a person shuts out others in that way they are beyond hope, except for miracles, if you believe in miracles.

There are ways to help alcoholics, workaholics, eataholics, sexaholics, and painaholics. But placeaholics? They are people who are irrationally addicted to the geography of the heart, operating totally on emotion. Reason becomes a lost art for them. They lose insight, and lose the ability to see themselves as others see them, or see themselves as they really are. They only vaguely remember, on an emotional level, how they used to be; and they try to claw their way back into the past. Such people die to the real world long before they are ever buried.

And so we live out here, torn between reality and *Heimat*, friendly by reputation but in reality deeply suspicious and defensive. Maybe poets are the only people who can help us; or we can help ourselves if we happen to be poets. For poets can mirror reality to us in such a way that we can see ourselves as others see us, and maybe then begin to see ourselves as well. I'm a poet myself. And writing about growing up in western North Dakota has brought me more pain than I ever imagined it would. It's been hard to show my work to others, or pursue its publication. I can't stand either letting it go, or being hurt by it anymore: for that work, in a broken way, is my *Heimat*, the geography of my heart. You well know how poets are. Prairie people, I think, are people who experience life somewhat the way poets do, but they do not have the poet's saving capacity for objectifying. And the more they lack that capacity, the worse it is for them. They feel but cannot see themselves or the world around them.

The prairie person's reaction to crisis can be sobering, whether the crisis is a severe depression in the general farm economy, or a disruption in a small local church. People who can objectify will see themselves mirrored in the irrational positions and accusations of others who are locked into *Heimat*. And if they are capable of responding with maturity, they don't respond with condemnation but say instead, "there but for the grace of God go I." But the insanity of *Heimat* is something that's very close to us all out here.

Sometimes I think I shouldn't even be here, because education has sharpened my objectifying skills too well. I know these people with a prairie heart and I love them with a prairie love, even those who have lost the capacity for objectivity. These divisions tear away at me; heart, soul, and mind. For beneath all the other exteriors I have I am one of them. I love tenderness and gentleness and peace. That is my hope for the prairies. I want to see tenderness and gentleness mature. But sin stands in the way, covering us with a bitterness that takes our inner eyes away. It make us selfish, narcissistic, and defensive. Outsiders are OK if they fit into our established patterns, whatever strangeness we have accepted as the norm. We can embrace all kinds of craziness *(Heimat* is an antinomian insane asylum) except the craziness of reason and objectivity. Especially when the chips are down.

When the chips are down we tend to retreat, like children, into that world that never was. We see puzzling reflections of its light side only, and not a glimpse of its darkness. True poets are dangerous to us then, for they will mirror the blind, dark side of prairie existence. A work like Larry Woiwode's *Beyond the Bedroom Wall* will be unbelievably unpopular in a little

Dakota town because it is so true. The power of *Heimat* is based on selective memory, the ability to wipe away whatever is too painful to recall.

Heimat is a world we've fabricated, one which outsiders—and even many insiders—cannot enter. It's a feudal society, our peasant heritage: the gift of the centuries, the downward draw of blood and bone. Progress is illusion and hope is folly. Acceptance would consume us. We are born, we live, we die. Leave us alone. We're aware of our terrible limitations. We bury our loved ones in deep dark holes in the blessed earth, away from the manicured grass of the Forest Lawns or the crematoriums of the East and West. We know we are going back into the earth, we all know that we belong there. We just don't want outsiders to make our days between the dust and the dust too unpleasant.

We don't even trust Jesus, really. We believe in him because we come from a long line of believers. His story is our story, hidden in our blood, buried in our bones. But he too is an outsider. And when we lose the capacity to objectify, we also lash out at him. Often we lash out at whoever is representing him in our midst. If Jesus can't make our sacred *Heimat* work for us, we reason, then what good is he?

The prairie mind is complex, filled with stubbornness and emotional inconsistency. The people can be surprisingly resilient, reacting with grace to changes they know are coming and will continue to come. They are capable of hoping for a place that doesn't change, where exploitation, decay, and death are absent and things can stay, instead of the way they are or used to be, the way they should be.

But inverted *Heimat* is the death of hope. Hope is real, but *Heimat* is a place that has no real existence. We need outsiders to give us hope, to hold up mirrors to us, mirrors of perception. As a minister I'd say we need the ultimate mirror of Jesus Christ the son of God; we need both words and the Word.

Prairie conversation can be beautiful, the abrupt music of it. But people suffering from inverted *Heimat* are inarticulate, and do not know how to express the emotions they experience. They tend to project the existential roots of their unhappiness outward onto outsiders, onto scapegoats. And any outsider who can't "fit in" is destined to take a beating among prairie people. Nonconformity in a closed, *Heimat* society is the unforgivable sin.

Outsiders complain that prairie people are hard to live with, and they are. The newcomer might receive a friendly reception at first, but true acceptance will almost never come. Small prairie congregations reflect this acutely: they've generally had parsonages with revolving doors. The average pastorate for many has been three to five years, and they've adjusted to the flow. In the first three years the congregation is usually non-committal. Year four is a time to prepare for the pastor's leaving. In year five they treat the pastor as if he or she had already left. And most pastors do. But the rare few who have stayed on have forced congregations into commitment. Some congregations even come to love their pastors and experience true sorrow, a lover's grief, when that pastor leaves. And that is good, that somebody cared about them enough once to hurt them like that. If they are spiritually mature enough, they can welcome a new pastor with their new-found commitment. But this seldom happens.

My theory is that we need a generation of pastors who will commit themselves to the squalid parishes of the prairie with no hope of reward. My wife says that the struggles out here build character. And Paul, in the fifth chapter of Romans, said, "We rejoice in our sufferings, knowing that suffering produces endurance, and endurance produces character, and character produces hope." Who am I to argue with that?

Perhaps in our encounters with prairie people we have to draw from the deepest wells of discernment and be overcautious about judging them. For prairie people, perhaps because they work a hard land, are almost overly sensitive to any form of condescension. We have to work extra hard to keep the relationship horizontal instead of vertical, with them on the bottom and us "intellectuals" on the top. After all, prairie people need what we all need: someone to understand their fears and observe their changes, to share their joys and sorrows; someone to be with them instead of above them, not a judge or categorizer but a friend.

This prairie society needs outsiders but it often ends up repelling them, especially professionals, especially ministers. I have heard glowing praise turn into bitter fire in a few short years. Prairie people know they do this. And hidden in their rejection of the outsider is a seed by which they set themselves up to be exploited and then abandoned, over and over again. They force outsiders to reject them, and when the seed they've sown is come to fruit in dissension and bitterness, they decide, "Well, these outsiders who hated us for what we did to them weren't worth spending the energy it takes to love them anyway."

And so we survive, despite the exploitation and our powerlessness, despite the craziness, despite the decay. And very early on we learn to befriend death, looking forward to the day when we will finally rest in some forlorn prairie cemetery with relatives and friends around us. The land and the weather force us to live in light of that reality. We belong to the land.

Also hidden in our response to outsiders is the most basic characteristic of minority behavior, the "us" against "them" mentality. This is a land of insiders and outsiders, friends and foes. Tom McGrath once commented on the latent Manichaeism of the prairies, contrasting it to the Pelagian sunshine of southern California. That makes sense to me, and is probably why I am more attracted to Martin Luther's passive picture of a person being like a horse over which God and the Devil fight to ride than I am to human potential movements and the power of positive thinking. It's not that such things are not attractive to us here. They are. And we wish we could embrace them. But such neo-Pelagian ideas always seem to stumble on our latent Manichaeism. And the outsiders who bring them to us tend to stumble too.

It is hard for the outsider professional to live on the prairie. Sometimes it seems you are struggling against an immovable wall, wasting your precious life and talents on unimportant things in this unimportant and ungrateful place. Maybe professionals with low self-images function better out here than well-adjusted, self-confident ones do. A touch of masochism doesn't hurt either.

Working with prairie people is like dealing with some families I have run across. They can say anything they want to each other, but let someone outside the family make a less-than-positive remark about one of the members, and the entire family rises up like a single organism to repel the invader. This is the way I found myself responding to your essay.

The essay is very good. It will be a sensation in St. Paul, Piscataway, and Poughkeepsie. But folks out here, if they read it at all, will only smile and unremember it. They'll remember only what a curious character this Kathleen Norris was or must have been. "It takes all kinds," one will say. Then the others will nod and go on.

Keith

Antony Oldknow

Field

I turn a corner and there is a field,
an ordinary gray field with a horizon
and trees, a couple of them in the mud,
and a silo and stables a little nearer.
Otherwise, blank graying grass.

However, to my astonishment, on it
there are mannequins, a group of them
with bright flesh-colored faces and arms:
in the foreground, a female model,
right hand on her elegant hip
as she stares ahead in a fury.

Behind her, together, are two young
girl models in going-to-church frilly
dresses and broad hats with flowing
ribbons. They are close together. A cow,
whose field it is, a gray cow, has her
head up from grazing and chewing
and stares curiously at the two girl
mannequins as they shine there,
stood as if staring worried at the woman
who is their model mother. She
is ready to stand on her indignant
dignity. I know that poise; the designer
has caught the mood excellently.

The little boy standing stiffly
a little apart from his stiff sisters
has his hands in his sailor-suit
pockets. The sneer on his face
is beautifully done, the kind of
mischievous cheeky sneer only an
eight-year-old naughty boy who
sticks pins in the girls' bottoms
on the Sunday-School benches ahead of him
could have—incorrigible boyhood!

It is a muddy field. Gray mud.
It ought to rain. I would feel
happier if it did, if the sides
of the cow smoked, and the trees
waved, and thrashed their heads
and shoulders and hidden passions
in the sudden gale, and you heard
the staccato drumming of hail
build to a deafening bedlam
on the corrugated metals of barns
and silos and the gray farmhouse.

I would feel happier if the paint
on the woman's face and the dye
in her hair ran down the plaster
in streams, staining the bright
clothes in patches, if their haloes
drooped, and all began to sink,
ankles and legs and hands in pockets
into the gray mud, like folks
in an open elevator going down.

Extra Mailman

A bird on a gate, a roof of snow on a hedge,
and a squall of footprints swerving round a gate
all the shivering winter, when you love the fire,
the shattered walnuts, and the maudlin dog,
when the sun comes through and shines though it shouldn't....

I get down a slick hill slowly, watching each foot,
careful to listen for cars behind me, pass the church
and post office, and enter the village which smells of coffee;
with snow falling from my feet, I ease up on a stool
and eat a doughnut and read the paper and watch.

This is a town with oddly-numbered street houses
in no order you can discern—all dotted about;
they say they numbered the houses in the order
they were put up; perhaps the mailman delivers there
in the order he thinks they'll all be pulled down again.

I remember delivering mail at Christmas in England,
an extra man to handle the extra mail, and coming on
an angry man who threatened to set his dog on me,
who swore and shouted after me because he had no mail
and kept on having no mail day after day for weeks.

I remember my cold hands among the letters, the mail from
    Milwaukee
from English brides of GIs now living in the Beer City
and sending home greetings to the old country—
maybe the packets were food parcels.... I remember seeing
miserable tricked brides from England out in the prairies.

The exchange rates had been miraculous, all Americans rich;
he had promised her he lived on a ranch; she thought of
venetian blinds and dry martinis, of four-lane highways,
skyscrapers, and doing deals; and, above all, she thought of
    Grand;
he must have come from the movies, one of the war-movie
    heroes:

he brushed his hair away from his freckles, standing
up in the turret of a mud-smeared tank that ground
down our street among the astonished horses; he had gunned
the black-helmeted troops with swastikas into their native soil,
and came like a fresh young saint among our old bricks.

But I know now they have mud tracks in North Dakota they call
roads, where the rats and the tumbleweed leap, and stores
where the oil lamp's brown light wavers in the wind, and cards
are bent and shuffled in the roar of the combines going by,
and they have International Harvester hats for the kids,

and she keeps a picture of the Queen on her bedroom wall
and wanders around the yard in her downtrodden old slippers
chasing after chickens, looking for their lost eggs under bushes,
sitting down round the hot tin stove in the evening,
and writing in ballpoint of all the joys of America.

I remember the proud old mothers and fathers opening the door
to me suddenly and holding out their hands
for mail, eyes opening wide when they saw the president
on the stamp, ripping the envelope open and beginning to
read aloud even before I'd gotten down the garden to the gate.

They were slouching around in slippers too, with big knobs
of fur on the ends above the pointed toes—dressing-gown folk
with bleary eyes. I walked in the snow carefully, watching
for the sudden cat-scratch and dart-away, the wild children
who would drop a huge snowball down a mailman's back,

and then it was into the house at the end of the block
with the scotch and Christmas cake, the lady with pearls
and a yellow bird in a cage, and her dead daughter's
picture in a gold frame, and her husband asleep
with his cigar burning beside him, and her gray hair and
    bright eyes.

The Sheep

Peterborough, England, 1945

The sheep come into town with the convoy,
the farmer and his collie driving them along
while a column of ragged prisoners under guard
heads back the way the soldiers and the sheep have come,
armed with spades and forks and hoes for the potatoes . . . .
The army convoy keeps on coming down the lane,
inching along between the prisoners and sheep;
the sheep are grubby, rheumy-eyed; one or two of them cough.

Small boys at a corner store
who have been gloating over candy in jars in the window
turn around and watch. One of them, who is bold,
yells out at the convoy, "Got any gum, chum?"—
a thing he's heard from people who go to the movies—
and he keeps on yelling this over the heads of the sheep,
the quarrelsome sheep which keep on trying to thrust up
their snouts in defiance and head off down a side street

until the busy dog rushes up and nips at the ankles
of one of them, as an example, while, in the meantime,
the brown trucks have halted for a slow coal train
crossing over the street ahead, and some of the soldiers,
who are eager, drop down and race across the road
between the sheep, and hammer on the shop door,
only to find it all locked up and the closed sign
perched discreetly in the window, and they swear;

but the brave little boy, who will go far,
inserting himself suddenly between the soldiers
and the sheep, yelps up gamely again
through spaced defiant teeth, "Got any gum, chum?"
And one irritated soldier, abruptly, to get away,
pulls out some gray gum from his mouth
and gives to the boy a piece he's broken off,
and the boy smiles with satisfaction before he swaggers.

He swaggers before his rivals, dancing about between
the nag and scuffle of sheep, chewing with mouth open,
panting with joy like a furious shaggy upright dog,
while the prisoners limp by sullenly in their column,
herded along to their captive gardens,
and the grumpy sheep under their burdens of wool
surge and panic, clumping their feet,
heading for a slaughterhouse they cannot imagine.

Janet Rex

Detasseling

Recruits at sixteen for Jung's Seed Company,
we were hired, along with Leroy,

to ride up and down the corn rows all day
plucking tassels for cross-pollination.

Leroy, our tractor driver for the season,
had a summer burn and broken teeth.

He leered at us girls growing through puberty,
who worked for cash and a tan, oiling our skin

each day before mounting the tractor baskets,
high, to either side of him.

I saw his eyes gleam as he looked over
his shoulder at the oiled young skin bending

over the corn rows and pulling the pollen feathers
from the tops of the ripening corn.

Some girls, silky white tassels in hand,
flirted from the side baskets

by tickling Leroy's ear or the slope
of his chin when he smiled at us

riding like two small harems in the pockets
of his large tractor. At noon,

we lunched, stretched on the grass,
then pushed deep into the stalks

of green leaves, where we lowered our shorts
and bent to wet the earth

before climbing back into place
to ride up and down,

up and down all day along the corn tops,
detasseling, for minimum wage.

On the Locked Ward

Here, residents lose their history
and become like trapped wolves
or rabbits behind glass.
Marvin paces the tile, or stands
transfixed in his tracks.
Melinda twitches and stares,
tucked primly on the couch.
Leonard, whiskery,
                howls and wanders.

As I watch them move,
I wonder what moons they meditate,
how the dust grazes their senses,
how light filters through their still irises.

Rarely speaking, only grunting,
repeating some locked-in phrase,
they hunger for contact,
and the mating of similar flesh.

Marvin took my hand one day
and I followed until he motioned
toward his bed.
Leonard exposed himself
in the lobby mirror, peed
at his reflection, repeating
strained undecipherable syllables.

At meals they shuffle together,
chaperoned toward the cafeteria
like a pack of balloons
bobbing, bobbing, in a tight grip,
before they eat routinely,
staring forward
with their silver spoons
stuck firmly in clenched fists.

CarolAnn Russell

Silver Dollar

Once we were safe for democracy
Dad bought a square black safe
which became the country he had fought for,
silently beating
back fire and flood
to guard against the multiplication of fate.
What divided us were the silver dollars
wrapped in green felt, heavy as stone.

I dreamed he dropped them in the sea
where he died, the flag folded like a napkin on his coffin.
I stashed one away like a war medal,
another sliver of his heart,
plunging it deep into the drawer next to the silky things
as the silver woman with her torch
slipped into my chest.

Thereafter on the day of his death
it throbs like a boji stone
or the shrunken heart of a child.
I hang it on a silver chain between my breasts:
men want to kiss me there,
tracing blue veins with their tongues, saying
my skin tastes of salt and metal
as if they know I have a keepsake
and they want to lay their hands on it.

Sometimes my heart moves
and I feel silvery cold, afraid
that I am lost in the middle of my life
because my father is dead.

Then it rolls toward me smooth as silk
like an act of love, an island,
and I feel the little craziness that is hope.
Hot days when a breeze bursts, then lingers
tracing faint haloes of watermarks on the countertops
and gently pushing the white paper napkins
onto the checkered floor where they flutter
like blank pages torn from some book,
somebody like me lays down hard silver from the past
among the green wings of dollar bills
sewn with tiny red and blue threads from invisible flags,
lifting it like a manhole
off the heart,
letting anyone who wants to
touch it for the moment,
for nothing.

David Solheim

Thirtieth Birthday

At the crossing headed west,
Engine number 1947.
I watch the year of my birth
Pulling a string
Of empty boxcars over the hill.

Son

When my father's father died,
The pastor told my father:
"You're never fully grown
Until your father dies."

When my mother's father died,
My uncle talked with me:
"I've been sorting through Dad's desk.
My letters don't say anything.
I never could please him; he couldn't tell me how."

The night before my father's surgery,
He lay ashen-gray, a banked fire flickering out.
I thought about the letters I hadn't written.
The poems my father has never read.

I've stood at my grandparents' graves.
The thriving grass, the distant homestead trees,
The sky arched over the prairie
Seemed fitting, appropriate.

I can't imagine my father's stone
Or grass healing that raw earth.
That absence is too vast to imagine
Until it exists for me.

My father seemed small that night.
As though he were disappearing,
But preacher or doctor, something held him
And my father was restored.

We know those powers will fail
And we will be alone in fact;
I will know what he knows,
Not this premonition.

Golden Anniversary

Gathered in this church basement
In this small town
Surrounded by strips of fields
And cattailed sloughs
In the center of North Dakota
Are my farming uncles, their hired hands and neighbors:
The heroes of my childhood.

I want to tell my son their feats,
But he sees only tired old men,
Balding heads unprotected by their caps.
Dry voices crack during the testimonials,
Bones show through where muscles used to bulge.

I see these shoulders could no longer carry me.
My son wonders how they ever could,
But I will think of them as giants
Even when they are in the earth.

Horsemen

As the clot hit his brain,
He slumped into the kitchen chair,
His hand hit the table like an axe
And the world fell away.

The meadow lark sang matins at evensong.
The moon rose like a bloody orange
Over and in the pond
Where every bird he had ever heard
Chirped, whistled and drummed.

He dreamed of dangerous horsemen
Charging through his camp and
Carrying him off.

His body awakened gradually,
But his useless hand still rides
With the horsemen who wished
To spirit him away.

Medicine Hole

I drop a pebble down the shaft.
It bounces along the net-fence ladder
Deeper than my ears can follow.

Out on the bluffs under a bush
That casts less shadow than my hand,
Nighthawks crouch like soap-stone effigies,
Locked in life, the totems of themselves.

To this place one should bring
Tobacco and kinnikinnick and let it drift
Through the limestone heart of earth.

This is where it all began.
Stones and clouds whisper
That I could live
Like a hawk on air.

Naomi Stennes-Spidahl

Walking on Water

The first time I saw her she was swathed in leaf-green and shivering. The second time I saw her we were surrounded by the material of my world, and we were both suffocating. The third time I saw her was the time she rescued me.

Our encounters happened during one of those inhospitable February cold snaps, when tires crunch on the biting snow and people run between cars and buildings, buildings and cars. When I saw Tabita for the first time, she was pressing her elbows against her side in a futile attempt to warm up. I had left my two daughters at home with my husband so I could go to a mission conference at our church. The speaker was Gelfou Bulus, the president of a Lutheran seminary in Cameroun. He was Tabita's husband.

I had been rushing around ever since I got home from work—talking to the girls, fixing supper, making scattered conversation with Sam, washing dishes, getting things laid out for bedtime, changing clothes and renewing my make-up—and then I tore out of the house into a stiff car and rammed through our town, which seemed to be more exhaust and smoke than substance. When I finally sat down in the middle of the church, just in time for the opening hymn, I took a deep breath. I was by myself, at last.

I wouldn't normally have gone to this kind of a meeting—I'm very protective of my evening time with my family—but I was afraid that if I didn't do something just slightly out of the routine, I would do something very strange. That morning, on the edge of my sleep, I had had a dream about a big family birthday party

for my husband. It was a nightmare. We hadn't planned anything special for his birthday because it was his thirty-eighth,
and there is really nothing remarkable about that, and because
his birthday came on a weeknight and I just couldn't imagine
getting everything together for a dinner party. But, in my
dream, when I came home from work, some relatives were
already there, and as I rushed in and out of the rooms, picking
up and rearranging, more and more came. Finally everyone was
there—about twenty-three in all—eating pistachios and pretzels
and joking about having to put candles in the store-bought
Pecan Sandies because there was no cake. I got icy and took Sara
and Kate into the bedroom. Then I woke up. But for a minute,
I just lay there, continuing the dream. My waking fantasy is
what really frightened me. After all, a person should be in control of fantasies, whereas you can excuse yourself from what
you dream. I imagined that Kate and Sara and I simply disappeared and began a new life. We left through the bedroom window, taking only a backpack, which I had conveniently left on
the bed with all the important things in it; we sneaked around
(in the thickly-falling snow) to the garage and took the car; I
somehow just happened to have several thousand dollars on me;
we drove and drove and then I couldn't quite decide on the
details . . . was it Anchorage where we found our new place? or
Quebec? South Carolina? All day my fantasy followed me. I was
afraid that I would do something a bit out of sync, like being
stark naked underneath my coat while showing the Dahl house
to a very proper retired couple, or going into the Salvation
Army and buying a wig and then wearing it to lunch with the
realty crowd. Mostly I was afraid because I didn't know I needed a new life. And yet I must have, if I could imagine it all so
thoroughly. So, I was relieved, when I scanned the paper in the
minute when the girls were in their rooms and supper was just
about ready, to see the announcement for this conference and
have my memory jogged. Just the thing, I thought. I'll get away,
just for an hour, I'll listen to someone with a different accent,
I'll see a bit of another life. Maybe that will cure me.

　　When the peripheral things were over and Gelfou got up to
speak, I was ready and willing to be transported. He was very

black and wearing a thick white cotton tunic with embroidery around the neck. He wore it over cotton trousers. His voice and the way he used English made his words seem more substantial than North Dakota talk. I listened intently, but when I realized he was giving a scripture-based sermon just like any I would hear on Sunday morning, rather than telling us something personal or giving us some glimpse of his real world, I started to drift. That's when I noticed Tabita. She was dressed in a patterned green fabric: a scarf, a blouse, a shawl, and a long wrapped cloth for a skirt. Someone had lent her some sensible Bass shoes which looked rather out of place, and she was very cold. I thought I could even see her shivering from where I sat. Her face was so shielded that I began to wonder what she was thinking. She seemed so out of her element.

After the service, I was thinking about talking with her, but a crowd quickly formed around her and Bulus. I noticed that Lisa, a member of our church, was interpreting for Tabita. Tabita looked very uncomfortable and I didn't quite trust my own college French, so I skipped the encounter, went home, and put my strange fantasy out of my mind. At least I took the girls with me, I thought. That night I slept in fits and starts, but without dreams.

The next evening, I had to go to Wal-Mart to drop off a film. I had the feeling we needed something I couldn't quite put my finger on, so I walked through the household aisles. When I turned the corner by the toilet bowl disinfectants, I just about ran into Tabita and Lisa.

"Lisa. Hello."

"Hello, Carol. Have you met Tabita?"

"Bon soir," I said, extending my hand to Tabita.

She smiled, looking briefly at my eyes and then resting her gaze on my top button.

"Bon soir. Merci," she said.

I stumbled along in French with Lisa stepping in at crucial moments. I said I had wanted to meet Tabita and her husband at church, but the crowd was too big. Tabita was so gracious and graceful in her manner and her words that I began to feel awkward and bumbling. We turned to the piles of things around us.

Tabita said she thought that, aside from gathering wood, her way of keeping hours and cooking was much easier, much more quickly done. Here we seemed to spend hours taking things from cupboards, putting them on the stove and table, taking them off again, cleaning them and rearranging them in cupboards. And several hours later, it was time to start all over again. As she said all this, laughing, the stacks of cleaners and plastic containers, cheap glass and bendable aluminum began to close in on us. Under the fluorescent light our faces turned gray, and I had the impression we were gasping for air. Five minutes later I was on my way into the blue evening, having invited Tabita and Bulus to our home for supper the next night. Lisa had another commitment; we would be on our own.

When Sam went into town to pick up our guests, Sara begged to go with him. Kate stayed at home with me. Lisa had said that Tabita was finding our food extremely rich, so I had decided to make stew and corn bread, with baked apples and chocolates for dessert. With such simple fare, I had little left to do. Kate helped me start a fire in the fireplace, we put "Love for Three Oranges Suite" on and then snuggled together on the couch, reading another Madeline story.

When we closed the book, we turned off the living room lights and moved to the porch to look at the lights of the clustered fish houses on our lake. The lights came to us in odd configurations and colors. Most of them were in motion. There was the brief rectangle of light when a door opened and closed—yellow from some fish houses, red from others. Sometimes there was a line of light that seeped out between the wall of one of the more rudimentary fish houses and its ice floor. And then were the lights of vehicles, red and white, crawling, speeding, turning.

Kate had stopped looking at the lights and was whirling and twirling to Prokofiev. In the half dark, I could look at her without her knowing it. She held up her ballet dancer's head and her eyes were steady, fixed on things I couldn't see. She had escaped the house, and I envied her. She was not hemmed in as I was by the knowledge of underwear and socks in the drawers, of stacks of dishes in the buffet, of the shape and size of our furniture, of the weighted hangers in the closet, of the numbers in our checkbook, or of the layers of preparation even of a simple stew. Kate glided off to the sliding glass doors, and I sat down on the floor, exhausted by my heavy life. From where I was sitting, Kate seemed to be dancing out on the ice amid the fish houses. I must have made some sound because Kate hesitated in a pirouette and then stopped. She had caught the glimmer of my eyes on her, and suddenly self-conscious, she sank, bobbing in the water once, twice. I would have to grab her hand.

"Do you hear that?" I asked, rising.

"They're here! They're here!" She ran off to the front door.

As I walked behind her, I sensed a spreading dark spot within me, but I had no time to pinpoint its cause. Sara bounced in, and behind her came Tabita, then Bulus and then Sam, who looked relieved to be home.

"Bon soir. Soyez le bien venu," I said. "Welcome, welcome."

"Merci," Tabita said, reluctantly giving up her coat and boots. It was again a cold night.

She was dressed in green as she had been the night I met her in church, but this was a different green, deeper and of a shimmering cotton.

Sam hurried them away for a tour of the house, the house that he had built, while I made last-minute arrangements of the food and table.

They lingered in the porch looking out over the lake. Tabita and Bulus were laughing and shaking their heads in incredulity, and Sam was enjoying this moment. Something from the darkness inside of me raised itself, but I pressed on, refusing to look at it, my goal the presentation of my meal. When I joined them to invite them to the table, I realized the source of laughter and wonderment: the frozen surface of the lake. Bulus was explaining something to Tabita. She turned to me.

Water strong enough to drive on?

I held my hands about two feet apart, one above the other. *"Comme ça,"* I said, "This thick."

Tabita did not quite believe me.

The conversation took place in snatches of gestures, French, English, Moundang. Around the stew we learned about their lives. They had ten children, the youngest was two. Tabita grew corn and vegetables with other seminary women. They sold some of it at the weekly village market. The older children took care of the younger children.

Sam told them about us: Carol sells houses, Sam sells cars. Two daughters, that was evident. What was left? So much of our lives are explainable in terms of calendars, meetings, memberships, arrangements, and lists, and it somehow didn't make sense to tell Tabita about all that. I wondered if they understood what this house means to Sam, the crowning achievement of years of moonlighting and stiff money management and that he had built it all himself, on weekends and vacations. I wondered if they understood how carefully I have to balance everything— work, housework, cooking, marriage, and our daughters—in order to survive. I wondered if anyone could sense, that deep inside some murky part of me, I really wanted to leave it all.

After clearing the table and arranging the dishes in the dishwasher, we gathered around the fire. Sara played her new piece on the piano, and then the conversation died. I was searching for an in—the price of the Welty house, the construction of houses in Cameroun, Tabita's fabric—when Sam brightened.

"We should go out on the lake."

Bulus turned. "The lake?"

"Yes. I'll drive us out to see our fish house. My neighbor might even be fishing. You can see what it's like. All of us—you, Tabita, the girls, Carol."

Tabita knew, without translation. She laughed, nervously. *"Non, non, non merci. Pas moi."*

"It's perfectly safe," Sam continued. "The ice is thick. It's been around zero for twenty days. One thing about cold weather in February—you know the ice is safe."

Tabita withdrew, shaking her head.

"Show her all those cars out there, Bulus," Sam continued. "They're all okay. It'd be the experience of your life. You could go home and tell everyone you've walked on water."

Bulus laughed and translated for his wife. "I'm ready," he said.

"You'll come too, won't you Tabita? The girls will come along. Just last Saturday, they came out to the fish house. Carol's coming. Aren't you?"

"Sure," I said. "If Tabita would like to. If not, the two of us will stay here. There's no need to push her."

Tabita turned to look out over the lake and the lights. "Okay," she said, her eyes lowered.

"Great. I'll warm up the car. You won't even have to get cold," Sam said.

Tabita was silent in the car as we drove down the road to the public access. Sam noted the exact moment we drove out onto the ice.

"*Kai, kai, kai.*" Bulus shook his head, laughing and elbowing his wife. Tabita was quiet.

The lake was busy. We met two cars on our way out to the first cluster of houses. Sam drove on to our fish house. A pale crack of light shone beneath the door; George was still there. We all heaved ourselves out onto the lake. Tabita looked down at her feet, at the ice, and beyond, to the thick seaweed and the hovering fish. The girls danced around us. Sam knocked and opened the door. The lamp swayed. George looked up in his slow way. We went in. He had already caught three northern. It had been a good night. Tabita stared at the gaping hole in the ice. Sam liked to cut a big square so he wouldn't have to reopen it. A car drove by. Waves moved the ice underneath us and the water from the hole lapped up onto the plywood floor. Tabita looked at me. We went outside.

The sky opened up above us and around us. The stars were thick.

"The stars are different where I live," Tabita said.

"Oh, of course," I said. I hadn't thought about that. The Southern Cross instead of the North Star.

"Do you fish?"

"Oh, sometimes. It's mostly men who do," I said.

"Where I'm from its the women who fish," she said.

"Oh."

"We use nets," she said. "We leave in the morning in *pirogues. . .* "

"Canoes."

"Yes, canoes, and we're gone all day. On good days we come home with full nets."

"And the children stay home with the older ones?" I asked.

"Yes. And the babies are on their mothers' backs, in the pirogues."

I thought of a fleet of *pirogues* on a choppy lake, and I zeroed in on one woman who was keeping the boat on course with a baby on her back. The cloth was slipping and the baby falling. And then I thought of my daughter and how she had started to sink under my watchful eyes. I was finally looking directly at the cancerous spot that had spread within me all evening. Even if I wanted to leave Sam and our weighted dream house and our hard-working lives, I had thought I would take my daughters with me to a new start and a freedom. Now I thought that my daydream was not only naive, it was mistaken. It may be too late to take Kate and Sara. Kate had seen me looking at her and she sank, no longer buoyed by her own imagination. I had made her drown.

A circle of silence settled around Tabita and me. From inside the fish house the murmur of men's voices expanded and receded. The ice boomed, first far off and then near by. The men laughed. Tabita and I moved closer to each other until we were standing shoulder to shoulder in the darkness. Beside her, a woman who fishes with nets and carries babies on her back, I took in deep breaths of the cold air and exhaled into the night. Leaving wasn't the question; how to stay was. Above us, the stars gaped. Below us, the fish weaved their way in and out of the weeds.

William Stobb

Night at the West Edge of
Grand Forks, North Dakota

There are only three buildings now, but I can imagine
a day when there will be ten or more of these unlikely,
secretive atriums called Centers for Aerospace Science,
where people can look west out black glass windows
at the absolute expanse of the wild prairie while being taught
how to fly planes and rockets.
           The interstate will have to be moved,
I suppose, as it borders closely this west edge, restricting
development like a belt holding the fat stomach of town
with red and white lights moving at speeds
some would consider fantastic.
           And this little convenience store,
hidden like a small bulb under those dark stair-cases of architecture,
what will become of it? Where, on any given night
you can walk by, look in from some distance and see
the blonde hair of the woman behind the counter,
so bright it lights even that fluorescent space.

With Kari's Family at Lake of the Woods

After dinner, before pinochle and drinks at the bar,
Jeremy pulls me down to the beach.
It has been cool, northwest winds bringing whitecaps
from a storm over Canada. I shiver and button my flannel.
Jeremy races down the beach barefoot, thirteen, all thoughtless
    action.
He stops only to wonder who captains the big launches
jumping waves across the horizon. Then he snaps
a driftwood log into a baseball bat and shows me swings—
Barry Bonds, Robin Ventura, names I know just vaguely.
I pitch him rocks and he slugs them out over the breakers.

I'm in love with his sister, and he doesn't mind. Who else
will follow him past the point where the beach dissolves
into piled up wood and rock? Who else will pitch him stones?
I remember thirteen, the certainty that I would hit
the ninth inning home run, trot the basepaths beneath a sea
of October lights. It always happened on TV. It would happen.
I don't remember the first autumn I felt a space inside.
I don't remember filling it in. But now there's wind off the lake
moving the trees along the shoreline. And there's Jeremy,
further down the beach, standing still, looking across the wide
    water.

Speculations

In the spirit of the woman siting in front of me whispering
to her friend all through the lecture on semiotics, whispering
and giggling about the speaker's brown-orange ensemble and
    the price
those of high intellect pay in terms of common sense;

for the boy I overheard at the top of Niagara Falls
tell his father he'd give anything
to plunge like that just once and survive,
and for the father who only nodded gently;

lastly, for the young protestant yawning through the Catholic funeral
of a suicide classmate he barely knew—the young protestant
who, walking back from the communion line, quickly swiped
    the inedible eucharist
from his mouth, stuffed it in his pocket and later
flung it to the air where it turned like an unimportant coin.

For the sake of all these, I feel we must all now speculate
as idly as possible, or commit ourselves
to an action of the least consequential nature.

It's like this: two friends of mine once drank so much beer
that they decided to roll down a nearby hill.
At the bottom, they both abruptly vomited, laughed
and climbed up for another go. Why shouldn't they?

There is a man waiting at the station two hours after
his girlfriend's bus passes through. He flips through his wallet.
He has seventy-five dollars.

There is a woman standing
on the Hennepin Avenue bridge, the Mississippi running below.
Upstream are her parents, downstream a thousand new places.
Her car is just a few blocks away.

What will they do? What will any of us ever do?

Consequences to the wind, I say. Like each May's cottonwood
    seeds,
their beautiful ride a brief reward for having grown
and having to grow again.

Donna Turner

Blizzard

Leaving work, I drive as though
I'm headed into
a storm, as though this windshield
were pummeled
with snow, the roads
deep with drifts
and cars slung in ditches.
These hands
knuckle at the wheel
the way they'd
grab for the hard bones
of friends. And I breathe with difficulty,
as if the air were too cold
to take in comfortably,

though the road is nearly drained
of its winter,
and my son has been released
early from school. He's probably
tapping out survival codes
even now in his computer games,
or else he's phoning
buddies as bored as he.
As long as he keeps

the lines tied, I won't startle
at the ring, I'll never
know if the one I needed
decided not to return
my call, not to resume
the roles we'd settled into
before I walked out
into what feels like a blizzard:
this chill at my throat,
the way my back aches,
the way I keep trying
to see, but everything
has turned white: my hands, the air,
the road in front of me—so white
that all I've ever known
has vanished.

Survivors

Today I threw the mangoes out.
Their bodies, heart-shaped and heavy,
brought back last night's dream
of Sister in labor,
her belly transformed into
fibrous red tissue, a heart
unwilling to let
this one go. *Call 9-1-1!*
I shouted. But phones never work
in my dreams, and so, bending into the dark
writhing on the bed, I pulled the baby,
a white wet seed,
from its womb, strands of its mother's
heart still clinging.
It has no legs, I whispered,
and then I saw them
anchored strangely to the body
and formed of hard plastic.

I've discovered through dreams
it is often those most damaged who survive:
the healthy twin died years ago,
and the one without legs grew them
and outswam the sharks
to shore. I heard the best looking kid in
high school is dead now,
but I imagine good things
for the girl we called retarded
who I last saw smiling,
two kids pressed against her ribs
as they waited for a doctor
to bring one a heart.

None of us can escape
a few moments of terror, a few deep
imperfections—this I tell the little girl
who comes to me in dreams: *It's okay to be*
scared, hon'; it's okay to be you,
and when I wake in a cold sweat, heavy
with the need to retch, I think of
the girl we dismissed
as handicapped, the way she
jumped so high
as we crowded the trampoline
to watch her emerging.

Benet Tvedten

The Healing of Father Albert

When the abbot posted the notice of Father Albert's return to the monastery, no one in the community was particularly pleased. The young monks knew him as a cantankerous old man whose needs they would be assigned to look after. The middle-aged monks expected to be tormented by their boyhood professor for conforming to the foolish ways of modern monasticism. For some of the elderly monks, Father Albert's return simply meant the occupation of another room in the infirmary. When one was no longer capable of service, he was put on the shelf to wait for eternity. Other monks of their generation appreciated retirement and for them Father Albert's coming back to the monastery meant the reign of peace was about to end.

Father Albert himself did not want to return to the monastery. Things had changed too much. It was not the same monastery to which obedience now called him. Holy obedience to the previous three abbots had sent him into the Lord's vineyard where he had labored untiringly for farming communities scattered over the prairie. And what reward did the new abbot hold out to the senior member of his community? The abbot wanted him to return. The bishop, likewise, was an accomplice in the conspiracy to remove him from St. Joseph's. They could both go to hell.

The abbot had hinted that time was running out when Father Albert observed the golden jubilee of his ordination. "I'm sure, Father, you'll want to come before too long."

Because it was his jubilee celebration and the abbot had driven the distance of two hundred miles from the monastery to pay his respects, Father Albert, though irritated, chose to ignore the suggestion.

"Father Abbot, would you like to look at my garden?"

"Why yes. You know, Father Albert, I was thinking that when you return to the monastery, the old garden plot could be plowed for you. We haven't had a garden since Brother Otto died and the younger Brothers aren't interested in gardening."

"I tried a new hybrid corn this year," said Father Albert. "Look at those stalks. You can get lost in them."

He hoped the abbot comprehended the subtlety of his response. There really was no need to respond. The abbot knew how he felt about moving in with those bastards.

Being a pastor, even in this rural place, was no easy thing these days, but it was more tolerable than living in the monastery. He realized most of the parishioners did not object to his presence because with parishes closing all around them, they were grateful to still have a resident priest. Some of the young couples avoided the parish and attended Mass elsewhere. They expressed a need for a more *meaningful* liturgy. Guitars, Father Albert surmised. Only a few high school students came to his weekly catechism class. He had banished several of them from class for repeatedly challenging the Church's dogma. The other absentees were outright truants. Although he could not cope with their rebellion, he was concerned about these young people who would soon be marriagable. He worried a lot about Protestants they might marry and birth control which they would surely practice. There was much to be alarmed about nowadays. New morality, new theology, new rubrics—he didn't like any of it. But, Father Albert was, for the most part, satisfied. At the age of eighty-seven, he expected to end his life caring for the souls under his charge at St. Joseph's. With only thirty families in the parish, he was not overworked. He could plant his garden, raise his chickens and shepherd his flock, knowing that he was fulfilling the will of God.

Actually, Father Albert had never wanted to be assigned outside the monastery. He had liked teaching in the monastery school. It was an uncontrollable temper that had ended his teaching career. Often he had leveled physical blows at his students. He believed that boys should be disciplined and this was the proven method. Unfortunately, he had broken the nose of an unruly boy whose father was a wealthy and generous benefactor of the monastery and school. At the termination of that school year, Father Albert was sent to one of the monastery's rural parishes.

Adjustment was difficult. Father Albert was convinced that he really belonged in the monastery. He had grown to manhood in a city and had never associated with country people. Even though the monastery was located in the country, most of his students came from urban families who could afford a private education for their sons. Expelled from academic life, he searched in vain among these rural folk for traces of culture and refinement. They were like the lay Brothers back in the monastery. Good, sincere, hardworking people, but very simple. His master's degree in Latin and the fact that he had studied in Europe did not impress them. "Useless credentials for this sort of work," he told his confessor.

The confessor suggested that he should make an effort to identify with the farm people. So he learned to plant a garden, procured some chickens and resigned himself to a life of exile.

*

The bishop's letter arrived on Ash Wednesday. St. Joseph's was being closed after Mass on the Fourth Sunday of Lent. His parish would be absorbed by two nearby parishes. The abbot's letter arrived the next day. It was to the point.

Dear Father Albert

His Excellency, the Bishop, has informed you of the decision regarding St. Joseph's. I must now ask you, under obedience, to return to the monastery. This may displease you, but it is necessary because of your age.

Please dispose of your chickens. Find someone to
help you pack. (You may bring the television set.) Two
of the Brothers will come with the truck to bring you
back to the monastery after your last Mass on Laetare
Sunday.
  Come home. Your old chums are anxious for a
card game.

Laetare Sunday! Hell! Old chums! Hell! His only classmates in
captivity at the monastery were Father Virgil, whose arthritic
hands couldn't pick up a deck of cards, Father Stephen who was
blind and Father Ladislaus who was so senile he didn't know the
Queen of Hearts from the Queen of Heaven.
  Father Clement, another peer, had been allowed to retire
away from the monastery. They said it would have been a crime
to bring that man back after all those years away. Well, damn it,
wasn't it a crime in his case? He thought it was. The blame could
be placed on the new abbot. Although the abbot had been in
office twelve years, Father Albert refused to acknowledge his
permanency. This one brought about all the changes. "The new
stuff." He had some crazy notion about drawing the community together, abandoning remote apostolates, withdrawing from
parishes. When the pioneer monks had established the
monastery a hundred years ago, they hadn't been content just to
sit in it. They'd gone out to serve the faithful who were crying
for priests. Now the new abbot wanted all of his monks back at
the monastery to concentrate on the development of the
damned school where, it was rumored, atheism was taught
openly. Incredible, but Father Albert was disposed to believe it.
He would not recommend boys from his parish to enroll there.
No discipline was enforced, he'd observed, and obviously the
students lacked piety. They weren't even punished for missing
Sunday Mass.
  He might have remained in the neighborhood of St. Joseph's
if Emma had not died five months ago. Emma Kraus had
responded to Father Albert's advertisement for a housekeeper
shortly after his arrival at his second country parish. They had
grown old together, she always moving with him when he was

appointed to another parish. It was their joke that whenever a letter mailed from the Office of the Abbot arrived, she would ask, "Are we being transferred again?" When Emma died, he did a shameful thing. He almost despaired of life. Alone in the rectory that evening after her burial, he cried like a child. It took him weeks to recover from his loss. She was more to him than a mere servant. None of the diocesan clergy in the area and certainly none of the monks could ever compensate for the relationship he'd had with Emma. Many years before these young priests began fussing about celibacy, Father Albert had experienced genuine loneliness. He could sympathize with those priests who became alcoholic. Living on the prairie drove them to the bottle. The long, cruel winters and the isolation were enough to break any good priest. Thank God a woman like Emma had come along even though she had not been the proper canonical age to assume housekeeping duties for a priest. In the beginning this had evoked unfavorable comments from surrounding pastors and a few gossips in the parish always complained because Emma did not sit in the back of the car when he and she went to town on shopping days.

He and Emma had discussed the possibility of his removal from St. Joseph's. After the abbot's return to the monastery on the jubilee day, Father Albert reported the threat to Emma as she served his supper. "Emma, what would become of you if I should ever be hauled back to the monastery?"

"I'd probably have to go to a nursing home," she said. "I don't think I could live alone."

"Emma, you and I are both doomed to end our lives in institutions. This afternoon the abbot indicated to me that he's thinking about bringing me back to the monastery. I'll fight it, but I'm damned by my vow of obedience."

She began crying and retreated to the kitchen. Father Albert, unable to finish his meal, went to the garden and began weeding the beans. Why should it end this way? The abbot's parting words were, "Consider coming back to the monastery, Father. You have earned your retirement."

All right, he would retire from St. Joseph's, when the time came, but maybe he could work out an agreement with the abbot. Father Clem and his housekeeper, Sylvia, shared a low-rent apartment until his corpse was brought back to the monastery cemetery.

The opportunity never arose. Emma died. The good Lord had given them forty-five years, but nevertheless, he felt cheated when she died.

*

Upon his arrival at the monastery, Father Albert suggested that the abbot could have moved him to another parish as an assistant. Although an octogenarian, he was still useful. "Or are you considering closing the three remaining parishes we have, Father Abbot?"

"Now, Father," the abbot replied, "there is an attitude in the community that monks should no longer be in parochial work. I'll do whatever is best for the community."

Yes, thought Father Albert, and to hell with individuals. He said, "I'm mentally alert, Father Abbot, and you know I'm capable of hard work. There was the garden and the poultry and . . . ."

"Father, I realize this. But, pastorally speaking, why should you even want to remain in a parish when you find the changes in the Church so difficult to accept?"

Making friends with mammon, that was how Father Albert regarded the implementation of Vatican II decrees. He had submitted to the bishop's ultimatum to begin offering Mass in the vernacular, facing the congregation, but he did not consider it a disgrace that St. Joseph's was the last parish in the diocese to introduce these changes.

"Father Abbot, the point is that I did go along with the bishop. I don't like the new liturgy, but I'm obedient."

"Good, very good. Now make the same application to your situation here. You will observe many changes in monastic life, but please try to conform to these new customs in obedience to me."

Brother Richard showed Father Albert to the infirmary, explaining that all the retired monks lived there because the rooms had private baths, not because all the occupants were infirm. His room was next to Father Ladislaus's. Discovering the newcomer, Father Ladislaus introduced himself and asked the identity of Father Albert. In the early days of their monastic life, they had been friends. Later they were both on the school faculty and in the summer of 1946 Father Albert had invited Father Ladislaus to preach a mission at his parish. Last year at the community retreat, Father Ladislaus had appeared to be somewhat forgetful, but that was understandable. Retirement, especially at the monastery, atrophied one's brain. Now poor old Ladislaus spoke like a babbling idiot.

He told Father Albert, "You'll like it here. Meals are substantial. Clean sheets twice a week. Liquor permitted in the room. But you know. Living in a boardinghouse is not like home." Returning to his own room, Father Ladislaus said, "We really should try to leave on the fifteenth."

"What do you mean by that?" Father Albert asked, but Father Ladislaus didn't reply. If the place becomes too unbearable, Father Albert mused, I might just run away with Laddie. It probably won't matter where.

He looked around the infirmary, trying to locate the displaced persons, his fellow castaways, but no one was in sight. It distressed him to read the place on the door two rooms from his. FATHER EDMUND. Edmund was not old enough to be senile and he had appeared in good physical health the last time Father Albert had seen him. No doubt Edmund was locked up because he'd gone crazy. Father Albert recalled Edmund's recent magazine article advocating the ordination of women.

Father Albert had been faithful about returning to the monastery for the yearly retreat, and in recent years he had come back more than once to vote on issues affecting the monastery. True enough, most of his votes had been negative, but the community could not accuse him of not having participated. He had not completely ignored the community all these years. Nevertheless, he did feel like a stranger. Even the appearance of the place had changed from when he first knew it. The wing of the monastery which had housed him at the start of his monastic life had been razed by fire in 1950. In its place stood an ugly hunk of modern architecture. The old austerity was gone too. Corridors were carpeted, the young monks in formation had their own rooms, equipped with stereo machines and other electronic gadgets. He remembered sweeping the wood floors of the novitiate with oiled sawdust from the carpenter shop. He lived in an open dormitory until ordination, and when his parents presented him with a radio as an ordination gift, the abbot refused to let him keep such a costly luxury. Life in the monastery had become too soft.

Some of the monks didn't even look like monks. Father Fidelis, ripe enough for the infirmary but still teaching English, affected the appearance of a fop. The old fool had grown gray mutton chops and wore a turtleneck sweater when he taught his classes. The monks in the school thought the holy habit was a detriment these days. They said modern boys could not relate to people dressed in medieval garb. At a chapter meeting four months ago, young-what's-his-name (the school registrar) boldly accused Father Albert of not living the monastic life when he had condemned some new monastic practice.

"By yourself, on that rundown farm, you're nothing but a malcontented old hermit. Don't tell us how to live our monastic life. Real monks, you should know, live in a monastery."

"May I ask, sir, are you a member of this community?" Father Albert had asked him.

"Of course I am. You know I'm Father Andrew."

"No, no I don't know that. I've always presumed that real monks wear the monastic habit." Father Albert had wanted to yank off the registrar's necktie and hang him with it from the ceiling.

Father Albert was a monk, no matter what the rest of them might think. Furthermore, he was not ashamed to clothe himself in the monastic habit every day of his life. If he were the abbot, monks would look like monks and he'd shave their heads. All these longhairs. Half the community looked sissified, including Fidelis.

Although the abbot excused him from community prayer, Father Albert attended in order to confirm his suspicions of irregularities. After praying his Latin breviary for so many years, it seemed almost profane to speak the psalms in the vernacular. He delighted, though, in the cursing psalms particularly, and prayed them with vocal enthusiasm, much to the annoyance of the monks beside him in the choirstalls.

Though parched and exhausted
with waiting, I remember your statutes.
How long must your servant suffer?
When will you sentence my oppressors?

*

The abbot reneged on the garden. The chapter had voted to build a new gymnasium and the site chosen for it was the old garden plot. "Find me another patch," Father Albert demanded. The abbot said no land was available. The school had a twenty-year expansion plan and buildings were going to be constructed on every inch of their property.

"I'd like to get some pullets," Father Albert said.

The abbot laughed. "Father Albert, relax. Enjoy your retirement."

"Does no one do any work these days?"

"Running a school is work. Hard work."

"What about the Brothers? Don't they work anymore?"

"Most of the Brothers are involved in the school as teachers or counselors."

Father Albert wondered why the Brothers couldn't be as simple as they used to be. He resented the young Brothers. They called him *Al.*

*

One evening after community prayer, several months after his imprisonment in the monastery, Father Albert remained in the church to meditate. He was curious when a small group of laity and monks entered the sanctuary. They carried folding chairs and arranged them around the altar—the picnic table which had replaced the magnificent old high altar. One of the women held a Bible from which she was asked to read. Father

Justin, a likable enough young fellow, but espousing some unorthodox opinions, appeared to be in charge. He said, "Sister Claudine will now read from the *Acts of the Apostles.*"

"Sweet Jesus!" Father Albert exclaimed to himself. "That, O Lord, is one of your brides?"

Sitting at the back of the darkened nave of the church, Father Albert could not hear the nun. He did not even want to look at her. No veil, dangling earrings and a skirt much too far above her knobby knees.

Throughout the reading some of the listeners rocked back and forth on their chairs. He heard a certain amount of mumbling. Then without warning, one or the other of them would shout the Lord's name or shriek, "ALLELUIA!" Father Albert had witnessed enough. He was about to leave but sat back when Father Justin announced prayers for healing. Good grief! Father Albert was stunned. The Holy Rollers had infiltrated the monastery.

He moved closer to the sanctuary. The freaks couldn't see him anyway. Their eyes were closed. Father Justin was speaking. "Brothers and sisters, let's pray for Father Albert. Pray for his change of heart. He's hurting so much. Lord deliver him from his misery. Father Almighty, send your Spirit to inflame Albert's heart with love. Jesus heal him, deliver him."

Joining hands and swaying from side to side, they sang over and over, "Heal him Jesus, heal him Jesus." He heard some of them chanting, "Albert! Albert!"

Such nonsense! Wasn't anyone going to come along and evict these unruly people from the church? Where was the porter? Where was the abbot? Such awful nonsense! He could no longer tolerate it. Bolting from the pew, he ran up the aisle. Shaking his fist at them, he tried shouting them down, but the words of condemnation would not come out of his mouth. All he could utter was, "AGAWA, AGAWA, AGAWA!"

The prayers froze. Then turned, startled to see him standing there. Father Justin cried, "He's speaking in tongues! Praise the Lord!"

They rushed to him. Surrounding him, all of them jabbering, they savagely grabbed at his body. He was knocked to his knees. Two of the monks, standing on the front of his scapular, had their hands on his head and were whispering into both of his ears, "Jesus, Jesus." One of the women was clasping his hand. They became even more excited when the tears began running down his face. He wept because of the pain. Sister Claudine was beating on his bald head and her ring was tearing away his skull. "PRAISE THE LORD!" she shouted hysterically. All the while Father Albert muttered, "AGAWA, AGAWA, AGAWA." When he tried standing, they forced him to his knees again.

Finally, he was able to break away. He collapsed outside his room and Brother Richard helped him into bed, cautioning him not to become so worked up the next time he attended a charismatic prayer meeting.

"A...ga...wa," responded Father Albert, feebly, and then fell asleep.

An hour before sunrise, he suffered another stroke. This one more massive. And fatal.

Mark Vinz

North of North

Today with no surprise
the wind chill sinks to 50 below.
The mailman slouches up the walk,
head down, the way we all learn how
to walk on this far edge.
You write to say how cold it must be here,
and thank whatever gods you have
this weather's north of you, far north.

But we say it too—
it's always colder somewhere else.
We praise our plows and furnaces,
fall back again on what we know:
there are no last words,
and what we speak of
is neither storm nor chill,
but what would happen if all letters stopped—
that other winter, directionless,
colder than ice, deeper than snow.

Country Roads

Leaving the freeway late at night,
stripped of all familiar landmarks
I know again I'd drive forever out there
under stars, utterly lost, ever
looping back upon myself.
Even in the broadest daylight,
disappearing into fields and dust clouds,
they still bewilder me.

How my country cousin laughed
at my confusion—he who knew
each farm and fence post, who
understood the angles of sun and crops.
It was he who taught me how to drive
the old grain truck, jolting through
wheat stubble, down the little draws,
spewing gravel on signless roads.
I've been driving since I was six
and you're more than twice that now,
he reminded me. But we'll make
a farmer out of you yet.
All I cared about was turning
that big wheel, amazed it took us
anywhere. Set the throttle,
watch ahead, I'll do the rest,
he'd say, and off we went in circles.
Some things never change, my cousin
told me later, flicking a grasshopper from
his shirt, squinting at gathering clouds.
Even a city boy can know that.

What I really knew was hopeless, even then—
that I'd never be a farmer,
that I was lost, dependent, driving nowhere,
that I couldn't get enough.

At the Funeral of the Poets

for Alec Bond

It would be an old house, I think,
somewhere past the edge of town—
40 good acres of oak and pine,
a little river with a boat for fishing
and deer to come and drink in waning light.
There would have to be birds
so we could learn the names and sounds again,
perhaps a pasture with a horse or two,
rooms with books and photographs
and crocks of homemade beer.

When the screen door creaks you'll know
they're going to call us in to eat—
roasted corn and ribs, three kinds of bread
thick sliced and warm, and soup so rich
you'll wonder where you've never lived
to taste such soup as this—and then the wine,
and all night long to sit in front porch swings
or stroll around the yard
listening to each voice from shadows—
quick small breezes bearing
scents of flowers and far-off ripening fields,
and lights in upstairs rooms that burn into the dawn.

The Last Time

for Jim White

I can't stop thinking of the last time I saw you—
how you looked so tired and so severe,
how I just wanted to hug you
and say it's all right, to lie a little
just to make us laugh again.
And I'd tell you if I could
that the last time should be different—
heat lightning on a warm night
and us just sitting on a front porch swing
to watch the families coming home
from the drive-in movie.
And we'd talk for hours in soft voices
till the rain started coming down near dawn.
Then you'd go in to shut the windows
and fix us a snack
and I'd light the last cigarette,
the one we'd been saving.
And we'd think of everything we shouldn't do
all over again, and maybe then
I could get to that place
where the weeping finally starts.
No, I don't know what it means to die.
It must be quite beautiful, you say.

The Last Time, Again

for Tom McGrath

Your room, the nurse tells me,
is the one with the scanner in it—
that, and not to be afraid to wake you.
Most patients here sleep too much anyway.

You seem to know me at first,
when you ask for a beer and cigarette,
but then all light fades and you
shudder beneath blankets, clutching
at the tubes that grow from your arm.

What are you doing here? you say.
We'll miss the dance tonight.
And how about those fences that
need mending? Have to keep them out,
you know–all of them trying to get in.

What can I do? I keep asking,
beside the small red numbers forming
on the screen above your bed.
Old friend, we've finally reached the place
each road leads somewhere else.

I'll be gone for awhile, you say—
but you keep on watching as I
bend toward you, closer and closer,
farther and farther away.

Sleepless, Reading Machado

I.

Beneath the desklamp
these small songs,
a sea wind bearing
tiny yellow flowers,
a sleeper moaning
in another room.

II.

Consider for this moment
the joy of solitude,
the grief of empty rooms.

So little changes:
not the ship, or the storm,
or the eternal hunger of
the waves. Only the faces,
the fear of going down.

III.

And this:
new snow in the night
covering the fresh
spring grass. Bird
tracks wandering alone
in the moonlight.

Some call it sorrow,
some call it love.

IV.

Toward morning
the words grow darker
against the page.
Darker and longer
beside the clock radio
humming to itself on a table,
and the wind
just moving the curtains.

Someone whistles
beneath the window,
and footsteps walk away—
my own song returning
as the first light
gathers in the trees.

Ron Vossler

Her Week of the Jew

Once a year the Jew came to town. It was in the fall that we always saw him: after the farm trucks brought their loads of grain to the town's only elevator. The train left him on the depot platform, where he would stand, holding his cloth-covered suitcase, and blinking his watery eyes. Then, he would make his way along the gravel road he called "My Via Dolorosa" to the Plainsman Hotel, a small, stuccoed building at the north end of mainstreet, not far from Eva's home.

The man's name was Mr. Mackovsky. He was old. A gold tooth gleamed in his upper jaw: evidence of the Jew's greed, or so Eva's husband told her. People saw that tooth a lot, since Mackovsky, who was somewhat exuberant by nature, often threw his head back in raucous laughter.

With her children finally away at college, the loneliness of her home had overtaken Eva, and so she began a job as chambermaid at The Plainsman Hotel. Soon, her face had color again. Her complaints about her ailments and pains had ceased. And she began to meet people whose paths would never otherwise have crossed hers. Sometimes campaigning politicians took an over-night room. And there were railroad men from across the state, with their leather satchels and strange hours. But of all the people who stayed at the hotel, her favorite was Mr. Mackovsky. During her week of the Jew, for that was what her husband called Mackovsky's annual visit, she was particularly happy. Often, while doing dishes or ironing, she sang aloud her favorite song, "All Over the World," by Nat King Cole, and her husband would turn away in disgust and say, "Don't you ever get tired of that darkie's song?" Afterwards, feeling guilty about her cheerful self-indulgence, she sang her version of "Gott isch die Liebe," the somber German tune that required a pious church falsetto.

Every year Mackovsky returned. There in the autumn he would stand, holding in his hand the cloth suitcase, threadbare with the years, and, as he walked to the hotel, calling out his optimistic greetings. Sometimes he cajoled people to speak with him, saying, "I hang my heart on a hook and no one bites," or, if he stumbled on the rough gravel road, shouting at a passing car, "A snake and a Jew could break their backs crawling the ruts of this low-rent Eden." Eva never got much chance to speak with him at length. But in their chance encounters, in the hallway of the Plainsman, or on mainstreet, he heaped her with praise. Once in the grocery store, while she stood at the checkout line, he pushed through the door and told everyone how Eva's soul was the peg that held the edge of town to the prairie, and how without her the twelve hundred souls of New Odessa would spill into the wild cattle country to the north, "like a skewered water skin," he said.

Though he sometimes embarrassed her, she enjoyed the attention. Often she wished he was a permanent hotel guest, there every morning to compliment her lithe figure and quick mind, and tell her again how her voice suited a Maria Callas, the great opera singer. Through the years he began to represent for her everything that was fine and noble. And when she looked at her husband she sometimes could see only the dark aura of all their years together.

Usually there was a balance between her and her husband, a precarious one: she sensed how much she could say, confide. Unimaginative, he often saw only the words she put before him, like a prepared meal. He said little, preferring to listen to her, to sit in silence, or to just speak in a dialect, in proverbs and "spruchworts," especially when he felt she had spoken too long. "You're trying to catch the rain in a sieve," he would say, or "An empty barrel makes the most noise."

Once, when her oldest daughter telephoned to confide in her about a new boyfriend, Eva was swept away with happiness, and told everything she knew about Mackovsky: how the man returned to the Plainsman every day after his lunch in the Magpie Cafe, and showed his appreciation for his clean room by calling her his veritable handmaiden of the azure heavens, or his own savory delight of this spinning earth. She told how when he saw her sweeping or vacuuming he said she was his "seraphim of the dustpans," and she related with an exuberance that seemed to her borrowed from Mackovsky, how in the afternoon after his nap, a big finned Plymouth belonging to his main renter glided to the curb of the hotel and whisked Mackovsky away like a dignitary, as he visited one of his many farms.

It was the week after Mackovsky had made his visit. He was gone again, and she threw herself into her work at the Plainsman, remembering how he had bowed so regally to her in the hallway, and his words came back to her with such force that she again basked in his compliments, "My Queen Mother of New Odessa," he'd called her, and "My incandescent Czarina burning wild in the forests of my dotage." That week a bearded geologist from the state university came to stay at the Plainsman. She was feeling particularly lonely, and surprising even herself with her boldness, she asked him about his business. He told her that several miles outside New Odessa he was studying some terminal moraines, glacial deposits from the last ice age. And one rainy day while she emptied the ashtrays and vacuumed the armchairs in the lobby, the professor told her about the ancient glacier that had once covered the town and the entire countryside. Over a long time, he said, the climate gradually warmed, the glacier retreated, and the flood waters from melting ice changed the face of the land: carving deep drainage channels and depositing rolling hills.

What the professor said gripped her imagination; why, she couldn't understand. But at supper that evening she tried to tell her husband about the glacier. As she told of the geologist describing the ice age and the glacier, as she talked excitedly about the incredible changes the melting flood water had made on the land around New Odessa, he became very angry.

After supper he left the house. Through the window she watched him walk along the sidewalk, his jaw still rigid, his angry silence turning over and over in her thoughts. She looked across the street, this last one on the edge of town, to the rusting farm equipment, the gleaners and rakes and combines abandoned in the open, weeded lot there, and saw past the grain elevator at the far edge, to the rolling pastures beyond New Odessa; and felt she knew what it was like under the weight and tremendous pressure of that ancient glacier that had once covered the land.

Though Eva was on the nervous side—she knew that, everyone told her so—after that incident she was worse. That next Sunday after church on the parsonage lawn, she watched a toddler put a fistful of dirt in its mouth. Stella Grobel, the choir director, was standing beside her. Eva turned and started telling her about a similar incident from her own childhood: how she could still almost feel the pebbles at the root of her tongue. "You would remember something ugly like that," Stella had said, "You're different you know." Eva's reply had come almost without her being aware of it, had erupted from her, and was a direct attack on Stella's refusal to pay the stipend the church council had recommended to Eva for playing the organ each Sunday. "And it looks like I'm still eating dirt too," Eva had said.

Of course she knew what townspeople said about Mackovsky: that he had quite a "gusch" or mouth, that it must be smeared with goosegrease, as the old saying goes, since he talked so much. And she also knew that many people didn't like his manner, or the disruption his visit caused. Edna Manke, the dishevelled cook at the Magpie Cafe, whom Mackovsky called his holy omnipotent angel of the cookstove because he liked her home-cooked meals and especially her sugar cookies, would sniff and reply, "An ugly old thing like me, with this big nose, an angel, forget it." And just the past year Mackovsky had created a stir. One Saturday night he'd stopped a child heading to get a bag of popcorn from Hiller's popcorn stand, a madeover ice-house squeezed between the hardware store and the bar on mainstreet. With a crowd of shoppers and onlookers watching nervously, Mackovsky asked the barefoot child if he wasn't glad there was a sidewalk beneath his feet; and asked him if he knew that it had been built by Franklin Roosevelt's WPA, despite the fact that everyone in New Odessa thought the President a communist; and told the boy that if it wasn't for the sidewalk, why at that very moment, everyone there would be ankle-deep in mud, "and Chinamen would be licking the soles of our feet," he said.

Mackovsky had grown louder through the years. At the slightest reply to his greetings of "Hail Citizen," or "Speak pilgrim," he grabbed people by their sleeves, and made wild motions in the air with his hands as he spoke, like he was trying to talk color and movement into all he could not see. It was thought he had some eye disease, some ventured glaucoma; but even Christina, the widow who owned the Plainsman Hotel, and the only person allowed to administer the eyedrops he needed once a day—even she didn't know for sure what his trouble was. Eva's husband just thought that was how Jews were. Loud. Needing attention. Trying to stare into your soul.

Even with her job, Eva still had time on her hands, so she did more church and community work. Sometimes she helped neighbors. Once she offered to help Mrs. Fetzer down the block with her chicken butchering. The old woman looked at her suspiciously and asked why she was helping, and Eva had answered in dialect, almost as Mackovsky might have, she realized later, "Well, someone has to oil the spokes of the world." And one evening, when she had served lunch for the Women's Society of World Service meeting in the church basement and so wasn't required to help with the dishes, she lent a hand anyway. It was then several women began to argue about the correct way to wash dishes, left to right as Edna Manke maintained, since it was the way they were done in the Magpie Cafe, or right to left as Stella Grobel insisted. She had stayed out of the argument, and, instead of calling her husband, decided to walk home afterwards. She walked through the early June fragrances of flowering crab bushes and lilacs. And halfway home, an emptiness opened in her that seemed as high as the dome of the sky overhead. She couldn't explain the feeling to herself, and as she crossed the highway that cut through town, with the last daylight seeping away and the air a peculiar shade of blue, it seemed to her as though the glacier had returned, that mountain of blue ice. And when she got to her house, she could not even look at her husband. She was waiting, she knew, for Mackovsky to come again.

Several months later, the Jew made his annual visit. But he mistimed his trip. Or perhaps there was a late harvest, for the evening he arrived, Eva saw trucks—a long line of them, with their tarpaulins stretched over bulging grain boxes, and backed bumper to bumper from the elevator ramp. This time, Mackovsky didn't walk. For the first time in anyone's memory, the renter's big-finned Plymouth was parked at the depot, waiting. The renter helped Mackovsky limp to the car; the renter's son, a hulking adolescent, hastily tossed the suitcase in the trunk, while Mackovsky, as always, rasped out his praises, saying, "This young man is a veritable prairie Adonis, and gracious too."

The next day at supper, the first day of Mackovsky's visit, her husband, who usually sat silently during the meal, immediately started telling about Mackovsky. Right there in front of the hardware store where he worked, he'd seen the man waylay Mrs. Springer, an elderly lady on her way to the grocery store. Mackovsky had fingered the embroidery of the woman's shawl, a "tuechla" from Russia, his fingers trailing inches from her sagging bosom, and asked if she too remembered the beauteous Russian sky, "Es war so shay," he said, or their German colonies on the edge of the Black Sea, the bursting white blossoms of the acacias, or those fine Bessarabian wines. Oh surely she remembered that land across the ocean where their childhood was lost, and surely, Mackovsky said, kissing the palm of Mrs. Springer's hand until she flushed, surely she must awaken each morning as surprised as he, "a fragile husk ready to be blown off the face of the earth by the first strong wind of mortality."

"And half the town was watching your Jew," her husband said, an accusation in his tone, for he had heard people talk about the way Mackovsky spoke to his wife.

"And what does that mean," Eva said.

"It means he wants too much. It's the way of those people," he said finally.

The week passed. Mackovsky kept to his room in the hotel. He turned visitors away from his unopened door, ignored trays of food that Christina brought from the Magpie Cafe, and even refused a dozen sugar cookies that Edna Manke had baked for him. There were rumors going around town. Some said he was "verruckt," and spun their fingers at their temples. Others talked about the incident with Mrs. Springer, or how Mackovsky had managed to slip out a side door of the hotel one evening and been seen tossing fistfuls of money into the air and shouting, "Let the wind eat it." And, of course, some said the old man was dead. And Eva wondered about that too, for every time she walked by his room during the week, only a pall of silence greeted her. One evening, after her husband had fallen asleep in his chair, she decided to visit Mackovsky. But on the way to the hotel, as she passed by the open lot, she saw the shining eyes of an animal sliding through the long grass and weeds. Startled, she turned back and went inside thinking, "There are no secrets in New Odessa."

The next day Eva checked out some railroad men, and watched them walk along the gravel road to the depot with their leather satchels and their long-billed caps. Then she started cleaning their rooms, scrubbing their bathtubs and changing their sheets, feeling like she wanted to go see Mackovsky.

As she went about her work, she began to hear sounds, at first low and indistinct, coming from the direction of his room. Listening carefully and approaching his door, she heard Mackovsky speaking in the dialect of the Jews, the words not that different from the German she'd grown up with and still spoke. He was saying that the people of New Odessa were one of the lost tribes of Israel, fashioning from the dust of the American plains the Promised Land. And how all his people in town, "Meine Leuta," were saints and frozen martyrs roaming the catacombs of North Dakota in chains of ice, holy mercenaries of some new millennial ice age. And he was claiming that he was their seer and prophet, their crippled messiah, trying to deliver them from despair and the dark nights of their souls. But now, he said, his world was shrivelling like a piece of fruit, his ancient heart was laboring and tumbling in the caged sorrow of his chest, and he, Joachim Mackovsky, born in the Bessarabian village of Mayoyaroslavetz, was weary with the travails of life, and now realized he had failed, and was but skin wrapped about wind, an orphan from the green flesh of God, longing for the thick sleep of the dead.

She'd never heard such outpouring, such a rush of grief, not even during the evangelical revival week, when everyone in her church confessed their sins out loud. And listening to Mackovsky now it seemed he was giving voice to her own faded dreams.

Finally she couldn't bear it anymore, listening without his consent, and she retreated to the end of the hallway, to fold pillow cases and towels in the linen closet, but his voice seemed to follow her. In desperation she returned to the room she'd been cleaning and began to scrub down the bathroom walls until the backs of her arms ached and her nostrils burned from the cleaner. It was then she heard Mackovsky calling from his room for help with his eyedrops. "Help an old Jew mired in darkness," he said, and "Water this withered old plant."

At first she hesitated, afraid of being alone with him in his room, and remembering what Christina had said, leaving for a funeral that afternoon, "Tell him to wait for his eyedrops until I get back." For an instant she thought it better to return to the front desk and pretend she hadn't heard; but she found herself at his door, and she heard him call out, "Enter the outpost of the lost."

She found him in his armchair by the bed, his head thrown back, his mouth open, his breath coming in sighs. There was so much she wanted to say to him: how his words and phrases had always given her strength to live another week, another year in New Odessa. But just as she was about to speak, Mackovsky motioned with a finger towards the dresser where among the bottles of liniment and salves, Eva found the small vial with the dropper. Mackovsky was staring blindly at the ceiling as she steadied her hand on his forehead, and fearful she might crush the fragile globe of his skull with her weight, she quickly squeezed a single drop into each eye.

Then he took her hand to his chest and covering it with his own, he said, "My warm gold of this world." With his chest rising and falling as though some great weight was pressing on it, he started whispering how as a child, accompanying his parents in steerage on the ship Kaiser Wilhelm der Grosse out of Hamburg in 1884, he'd eaten moldy bread, scratched lice until the blood ran in gouts from his body, watched the high waves of the Atlantic beat against the ship, and seen—"Es kummt mir nicht aus dem Sinn," he said, —I can never forget it—the immigrants' dead children, Jews and Germans alike, buried at sea. And he had seen too, he said, the grief-stricken parents scooping a handful of Russian earth from a box carried on the ship for that purpose, and depositing this in the shroud, so their offspring would not be separated forever from the place of their birth, their homeland. And he told her about the visions and dreams he had of those children, lost beneath the turbulent waves, mating with whales and creating their own race there in the ocean, without their parents' love. Then, as he lapsed into sleep, he released her hand and gripped the arms of the chair as though he too were now sliding into the same watery grave.

Eva left him that way, returning to the lobby where she sat in one of the armchairs, waiting for Christina to return. Mackovsky would need his rest; in an hour or so he would be boarding the evening train. And she felt like she needed her rest too. There was a heaviness in her limbs as she stared out the lobby window: the shadows were lengthening across the lawn, the light of day was draining away. Later, when Christina returned, Eva left the hotel, crossing mainstreet on her way home, remembering how Mackovsky always shouted out "Back to my Via Dolorosa," whenever he was leaving town. She found herself taking the same path, this unpaved road where the gravel was pulverized into dust from the heavy grain trucks, this same path that led to the depot and the railroad tracks.

Jack Natterud, the hard drinking depot agent, was busy behind a barricade of boxes, sorting freight and tossing boxes around in his usual cranky manner. When he didn't look up or even notice her in the waiting area, she was relieved; at least she wouldn't have to explain her presence there. She couldn't explain it to herself except that it was Mackovsky's last day, last week, last year in New Odessa—but she didn't know if she could put it into words for anyone else. Waiting, she watched the rays of the dropping sun move over the polished bench she sat on, over the whorls of oak grain that seemed themselves like suns buried in the wood.

Then the renter's son brought the suitcase into the depot; and groping his way through the entrance and fending off the closing door, Mackovsky followed, saying to the young man as he left, "Bless your ripening eyeballs my Dakota Argus, bless you." As the bench beneath her shifted and trembled, and as Eva watched Mackovsky exchange a few last words with Natterud, she knew his train had arrived.

With his suitcase in hand, Mackovsky turned to leave. It was then he seemed to see her, and throwing his head back in laughter, and his hands into the air, he called her his apocalyptic spouse of the American steppes, his Moghul princess, his high plains siren who'd shipwrecked his soul, and a host of other phrases that fell from his dry lips like rain. So this is the end of it, she thought, as he put his arms around her and slid his lips across her cheek; she felt the same as when she'd put in the eyedrops, now almost afraid that if she held him tightly his ribs might buckle or he'd crumble into dust in front of her.

After she'd watched his frail figure board the train, his suitcase pushed in front of himself as though finding his way, Eva walked home through the autumn dusk. Her long shadow moved over the rutted gravel road ahead of her, and she could hear behind her the protesting metal of the railroad tracks beneath the heavy train, and the grain cars coupling and uncoupling, their clanking sounds losing themselves in the broad meadows and carved hills beyond New Odessa. Leaving the gravel path, his path she thought, and turning onto the street that led to her home, Eva started walking more quickly, as if being carried back on waters that had once been blue ice.

Larry Watson

Shoveling Snow

For God's sake, bend your knees
and keep your shovelsful small.
You don't want to be like those men
you read about every year who explode
their hearts with one wet burden.

Watch the old women, widows usually,
who push rather than lift,
and scrape away the snow five times
a day—what is time for if not
keeping the sidewalk clean?

But the body is not the real problem.
Once you have your rhythm you could do it
all day. It's the mind, faced
with the puzzling blank of all
that white, that needs special care.

Keep your thoughts along cleared paths.
If they stray into drifted fields
they may never find their way back
and could become lost in the five ways
we are like snow:

children are happy when we return;
we slant with the wind;
we are born to fall;
we live to conceal;
when earth rises through us we are gone.

Hot Soup

"The meaning of soup has been lost."
—Andre Gide

Last night my daughter and I were up late
quarreling the old forever quarrel,
disagreeing as we do on her life's denomination.
Yet today in my weariness and dejection
the delicious taste of soup can still find me,
soup I made for myself by boiling tap water.

My grandmother made soup by packing snow
in a kettle, melting it on the stove,
and throwing in last summer's vegetables,
herbs, and bones of meat no one remembered
eating, and soon it didn't taste like snow
but hot soup to keep you warm against snow.
This was easy with December's snow, pure
and loosely packed, but in March!—March
when there was still no open water down the hill
where the Sheyenne River stubbornly sat,
March, when she had to hack through the dirty
crusted top layer of snow and reached months down
to December where the best soup lay.

Yes, this is the same grandmother who went blind
and this is the same daughter, who, at three,
balanced on a chair and danced for a woman
who clapped time to a dance she couldn't see.
Or so I wish to remember. Memory,
this thin, thinning broth I live by.

The Population of North Dakota

In fact, North Dakota's population numbers
in the millions yet every census counts it
not much more than six hundred thousand.
How can this discrepancy be explained?

Perhaps the census taker couldn't see
the Indian population—that the Sioux, Mandan,
and Chippewa are still invisible, as they were
when whites first came and took what *they* saw
no one else claiming. It may be that because
North Dakotans are hard-working, when
the census taker came they were on the job,
and when he visited the fields to see if they
were there the dust from four years of drought
obscured both tractors and the men and women
riding them. Or the census taker might have
stood outside Fargo, looked north, looked south,
and assumed that should anyone be living
within sixty miles he'd be able to see them
(since nothing blocked his view), and seeing
nothing, marked down zero, neglecting
to look inside those seven groves of trees.

Maybe he took one look at the Badlands,
became badly frightened and simply turned back,
leaving uncounted all those millions living
up and down the banks of the Little Missouri.
He might have seen the endless miles of sagebrush
south of Dickinson, assumed he was in South Dakota
and quit for the day. Maybe he took the lazy way out,
climbed to the top floor of the capitol
and from there simply counted houses, forgetting
that North Dakotans will sometimes take brothers,
cousins, aunts, or uncles into their homes
until they can get back on their feet.

Perhaps he came during a tornado warning
when most people were in the southwest corners
of their basements and did not hear the bell.
Or finding someone home he may have met with denial—
"Oh no, we're just visiting, here from Minnesota."

Or perhaps he came in winter.

Ray Wheeler

The Thirteenth Spring

There was still three foot of snow that April. But spring doesn't mean anything up here. One day it's winter, the next it's summer.

"We're almost there," Grandma hollered. She gripped the steering wheel out at the sides like it was the horns on a runaway steer.

I didn't say anything. She was talking for her own benefit. She couldn't hear anyway, because there was a hole in the floor on my side of the pickup, and the wind coming through there made a noise only she could talk over.

"The spot ain't marked," she said.

I was too cold to talk. My nose ran. Where it dropped on my coat, it was ice.

"It's a goddamn crime it ain't marked." She got a Camel out of her coat, pulled her thumb over a big kitchen match and put it to the cigarette before the wind got it.

I looked out the window and tried to think up a place where there was real spring, but it was too cold every place I thought. About a hundred yards out, a herd of pronghorns stood in the snow. They could have been ice for all they moved. I wondered if they wondered about the cold.

Grandma looked over at the pronghorns. "They're just lucky I left Mert at home," she said. Mert was her Winchester lever action. Those pronghorns *were* lucky. At that range she could put a third eye in their heads.

"I s'pose you want a smoke?"

I nodded. I thought it would feel good to drop a match in my lap and set my pants on fire. I wouldn't even mind being dead if it was warm.

One night about a year ago when we couldn't get the television to pull in anything except snow, she taught me smoking.

"Ever try one of these?" She held up a Camel like it was something from a church.

"No ma'am," I lied. I had tried lots of times, but never could get the damn things to work.

"You don't know what you're missing." She lit her cigarette with one of those wooden matches she struck by making a big arc on the linoleum. She took a drag and let a whopper, crazy cloud out of her mouth and nose. It hung in the air like a white anvil.

She pinched some tobacco off her tongue and held the cigarette out to me. "Have a drag?"

I didn't want to seem too anxious, but I was across the room damn fast. I blew on her Camel, but no smoke came out of me.

"Kids ain't so smart," she said. "*Suck* on it, boy."

I did. And it's been two packs ever since. Other kids get warnings. Their heads spin and stomachs roll. Tip Hutzenbuhler even threw up his first drag. Happened so fast he didn't even get out of the way.

But with me it was just good. I was made for forty Camels a day.

That night, after Grandma fell asleep, I smoked the other ten cigarettes in her pack. I spit flecks of tobacco all over her living room, gave birth to all kinds of white critters by pursing my lips or putting on the pressure at my mouth or nose. Damn few times I've felt better than that evening.

She handed me a Camel now, but the wind snuffed out my match every time I got one started. I had the paper ones.

"You need to start buyin' your own," she said. I had a fresh pack of Camels in my coat, but was saving it for when I couldn't get one from her. She struck a match, got her hand around it like a shell and held it over to me, her eyes all the time on the road.

I blew the first drag down my shirt, hoping it would be warm. But it wasn't. All smoke and no fire.

"You have to go, don't you?"

"Really!" I tried to make it sound like the most urgent word I ever said. She stopped the truck so fast I had to brace myself against the dashboard to keep from going through the windshield. I tried to think if I had grabbed my pecker or something. How else could she know I had to go? She looked out her window, and I got out.

I got just behind my door, so I couldn't see her. But I couldn't get things going. I never could if I thought someone might be looking. Just because you can't see somebody doesn't mean they can't see you. You learn that if you go looking for deer. She probably wasn't looking, but I thought somebody out there might be. I rocked my butt a couple of times, but it didn't help.

Over past the other side of the truck maybe a half mile, cars were flying down the interstate. We couldn't drive over there. We drove on the old road because her truck wouldn't go fast enough for over there.

She revved the engine a couple of times to tell me to hurry. I got one quick burst out on my boot. Thirteen years of practice and that still happened half the time. Especially in the morning when you woke up with a boner. I banged on the truckbed with my fist so she'd know I was working and raised my aim.

She always said people over on the interstate never saw a damned thing except each other. We almost never saw anybody on the roads we drove except critters. The piss melted right through the snow to the blacktop and steamed. It made me wonder how it could be so hot—cold as I was.

When I got back in, she said, "You didn't get any on the truck?"

I shook my head and we spun out of there, fishtailing all the hell over the road. It wasn't too old, beat up, or shit on to spin the wheels. I don't know how old that truck was, but she never had washed it. There was goat shit in the bed from ten years back I'll bet, and there were holes in the fenders big enough for a jackrabbit to jump through. But she didn't want you to piss on it.

"It won't be long now. If they had a goddamn sign . . . ."

That second part was a sign for me. It reminded me of when we went looking for the Four Corners. It was winter that time, and she spread half a foot of straw on the floor of the pickup so our feet wouldn't freeze. We had two quarts of Schnapps under the seat.

Ever since I could remember she had talked about a single spot where Montana, Wyoming, North Dakota and South Dakota all touched. But not a damn soul out there in any of them knew exactly where. In fact, no one we ever talked to out there even said there was such a place. They looked at us like we were half damn crazy, but that was nothing new.

So we drove around for days until we ran out of food and ranchers who'd give us gas. We damn near froze. Then she just stopped and got out.

"Stand on the SPOT and you'll feel something gawdawful," she said. Sparks came out of her eyes.

I felt something gawdawful. Then, I thought it came from imagining the Four Corners. Now, I know it was the Schnapps.

When she stood on the SPOT, a rock big enough to be above the three foot of snow we walked a half mile off the road in, her teeth clacked like she had finally gotten too cold. She whimpered and breathed heavy. I thought maybe she was going to die right there.

"You won't know about this feeling till you get with a woman," she said.

When I got up on the rock, I didn't feel anything except cold and the need for a Camel.

While we were walking back to the truck, a snowy owl came gliding in at us. Except for the eyes, he could have been a slice of snow changing places in that field without making a sound. The eyes went so far inside me I thought he would rip something out of me with them. There wouldn't be any blood or pain. Just a scarlet heart sailing away in all that white.

"That damn critter ain't going to bother you," she said. "He came down to this country to get warm."

That was something to ponder, since her place was a long way north of where we were. Still, it wasn't warm down there either. But what do owls know?

She took the truck out of gear and let it coast over to the side of the road. She slumped over the wheel and gripped her head with her hands.

"You okay, Grandma?"

"I can't see the map."

"What map?" I loved the woman, but she was getting old. There wasn't any map.

"We'll ask in Steele," she said, popping the clutch.

We turned south on another road, and there was a town practically in front of us. She pulled up to a place called the Canoe Bar, a great big plastic canoe with an Indian in it over the door. There was a hole in his hands where there was supposed to be a paddle.

"There water around here?" I said.

She looked at me like I was a fool and got out without telling me what to do. So I followed.

The bartender was so short all you could see over the bar was his head like it was floating back there. He put a napkin down in front of Grandma.

"What'll it be today?"

"Two Wild Turkeys." She turned around to see if I was there. "Make that three and a Coke."

Way to the other end of the bar was another man. The light wasn't good down there, so you couldn't make him out very good. He was rocking back and forth, either drunk or crazy.

"Musta been a hell of a night," he said.

"When you're my age, *every* night's a hell of a night," Grandma said. She didn't look at him.

"I know what you're talkin' about, lady."

"You don't know shit, Olaf," the bartender said, "So you can leave the lady alone." He didn't look at the man either. He put three shots and the Coke in front of Grandma and took her money. When he turned around to the cash register, she slurped down some of my Coke and dumped one of the shots in it.

"He's no bother," she said. She handed me the Coke.

"What I don't know about old, ain't worth knowin'," Olaf said. "It's all I do."

"Drink cheap wine and have free use of the can is all you do," the bartender said. He put Grandma's change in a neat pile in front of her.

Grandma took up one of the shots and downed it. She wiped her mouth with the back of her hand and pushed the two empties toward the bartender. He gave her one of those strange looks that I'd seen her get so many times in bars. It was like he wanted to turn the lights up and look closer. Instead he picked up the empties and took them down to the sink.

While he was down there I bolted the top half of the Coke. That way you got the whiskey and had the rest of the Coke for a chaser. I knew in a few minutes I'd feel warm for the first time today.

"I don't reckon you'd know where I'd find the hunderth meridian?" Grandma said. She didn't seem to be asking anyone in particular.

"Hunder what?" the bartender said. He said it like he was pissed off. He came back over to Grandma.

"Hunderth mer-rid-i-an," she said.

The bartender scratched at his temple with a little stub that should have been a finger. It was only one knuckle's worth. When he saw that I was looking at it, he stuck it up to his nose. It made it look like he had a whole finger up there, which you couldn't do. Then he held it up and wiggled it at me. "Grain auger," he said. He laughed like hell and coughed at the same time. It sounded like he had gravel in his lungs.

"Goddamn birth defect," Olaf yelled.

"Mer-rid-i-an?" the bartender said, his face pursed up like he'd just tasted something rotten.

"Three more," Grandma said, gulping her last shot. I threw down the chaser so as to stay in stride. "And another Coke." She didn't see me, but she'd heard the ice. "Hunderth meridian."

"You're askin' the wrong person," Olaf said.

"Goddamn it, Olaf."

"Then if you know, tell her."

"I'll tell her I'm going to kick your ass out of this establishment." He put the shot glasses on the bar in front of Grandma,

filled them, and left the bottle. He set my Coke there, and I wondered where the hell it came from. Wild Turkey!

"Get him one, too," Grandma said, tipping her head Olaf's
way. The bartender looked down at Olaf. In the time it took him
to cop that look, Grandma dumped part of my Coke on the
floor and tossed a shot into it.

"You'll be sorry," the bartender said, heading down to Olaf.

"You'll be glad," Olaf said. "Because I know where the goddamn hundredth meridian is."

"Total bullshit," the bartender said. He came back over to
Grandma. He had some kind of wooden box or something he
scooched on the floor. He stood up on it and got himself right
up to Grandma's face. "He hasn't been sober once for twenty
years. He talks out his ass."

She didn't move. She looked straight into his eyes. I had the
strangest notion for a minute they were going to kiss.

They held that way so long I felt like I was intruding, so I
took my drink and headed down Olaf's way. I knew he was
watching me even though he didn't look at me.

When I got behind him, he said, "You have any idea what
they do when they catch a kid drinking in this town?"

I took a good swallow of my Coke and looked right at him.

"I asked you a question."

I took another drink.

"I saw her put whiskey in your glass."

I took out a Camel, but before I could find my matches, he
swung around and fired up his Bic.

"You ain't old enough to smoke either, are you?"

I looked him in the eyes, but he couldn't take me. He lit a cigarette and took a drink, and when he looked back, I was waiting for him.

"You just escape from the nutfarm, or you just hauling coal
for the Devil?"

I had him. I finished off my Coke and headed back to
Grandma.

"Start *this* early, boy, and it don't leave you any place to go,"
he said. He wanted to make peace.

Grandma was bent over a map with the bartender. She tapped on it with an empty shot glass. "What the hell good do these do? They don't put meridians on them."

"Nosir, they don't seem to," the bartender said. He followed a road or something with his stub.

I was feeling pretty good. I stood up close to them, but it was like I wasn't even there for all the attention they paid me. So I took a shot of her whiskey off the bar, threw it down, and put the glass back. They didn't notice it at all.

"There probably isn't much call for meridians," the bartender said. He took some eye glasses out of his pocket and put them on. But he was looking over them, so I couldn't figure out why he put them on in the first place. Maybe to look smart. I felt sort of dizzy.

"Meridians," Olaf laughed. "You're such a goddamn idiot."

The bartender looked up from the map. "Watch your mouth, Olaf, or I'll cut you off. Understand?"

I went back to the can. Maybe I staggered back there a little. Instead of saying "MEN" on the door, it said "OLE." Instead of a pisser inside, they had a piece of guttering wired to the wall that ran at an angle down to a drain in the floor. But by god it was clean in there. The shitter didn't even have a seat on it, but it was clean. It sparkled.

Next to Mom's house in the old days, this was the cleanest place in the world. But for some reason I peed on the floor over in the corner. I couldn't say why.

In Mom's house you could put your bacon and eggs right on the floor under the table where we put our feet, and eat them. You wouldn't get any dirt on them or you, it was that clean. Until I came home from school one afternoon and there was a man in a dark suit sitting at the kitchen table who was as clean as her house. Mom was awfully agitated. She was wild. She was hopping all over the cleanest kitchen in the world like someone just poked her in the butt with a branding iron.

"Now the thing that's so tragic about all this, Mrs. Jesen," the man said, "is that they're going to steal your mother's oil."

Mom let out a little cry, sort of grabbed herself by the throat, and sat down.

"*Steal* it?" She was a frail, soft lady in those days, lost in my Dad's big shadow.

"Oh absolutely! What with the technologies they have today, they can drill in any direction down there. The rig is straight up and down, but they're drilling at any angle they please."

Mom winced and looked down at the floor like maybe someone was drilling under us that very minute. "I better call my husband."

"But they don't have to resort to that, Mrs. Jesen. Usually. Usually they just pump the puddle dry at the place next door, and then the oil runs from your place over to their place."

Mom sweated above her eyebrows. She daubed at it with a Kleenex. "I better call my husband."

She started to get up again, but the man reached across the table and touched her arm. "Call your *mother*, Mrs. Jesen. Your *mother* is the one with the lease. It's your *mother's* land." He patted her arm.

"She never told us anything—"

"She probably didn't know, Mrs. Jesen. And the people who do know keep quiet. It's the way things work in the oilpatch. They just tiptoe around buying up leases for a song." He shoved his papers into his case and let out a big sigh. "They're going to drill on her neighbor's land, Mrs. Jesen. Soon. Set your clock on it."

"Come here, Lucas," Mom said. I went over to her, and she pulled me up close. She was shaking all over, and she was hot. She squeezed me, but it wasn't a good feeling, though I couldn't say why. I knocked a piece of sugar cookie off the table, but she didn't dive after it. She wasn't even interested!

The man slid away from us and was nearly out the door. "They're drilling *everywhere*, Mrs. Jesen. Think about it, and we'll be in touch."

"Wait, " she said. I never heard a sound so hopeless. It wouldn't have stopped anybody, but the man was gone anyway.

If I had known what was going to happen in the next couple of weeks then, I would have put my old man's .357 in my mouth and pulled the trigger. For damn sure.

Grandma lived so deep in the Badlands they used to say her mail was brought in by a rattlesnake. You could sit on her back porch and hear the grouse cackling in the draws. You wouldn't see them, but if you walked down there, they'd explode up out of the ground and surprise the hell out of you. It was the same kind of feeling people got when they drove around the butte and saw her house: what the hell is that thing doing out here?

We lived forty miles away in Dickinson where Dad was a clerk at the Hardware Hanks and a missionary to the Catholics, but when he found out about the oil, he went crazy. He couldn't think about anything else. He couldn't even sell hardware after a couple of weeks. I've never seen such a thing. He kinda sat around the house shaking and mumbling things about "God's bounty." When Hardware Hanks let him go, he didn't even seem to notice.

We went out to Grandma's place on a Sunday morning. He wanted to catch her by surprise, since we'd usually be in church until well after noon. It's the only time I can remember that I'd have rather been in a pew than at Grandma's.

"You want to go out on the porch," he said to me. We were all standing in Grandma's living room, and she hadn't asked them to sit down.

"You goin' to swear?" Grandma said. She grinned. She knew better.

"May and I have important business with you—"

"Any business you got here ain't goin' to take long enough for that boy to get to the porch."

"Mother," Mom said, "the Lord . . . ." She was so sad looking, so frail against her mother, who a couple of hours earlier had probably shooed her four horses into the corral and given them some hay.

"Don't talk your goddamn religion to me. I ain't even had any coffee yet."

Mom kinda ducked on the "goddamn." It was like someone threw something at her.

"You really don't have to talk that way," Dad said. He had a way of scolding that could make anybody feel awfully low except Grandma.

"I'll talk any way I damn well please," she said. "I'm goin' in town for a newspaper."

"Mother, the oil—" my Mom blurted out. Grandma stopped and waited for her to finish, but she froze up.

"It's none of your business," Grandma said.

"It *is* her business. If you don't let them drill on this land, your neighbors are going to walk away with your fortune," Dad said.

"And yours," Grandma said. She winked at me. "Let 'em walk."

"Your daughter—"

"Can have this place when I'm dead. But until then every goddamn rock stays where it is."

"It wouldn't hurt a rock—"

"You don't know what the hell you're talkin' about." She headed out the front door.

Dad started after her. "When the Lord gives you this kind of bounty, you don't dare say no."

Grandma turned around and tipped her hat. "That's my living room you're shittin' in," she said. She hurried out to her pickup. Through a tear in the curtains, I watched her circle it a couple of times. Then she stopped, opened the door and came out with her rifle. When she fired the first round, Mom let out a terrible cry that got down so deep in me I almost cried. And if I hadn't seen that Grandma was shooting up in the air, I'd have thought Mom was shot.

"She's insane," Dad said without looking at Mom. Judging by the look in his eyes, he branded the wrong person.

Grandma dug out of there, throwing scoria all over Dad's Plymouth.

When I looked at the smashed and burned shell of that Plymouth two weeks later, I wondered if Mom saw what was going to happen and let out that same kind of cry before they crashed.

Two things bothered me powerfully. What the sound of those two things coming together must have been like. And what had been the *particular* thing that took Mom. A piece of glass, a splinter of steel, or the fire that came out of the Plymouth and burned everything.

"It don't matter," Grandma said. She picked at the one piece of blue paint that hadn't been burned off that car. "They're just dead. They were dead real fast. And not another thing in the world matters where they're concerned. Just dead."

She was calling "Lucas" and I was saying "what." Then there was the floor, clean but cold. Except I slid my hand forward into where I had puked. It was starting to come back. I was in a shitter someplace.

"You okay in there, Lucas?"

"I'll be out," I said. I got to my feet but it was shaky. I slid a paper towel under the puke and dumped it in the trash can.

"I was beginnin' to think you had croaked on me," she said when I went out there. "You look poorly."

"I'm okay." The windows up front were dark. And there were lots more people in the bar than there had been earlier.

When we got up even with Olaf, he reached out and grabbed Grandma's shoulder.

'The hundredth meridian, Madam," he said, pointing down to her feet with his other hand, "is right there. You just stepped on it!" He let out a little giggle.

Grandma pulled her foot back like there was a snake under it.

"You're outa your goddamn mind," she said. But she had the biggest grin on her face I'd ever seen, and she kept her foot back like the snake was going to strike.

"No ma'am, I ain't. I been sittin' on the line for thirty years. I know it."

She looked down, and her face seemed to warm up like she was really seeing an actual line down there. "If it is, partner, then it's the actual start of the West! Right here!"

"Sweet as bagbalm on a dry tit," Olaf said. He smiled so brightly you hardly noticed all his missing teeth. I don't know why, but I wanted to hug him.

On the drive back home I slept until we hit the scoria on West River Road. I opened my eyes just as the sun popped above the horizon, showering two cock pheasants near the side of the road ahead of us.

"You have a good one?" Grandma said.

"We been driving all night?"

"I have. You been sleeping."

"I got a headache."

"I wonder why."

We wound through the Badlands spewing the scoria dust out onto the snow along the road. Maybe some kid from town would come along this road and ask its mom why the snow was red.

We passed Dutchman's Chimney, and a mule deer leaped in front of the truck. Grandma hit the brakes and swore at him. He put out an extra burst and the left fender brushed him on the rump. He sprawled down into the scoria, but was back up in a second, racing into the sage.

"I don't know why they have to do that," she said.

When we got to the ranch, Grandma got out very slowly. I guess I had never noticed before how old she had gotten. Maybe it was just the way she looked without a proper night's sleep. I wanted to offer to carry her into the house, but with someone like her a silly stunt like that was out of the question.

When we got on the porch, she pushed open the door and grabbed Mert.

"They're probably not up over there yet," she said. "I wouldn't want anyone to think we'd given up." She pointed it toward Herbeck's Number 47, a hellaciously big pumping rig a couple of hundred yards up the rise on her neighbor's spread.

She fired a round, and it pinged off of one of the big metal surfaces. "Maybe if I didn't have to look at the sonofabitch every morning of my life." She shucked another shell into the chamber and fired again. The counterweights hit bottom and then rose again just as they had before, thank you.

It didn't take much to imagine it was a dinosaur or some such thing lumbering over the rise about to come down on her house.

"Could I try one?" I said. I hadn't asked for a long time, because the answer was always the same: "When you're a little older."

She lowered the rifle and studied me for a minute. She seemed to measure me against something, then she handed me the rifle and smiled.

"Blow the goddamn thing to smithereens," she said quietly. I sighted on it, took a deep breath, and gently squeezed the trigger.

When I lowered the gun to see what damage I'd done, the monster let out a hell-piercing squeal. Its paunches drooped near the gravel pit below it, and a little steam geyser spurted out of its side.

"You wounded him!" Grandma screamed. "Goddamn! Bless you, boy!"

She grabbed the rifle and sent three quick rounds up there to finish him off. The report of the third one was still knocking around the buttes when that thing went up in a fireball straight from the heart of hell. Even this far away, the heat drove us to cover.

Larry Woiwode

Beyond the Bedroom Wall

At the age of nine I wasn't afraid of the dark. When I ran down
a deserted street at night, I knew the chilling pursuer I felt at
my back was put there by my own act of running. and would
disappear—like any creature of the imagination when put to a
test—the second I slowed to a walk. The gray hands that reached
for me as I lay in bed were of my own creation, too, and once I
had proved my power to summon them up, for the sake of a
safe, enjoyable scare, I could destroy them.

When the change came, it seemed to come in a moment, but
I believe I was being prepared for it. I believe it began one
morning when my father read a letter at the breakfast table. The
letter was from his father, a prosperous contractor in Illinois; a
new school district was being formed in the town he lived in,
and they were looking for a high-school principal. For the large
and muscular, leathery-faced man my father was—strong-mind-
ed about his beliefs, uncompromising in carrying out school
policies—he was surprisingly unaggressive when it came to family matters. He seemed to dread the possibility of making the
wrong decision. He turned to my mother.

Wasn't he satisfied with the job he had, she wanted to know.
Of course, but there wasn't much chance of getting ahead in
North Dakota. Wasn't he the superintendent of a high school
now? Yes, that was true, he said, speaking as calmly and as reasonably as she did. And didn't he make enough to keep them
happy? More than enough. Then would it be wise to give up the
job he had, and sell the house, and move to Illinois, where it was

so hot and so humid, when a job hadn't actually been promised to him yet? Didn't she like Illinois? Not especially. Well, they had only been there in the summer, and he imagined that was why. His father hadn't liked it at first, either, but now he called it God's country. Then why did he so often come back to North Dakota? Well, probably because North Dakota was his home state. And wasn't it theirs? Yes, but his father had done well for himself down there, and maybe he could, too. Wouldn't she like a nicer house? This was the house she had always wanted—how could there be a better one? Well, his only reason for considering the idea at all was that his father was getting old and wanted the family reunited. She knew that, didn't she? Yes, she said, and leaned to him and kissed him. He took both her hands in his. Wouldn't she like it if they were in a bigger town where he could make more money and she could have more friends? She bowed her head, as she did only when she was sad or very ashamed.

And so, in the early summer of that year, we moved from North Dakota to the small town in central Illinois where my grandfather lived. While my father was waiting to hear about the appointment, he bought and started remodeling a duplex that had originally been a gasoline station. He ripped up the twelve-inch baseboards and tore stucco off the inside walls, knocked down a small enclosure in one corner of the living room (what it was, no one knew), sawed a long rectangular hole in the kitchen floor and put up a partition in front of it, creating a new stairway to the basement, and converted the concrete island that had once held the gasoline pumps, a car's breadth from the front door, into a flower planter. Setting aside his usual calm and reserve, he went at the place with such a passion that I was inspired; I learned to use a hammer like a man and started to have at the old house, too.

The bedroom I was given had no window. It was a small upstairs room with a ceiling that took its sharp slant from the pitch of the roof. There wasn't any floor in the rest of the attic, so the room was surrounded by bare ceiling joists, and felt as isolated as I did in this place we had moved to. There was no daylight and no light fixture in the room, no smell but the smell of dust and old lumber (the previous owner had used it as a storeroom), no color, no company; the seasons outside were merely changes in temperature. When my father first showed me the room, he said he would add a dormer and fill it with daylight as soon as he finished remodeling the downstairs, but, for the time being, all he did was move a dresser into the room and set up a narrow cot against one wall.

Lying on the cot, I learned the secrets of the dark. A wooden catwalk with a banister ran from the door of the bedroom to the head of the stairs. If I got out of bed, feeling my way to the steps, and went down them, I entered a house deep in sleep. A low hallway (I could hear it!) led from the foot of the stairs in one direction, to the left, past the bathroom, and ended at the living room. If I snapped the wall switch, the whole living room was caught off guard—the windows blinked, rugs stretched out flat, and chair backs straightened. To my right, in the far wall of the living room, the door of my parents' bedroom guarded their sleep; to my left, an arch leading to the kitchen—a high, wide arch—yawned. Utensils on the stove and the glass knobs on the doors and drawers of the cabinets, picking up the light from the living room, were like half-opened, protesting eyes.

Back in bed, hearing the whole house creak and sigh in its heavy sleep, I also learned about the one element that stays awake: the air. Long after the house was asleep, and long after I should have been, the dark air was alive with excitement. Because there was never any light in the room, from the sun or the moon, the air was my gauge of time and events. A disturbance outside—a passing train, a car, the lashing of a tree—caused it to ripple. When the sun rose, the air became angry, agitated, and some nights, for a reason I could never understand, it thickened and pressed against me.

Before the state of Illinois officially certified my father as a teacher, all the administrative and even the teaching positions in the new school district were filled. He had to start working for my grandfather, as a carpenter. My father wasn't one to go back on a promise or leave a job unfinished, but his remodeling of the house slowed to a stop; gray rock lath rose to shoulder height, and above that the bare studs, black with dirt and age, stood exposed. My room remained without a window.

My mother did not like the house we were living in, and was troubled that my father had to give up teaching, the profession he loved, and become a common laborer. She was also in her last months of pregnancy. She became silent and secretive, and kept her eyes lowered. My father watched her from the time he came home from work until he went to bed. How was she feeling today? Fine. Was there anything he could do? No. Would she like to go out—to a movie or somewhere? No. When her answers turned from single words to shrugs, and when his smile and his time-honored burlesque of the schottische, with the broom as his partner, failed to cheer her up, he became silent, too.

One afternoon I stood near the top of a stepladder and nailed lath to the partition in the kitchen. My mother sat at the table, paying little attention to the noise I made, and embroidered on a dish towel. Once when I missed the nail completely, and the stud, too, sending a circular hole through the rock lath with the head of the hammer, I cursed. Still she didn't look up. When I had first started using foul language, she had washed my mouth out with soap. I had never heard my father swear, and now she was letting me get away with it. I felt manly and arrogant, and made even more noise.

But then I realized how much she must have changed, to ignore what she had once disapproved of, and I studied her from the top of the stepladder. Her face had lost all its beauty. It was dry and chapped, and her dark-brown hair, which usually hung loose, was pinned back behind her ears. At her temples, just above her eyebrows, I could see the bones of her skull. She had paused in her sewing, and was looking at her hand—first the palm, then the back.

"Mom? Are you okay?"

Without looking up, she said, "Yes," and quickly continued sewing, as if I'd caught her at something. "Don't worry about me," she said. "Do your job."

Her manner upset me. I came down from the stepladder, marked a piece of lath, and cut across it with the razor knife, shakily curving off in the wrong direction a couple of times. I snapped the lath across my knee, broke off the hinged endpiece, and started up the ladder, when an emotion spread from her and pressed on me like a hand. I stopped, my eyes on the grooves of one of the steps, and tried to figure out what she was feeling. Then I turned to look at her, and the grooves seemed to lift with my eyes, stretch through the air, and link us. She raised her face and I felt weak; I'd never been so close to her. At any other time she might have smiled, or told me, with a blush, to quit staring, but now she stared at me until I was the one who blushed, and so badly I had to start hammering again.

"Don't," she said.

"Don't what?"

I turned to her and she was running her fingertips over the embroidery.

"Don't work anymore."

"The hammering bothers you?"

"No. I don't want you to work."

"Why not?"

She wouldn't look at me. "Go and play."

"Who with?" I took a nail out of my mouth and pounded it in place. "Dad told me to do this wall."

"I don't want you to work with your hands! You're too young to work."

"No, I'm not!"

"Don't argue. Go outside."

With her head lowered, her voice didn't seem a part of her. I came down the ladder angrily, determined to make her look at me, and saw that the length and breadth of her cheeks were wet with tears.

I went out the back door and sat on the steps. It wasn't right of her to go against my father's word, and she never had. She was even going against her own! She wouldn't talk to you, and when she did she wouldn't look at you, and then she cried. If something was wrong and she didn't want me to know what it was, I wished she would simply leave me alone. Then I remembered the long, unguarded look she had held me with.

*

One January night I woke, for no apparent reason, and felt the air above my cot had thickened. It was denser than it was when the sun rose, and some sound was trying to make its way through the denseness. I listened so intently my eyes joined in the effort, searching the volume of dark air, and then I heard (coming from the ground floor? from somewhere above the roof?) a sound like the breathy creak of a pigeon's wings, rising and falling, reaching for me and then falling away again. I rolled over and my shoulder struck the wall.

Light switches clicked downstairs, there were footsteps, the telephone jingled as it was cranked, and I felt the heavy throb of my father's bass voice. After a number of throbs, punctuated by silences that seemed humming question marks in the dark air, the receiver slapped into its holder, my father's footsteps crossed the kitchen, and another switch clicked. A white rectangle, its top end bent up against the foot of the wall, gripped the floor; he had turned on the light in the hallway downstairs. He made several quick trips from the bathroom to their bedroom and back again. I went to the banister, looked down the stairwell, and saw his shadow cross the bottom steps.

"Dad?"

After a silence, a pause in the footsteps, his head appeared around the corner. "What are you doing up at this hour?"

"Nothing."

"You'd better go back to bed."

"Who were you talking to on the phone?"

"The doctor. Do you realize it's three o'clock?"

"Is somebody sick?"

He stared up at me, and finally said, "Go to bed. Please."

I did, but I couldn't sleep. The birdlike sounds rose up again, his footsteps crossed the house, in long strides this time, and the jingling of the telephone was harsh. I got out of bed and was nearly to the bottom of the stairs when I heard my father's voice: ". . . realize it's practically a half hour since I called? You can't be more than a block away, and . . . *What?* How in the world can a man read at a time like this? . . . Well, I don't give a damn about your—your *damn* family doctor's book! . . ."

The profanity, so wrong on my father's tongue, scared me. And his voice was usually under control; I had never heard it like this. I went to the kitchen doorway and saw that he was trembling, holding on to the wooden box of the wall telephone to steady himself. "Are you listening? You get over here this minute or I'll come and get you!"

He hooked the receiver into its metal cradle, leaned a shoulder against the wall, and whispered, "Oh, God! What next?" Then he gathered himself and drew his body erect, and when he turned his face to me it wasn't my father's face. It was so white it looked as if his day's growth of beard had caved it in, and his large eyes were glazed.

"I thought I told you to go to bed."

"Are you sick?"

"What are you *doing* down here?"

"I have to go to the bathroom."

He bowed his head, gripped the bridge of his nose, and let out a moan of someone deathly ill. "Go," he said.

"What's the matter?"

"Do as you're told."

I decided I would go to their bedroom before I went back upstairs, to find out from my mother what was wrong, but when I stepped out of the bathroom he stood blocking the hall.

"Hurry up," he said. "I'll turn out the light."

"I want to see Mom."

"Not now. Not tonight."

"Why not?"

"She's too sick."

"Let me *see* her!"

"Maybe tomorrow. Go now."

"She's sick?"

He nodded his head with such finality I wasn't able to ask anything else, or disobey—run past him to their bedroom—but as I climbed the stairs I was sure I had done something wrong. Because I didn't know what it was, and at the same time realized it was my *mother* who was ill, I started to tremble, and when I settled into bed and the rectangle on the wall vanished, darkness pressed on me as it never had before. It took my entire imagination, and closed eyes, to keep it away, and just as I heard strange voices—several of them, it seemed—I gave in to the dark.

I dreamed I was walking with my mother through a department store. The walls and ceiling were white, and the floor of white marble, with low display cases set at great distances from one another. My mother held my hand in a firm grip. She wanted to go upstairs, and I wanted to stay where we were, on the ground floor, and look in the display cases. I pulled away from her and ran to one. *Don't. Don't look!* she called after me, and her voice echoed through the empty store.

The case was filled with blue china figurines. There was a blue swan, similar to the one in our kitchen, with a hole in its back, so that it could be used as a flowerpot, blue angels, and small blue busts of children. My mother put her hand on my shoulder and said, *Come away.* I turned to say no and couldn't breathe. She stood far above me, taller than she had ever been, her face made of blue china and her eyes alive and staring at me as they had in the kitchen. She pulled her coat close around her throat, turned and walked away, and when I tried to run after her, my feet wouldn't move.

I woke to darkness, twisted in the blankets, my heart beating hard against the cot. I had to see my mother. I started to get out of bed and struck the wall. I was stupefied; the wall was on the other side of the cot. I tried again. I knew there was no wall there, and not all the logic in the world, or the wall itself, could convince me otherwise. Nothing as simple as getting reversed in bed occurred to me. I tried again and again, and finally fell back onto the cot, and my left arm extended into open space. If there was a wall where I was convinced there was none, I couldn't imagine what waited for me in that emptiness where the wall should be. I pulled my arm back and held it over my chest, afraid to move, afraid of the dark.

*

In the morning, without having to be told, I knew my mother was gone. My father, who had had no sleep, said she had been taken by ambulance to the hospital. Without being able to confide in him, or in anyone (once the sun has risen, the dark seems partly our imagination), I knew I would never see my mother again, and started preparing myself for her death.

Biographical Notes

Clark Blaise was born in Fargo and graduated from Denison University. His works include the collections of short fiction *A North American Education* (1973) and *Tribal Justice* (1974), the novel *Lunar Attractions* (1990), and *I Had a Father: A Post-Modern Autobiography* (1993). Head of the International Writing Program at the University of Iowa, he is represented here by a section from "Memories of Unhousement," in *Resident Alien* (1986).

Ron Block, born and raised in Gothenburg, Nebraska, holds graduate degrees in English and in Telecommunications/Film from Syracuse University. The author of *Dismal River: A Narrative Poem* (1990), he taught for eight years at North Dakota State University and currently is on the faculty at Marquette University.

William Borden, a graduate of Columbia University and the University of California, has taught at the University of North Dakota since 1962. He is the author of the novel *Superstoe,* several short stories, a poetry chapbook, and a number of plays that have been widely produced; an adaptation of his play *The Last Prostitute* was presented on television.

Peter Brandvold was raised in North Dakota, and holds a B.A. from the University of North Dakota and an M.F.A. from the University of Arizona. His has published poetry and fiction, and he is currently writing articles for *Backpacker, Grit,* and *Montana Magazine.* He teaches at Stone Child College in Montana.

Madelyn Camrud, born in Grand Forks and raised in rural Thompson, has degrees in visual arts and creative writing from the University of North Dakota. She is the author of *This House is Filled with Cracks* (1994), and is the Director of Audience Development at the North Dakota Museum of Art.

Barbara Crow was born in Christchurch, New Zealand, and graduated from Christchurch Teachers' College. Now a resident of Grand Forks, she has published poems in several journals and anthologies, and is the author of *Coming Up for Light and Air* (1995).

Christine Delea has studied at Marietta College and Marshall University, and is now completing a collection of poems as her dissertation at the University of North Dakota. She has published poems in numerous small press journals, and last year was a participant in the Ruth Lilly Poetry Convocation at Indiana University.

Tom Domek, from Jamestown, works for the United States Forest Service in Custer, South Dakota. A graduate of the creative writing program at the University of North Dakota, he has published poems in *The Gettysburg Review, Intro,* and *North Dakota Quarterly.* He is the author of a monograph on the sanctuary movement, and of a biography of Father Richard Sinner, *Striving for Justice* (1992).

David Dwyer, who studied classical languages at LeMoyne College and the University of Chicago, lives in Lemmon, South Dakota. He has published poems in *North Dakota Quarterly, Virginia Quarterly Review,* and *The Count Dracula Fan Club News Journal.* His books of poems are *Ariana Olisvos: Her Works and Days* (1976) and *Other Men and Other Women* (1988). He is the recipient of a grant from the Bush Foundation.

Heid Ellen Erdrich, raised in Wahpeton, graduated from Dartmouth College and the writing seminars at The Johns Hopkins University, where she also served as an instructor in English. She lives in St. Paul, and is working on a novel based in North Dakota.

Louise Erdrich was born in Little Falls, Minnesota. She is the author of two books of poems, *Jacklight* (1984) and *Baptism of Desire* (1989). Her novels include *Love Medicine* (1984), *The Beet Queen* (1986), *Tracks* (1988), and *Bingo Palace* (1994). At different times a beet weeder, waitress, and teacher, she is a graduate of Dartmouth College and The Johns Hopkins University. Her first novel received the Best First Fiction Award from the American Academy and Institute of Arts and Letters. In 1985, she was awarded a fellowship from the John Simon Guggenheim Memorial Foundation.

Jeff Falla grew up on the North Dakota prairie, and has degrees from the University of North Dakota, where he studied in the creative writing program. He has published poems in a number of journals, including *Cincinnati Poetry Review, Minnesota Review,* and *North Dakota Quarterly.* He is completing a doctorate at the University of Minnesota.

Roland Flint, from Park River, has degrees from the University of North Dakota, Marquette University, and the University of Minnesota. He is the author of *Resuming Green* (1983), *Stubborn* (1990), *Pigeon: Poems* (1991), and of translations from the Bulgarian poet Boris Xristov, *The Wings of the Messenger* (1991). The recipient of grants from the National Endowment for the Arts, he is on the faculty at Georgetown University.

William Gass, born in Fargo, is the author of *Omensetter's Luck* (1966) and *In the Heart of the Heart of the Country* (1968). Since 1969, he has taught philosophy at Washington University, and since 1979 he has been David May Distinguished University Professor in the Humanities. In 1986, he was awarded the National Book Critic's Circle Award for criticism, for *The Habitation of the Word.* He has received grants from the Rockefeller Foundation (1965) and the John Simon Guggenheim Memorial Foundation (1969).

G. Keith Gunderson attended Hettinger High School and Dickinson State University, and is the minister of a Lutheran church in Garden City, Nebraska. He has long had an interest in the literature of the Great Plains.

Elizabeth Hampsten divides her time between homes in Uruguay and North Dakota, where she teaches at the University of North Dakota. From 1981 to 1989 she edited the magazine *Plainswoman.* She is the author of *Read This Only to Yourself: Writings of Midwestern Women 1880-1910* (1982), *Settlers' Children: Growing Up on the Great Plains* (1991), and *Mother's Letters* (1993).

Jon Hassler, writer in residence at St. John's University, is the author of six novels, and of two other novels for young adults. Among his best known works are *Staggerford* (1977), *A Green Journey* (1985), *North of Hope* (1990), and *Dear James* (1993). A graduate of St. John's University, he completed a Master of Arts at the University of North Dakota, which awarded him an honorary doctorate in 1994.

Gordon Henry, Jr. completed his Ph.D. at the University of North Dakota, and is teaching in Spain this year. An enrolled member of the White Earth band of Ojibwa, he is a poet and fiction writer whose poetry has been represented in the chapbook *Outside White Earth* and in the anthology *Songs from This Earth on Turtle's Back.* He is represented here by two sections of his novel *The Light People* (1994).

Lois Phillips Hudson, from Jamestown, completed her studies at Cornell University, and has taught for many years at the University of Washington. *The Bones of Plenty* (1962) and *Reapers in the Dust* (1965) are important books about life on the Northern Plains. She has received an honorary degree from the University of North Dakota, and is currently at work on "a very long novel" covering the decade 1850-1860.

Jan Huesgen, born and raised in Devils Lake, received her Ph.D. in the writing program at the University of North Dakota. She has published her poems in *Grain, Sidewalks,* and *South Dakota Review.* Dacotah Territory Press published her chapbook, *Those Who Follow* (1992).

Dale Jacobson, a graduate of Moorhead State University and the University of North Dakota, has published several poetry collections, including *Dakota Incantations* (1973), *Poems for Goya's "Disparates"* (1980), *Shouting at Midnight* (1986), and *Blues for Tom McGrath* (1991). He is a senior lecturer at the University of North Dakota.

Jeff Jentz, from Wahpeton, completed his undergraduate and graduate degrees at the University of North Dakota and the University of Arkansas. He has published poems in *Dacotah Territory, New Voices, World Order,* and *Pemmican.* He teaches at the University of North Dakota.

Robert King has been a faculty member since 1968 at the University of North Dakota, where he teaches in the English Department and the Center for Teaching and Learning. He earned his doctorate at the University of Iowa, and has two chapbooks of poems, *Standing Around Outside* (1979) and *A Circle of Land* (1990). He directs the UND Writers' Conference.

Louis L'Amour (1908-1988). Born in Jamestown, he is noted as a writer of western romances. Among his earliest work, the poems in *Smoke from this Altar* (1939) display the same spirit of enchantment and adventure that characterizes his more than one hundred novels and short story collections. Self-educated, he worked as a longshoreman, lumberjack, miner, elephant handler, and boxer. He was awarded the Congressional Gold Medal in 1983, and the Presidential Medal of Freedom in 1984.

John Little, from Brandon, Mississippi, graduated from the University of Mississippi and the University of Arkansas. The author of *Whistling Dixie* (1979), a chapbook of fiction, he has taught since 1969 at the University of North Dakota, where he founded the UND Writers' Conference. Currently, he is writing outdoor articles for regional publication.

Stephen Shu-Ning Liu, born in China, completed a Ph.D. at the University of North Dakota. He teaches at the Community College of Southern Nevada, and has been honored as Nevada's poet laureate. His poems have appeared in the anthologies *The Pushcart Prize VII, New Worlds of Literature,* and *An Introduction to Poetry* .

Richard Lyons, Emeritus Professor from the English Department at North Dakota State University, where he taught for thirty-two years, lives along the Kennebec River in Maine. He is the author of several chapbooks, and of *Scanning the Land* (1980), a full-length book of his photographs and poems.

Debra Marquart, born in Bismarck and raised in Napoleon, has studied at Moorhead State University, and is now completing a Master of Arts in the writing program at Iowa State University. She has published fiction and is the author of a book of poems, *Everything's a Verb* (1995).

Lise McCloud comes from Wahpeton and received her education at the University of North Dakota and Mankato State University. Her fiction has appeared in *Four Directions, Tamaqua, North Dakota Quarterly,* and other journals. She works in community health education and chemical dependency programs with the United States Indian Health Service.

Jacquelyn McElroy is currently professor and chair of the Visual Arts Department at the University of North Dakota. Since 1982, she has exhibited work in more than three dozen invitational and solo shows, and two dozen juried national shows and regional shows. Her serigraph that provides the title for this collection is one in a series of delightful images she has made of the northern plains.

Thomas McGrath (1916-1990). Born near Sheldon, he graduated from the University of North Dakota and Louisiana State University, before he attended Oxford University as a Rhodes Scholar after his army service in World War II. For his writing, he received fellowships from the National Endowment for the Arts (1974, 1982), the Bush Foundation (1976, 1981), and the John Simon Guggenheim Memorial Foundation (1967). His works include *New and Selected Poems* (1964), *The Movie at the End of the World* (1972), and *Letter to an Imaginary Friend* (1984). He taught at North Dakota State University and Moorhead State University; in 1981, he was awarded an honorary degree by the University of North Dakota.

John McKenzie was raised in Grand Forks. He is a graduate of Macalester College and Syracuse University, where he held a university fellowship in creative writing. His fiction has appeared in several journals, including *Gopherwood Review,* and in the anthology of midwestern fiction, *Stiller's Pond* (1991).

Anna Meek is a graduate of Yale University and the writing seminars at The Johns Hopkins University. For the past two years, she has been the director of instrumental music at the Williston-Northampton School in Massachusetts, and is currently studying at the University of Michigan. She has published a chapbook of poems, *Familiar Places* (1991).

Jay Meek joined the faculty at the University of North Dakota in 1985. He has published five books of poems, including *Stations* (1989) and *Windows* (1994). He is co-editor for poetry of *The Pushcart Prize, XIII* (1989) and of *After the Storm: Poems on the Persian Gulf War* (1992). He has received grants from the National Endowment for the Arts, the Bush Foundation, and the John Simon Guggenheim Memorial Foundation.

Martha Meek is a member of the English Department at the University of North Dakota, where she regularly teaches courses in modern literature. She has published commentary on many contemporary writers in *American Literature, The Massachusetts Review, North Dakota Quarterly, Plainswoman, Prairie Schooner,* and elsewhere. A chapbook of her poems is forthcoming from Dacotah Territory Press.

John R. Milton taught at Jamestown College between 1957-1963, before teaching for much of his career at the University of South Dakota, until his death this year. He was the author of several collections of poems, including *The Loving Hawk,* and a number of studies on western writing and plains literature. for more than three decades, he has edited the *South Dakota Review.*

Harold Nelson, born in Edgeley and raised in Jud, graduated from Concordia College, and completed advanced degrees at the University of Chicago and the University of North Dakota. On the faculty of Minot State University, he has published poems and articles in numerous journals, including *Bloodroot, Dakota Arts Quarterly,* and *North Dakota Quarterly.*

Kathleen Norris works her family farm in Lemmon, South Dakota, and has often served as artist-in-residence in North Dakota. Her poems and essays regularly appear in *The Hungry Mind Review, The New Yorker,* and *North Dakota Quarterly.* She is the author of a book of poems, *The Middle of the World* (1981), and a book of essays, *Dakota: A Spiritual Geography* (1993). She has received grants from the Bush Foundation and the John Simon Guggenheim Memorial Foundation.

Antony Oldknow was born in England and lives in Portales, New Mexico, where he chairs the Department of Languages and Literature at Eastern New Mexico University. Between 1966-1976 he made his home in Fargo and Grand Forks, completing his Ph.D. at the University of North Dakota. He has published numerous poems and translations from French and Italian poetry, and is the author of two chapbooks in addition to a book of poems, *Consolation for Beggars* (1978).

Janet Rex lives in Grand Forks where she has most recently served as reference librarian at the Chester Fritz Library of the University of North Dakota. A graduate of Ripon College and the University of Wisconsin, she completed a poetry thesis in the writing program at UND.

CarolAnn Russell was born in Fargo, and raised on a farm near Kindred. She graduated from St. Cloud State University, and completed graduate degrees at the University of Montana and the University of Nebraska. A member of the faculty at Bemidji State University, she is the author of *The Red Envelope* (1985), *The Tao of Women* (1991), and *Silver Dollar* (1995).

David Solheim, born in Elgin and raised in central North Dakota, chairs the Division of Fine Arts & Humanities at Dickinson State University. He is a graduate of Gustavus Adolphus College, Stanford University, and the University of Denver. He has published two chapbooks and a full-length collection, *West River: 100 Poems.* In 1989, he was named the North Dakota Statehood Centennial Poet.

Naomi Stennes-Spidahl, born in Jos, Nigeria, is a graduate of the writing program at the University of North Dakota. She has taught at Fergus Falls Community College and now resides in St. Paul, where she is working on a novella. "Walking on Water" is her first published story.

William Stobb comes from Little Falls, Minnesota, and holds degrees from the University of North Dakota, where he finished a creative thesis in poetry. He has published poetry and fiction, and while living in Denver at the present time he will continue to advance a collection of poems, *Light Sketches.*

Donna Turner completed a graduate degree at the University of North Dakota, where she wrote a creative thesis in poetry. Her poems are now appearing in journals such as *Kansas Quarterly* and *The Minnesota Review,* and she has a manuscript, *Levitations and Other Uprisings,* ready for publication. She is a lecturer at the University of North Dakota.

Benet Tvedten was raised in Casselton, and graduated from St. John's University. He is the author of a novella, *All Manner of Monks* (1985) and *A Share in the Kingdom* (1989), a commentary on the Rule of St. Benedict. For twenty years, he edited *The Blue Cloud Quarterly,* which gained an international reputation for its poetry chapbooks by American Indians. He is a Benedictine monk at Blue Cloud Abbey.

Mark Vinz, born in Rugby, teaches at Moorhead State University, and has co-edited *Inheriting the Land* (1993), *Beyond Borders* (1992), and *Common Ground* (1988). A poet, he has written several chapbooks and full-length collections, including *Climbing the Stairs* (1983), *Mixed Blessings* (1988), *Late Night Calls* (1992), and, in collaboration with photographer Wayne Gudmundson, *Minnesota Gothic* (1992).

Ron Vossler was raised in Wishek and attended Arizona State University and the University of North Dakota, where he now teaches. He is the author of a collection of short stories, *Horse, I am Your Mother* (1988), and has completed a new manuscript of stories, *Reindeer Armies*. He is currently at work on a novella, *The Drowning of Indian Ponies*.

Larry Watson, from Rugby, received his undergraduate and graduate degrees from the University of North Dakota, and completed his Ph.D. at the University of Utah. He is the author of *In a Dark Time* (1980) and *Montana: 1948*, winner of the Milkweed Fiction Prize (1993). His stories and poems have appeared in *The Gettysburg Review* and *New England Review*, and a chapbook of his poems, *Leaving Dakota*, was released by Song Press. He teaches at the University of Wisconsin at Stevens Point.

Ray Wheeler is a graduate of Kansas State University and the University of North Dakota, where he completed his doctorate. His fiction has been published in *North Dakota Quarterly*, and he has had several plays produced. He teaches at Dickinson State University.

Larry Woiwode, born in Carrington, spent several childhood years in Sykeston, and currently lives in rural Mott. He is the author of *What I'm Going to Do, I Think* (1969), *Beyond the Bedroom Wall* (1975), *Poppa John* (1981), *Born Brothers* (1988), *The Neumiller Stories* (1989), *Indian Affairs* (1992), and *Silent Passengers* (1993). His first book, *What I'm Going to Do, I Think*, received the William Faulkner Award and an award from the American Library Association; *Beyond the Bedroom Wall* was nominated for both the National Book Award and the National Book Critic's Circle Award. In 1971, Larry Woiwode was granted a fellowship from the John Simon Guggenheim Memorial Foundation.

Acknowledgments

CLARK BLAISE: "Memories of Unhousement" from *Resident Alien*, published by Viking-Penguin Canada, 1986. Reprinted by permission.

RON BLOCK: "The Apocalypse of Duluth" first published as a broadside by *Aluminum Canoe*, 1990. This poem and "My Egypt" printed here by permission of the author.

WILLIAM BORDEN: "Joining the People Tribe" first published in *The Phoenix* 6, nos. 1 & 3 (1986). Reprinted by permission of the author.

PETER BRANDVOLD: "The Spurge War" first published in *North Dakota Quarterly*, 1991. Reprinted by permission of the author.

MADELYN CAMRUD: "Those Other Worlds," "Just After East," and "Funeral: Holmes Church," from *This House Is Filled with Cracks*, published by New Rivers Press, 1994, copyright © Madelyn Camrud, reprinted by permission.

BARBARA CROW: "In This Room" and "Flight" first appeared in *Clearing Space*. These poems and "Visitation" from *Coming up for Light and Air*, published by New Rivers Press, 1995, copyright © Barbara Crow, reprinted by permission.

CHRISTINE DELEA: "The Rug Men Come to Town" printed by permission of the author.

TOM DOMEK: "After Chief Joseph" first published in *New Voices 1984-1988* (The Academy of American Poets, 1989). "The Medicine Bow Mountains" first published in *North Dakota Quarterly*, Fall 1988. These poems and "Holding" printed here by permission of the author.

DAVID DWYER: "The Higher Arithmetic" first appeared in a broadcast sponsored by the Seattle Arts Council, 1987. "Love and Poetry at Ground Zero" first published in *Prairie Schooner*, 1987. This poem and "The Middle of Nowhere" later published in *Other Men and Other Women* (Sand Hills Press, 1988). Reprinted by permission of the author.

HEID ELLEN ERDRICH: "The Red River of the North" published in an earlier version by *TAMAQUA* 2, no. 2 (Winter-Spring 1991). This poem and "Translation" printed here by permission of the author.

LISE ERDRICH / MCCLOUD: The author wishes to express thanks and appreciation to *Sing Heavenly Muse!* in which "Peace Turtles" first appeared ("Earth" issue, 1991). Reprinted by permission of the author.

LOUISE ERDRICH: "A Love Medicine" and "Indian Boarding School: The Runaways" from *JACKLIGHT* by Louise Erdrich. Copyright © 1984 by Louise Erdrich. Reprinted by permission of Henry Holt and Co., Inc.

JEFF FALLA: "In the Ditch," "Limitations," "World Imagineless," and "Forming the Language" printed by permission of the author.

ROLAND FLINT: "First Poem" first published in *North Dakota Quarterly*, Winter 1991. "Austere" and "Strawberries like Raspberries" first published in *Southern Review*, January 1992. "Easy" first published in *The Plum Review*, Spring-Summer 1991. "Varna Snow" first published by Dial Press, 1983. Reprinted by permission of the author.

WILLIAM GASS: "Order of Insects" from *In the Heart of the Heart of the Country* published by Harper and Row, 1968. Copyright © William H. Gass. Reprinted by permission of International Creative Management, Inc.

G. KEITH GUNDERSON: "Letter: A Reply to 'Gatsby on the Plains'" first published in *North Dakota Quarterly*, Fall 1985. Reprinted by permission of the author.

ELIZABETH HAMPSTEN: "'Where Are You From?'" from *Mother's Letters*, University of Arizona Press, 1994. Reprinted by permission of the author and the University of Arizona Press.

JON HASSLER: "Anniversary" first published in *Redbook*, July 1978. Reprinted by permission of the author.

GORDON HENRY, JR.: "Arthur Boozhoo on the Nature of Magic" and "Oshawa's Uncle's Story." From *The Light People* by Gordon Henry, Jr. Copyright © 1994 by the University of Oklahoma Press. Reprinted by permission.

LOIS PHILLIPS HUDSON: "The Dispute over the Mountains" printed by permission of the author.

JAN HUESGEN: "On the Burden of Expectation: first published in *Nebraska English Journal*, Fall 1991. "Life on the Prairie: Those who Follow" first published in *North Dakota Quarterly*, Fall 1988. "Living with What Belongs to Us" first published in *South Dakota Review*, Autumn 1989; reprinted 1991. These poems and "Reflection of Me, My Sister" reprinted by permission of the author.

DALE JACOBSON: "Hitchhiker" and "The Alphabet Mongers" printed by permission of the author.

JEFF JENTZ: "Wiping the Eyes of a Horse" printed by permission of the author.

ROBERT KING: "Walking at Dusk" first published in *Kansas Quarterly*, Summer 1988. "Fourth of July" and "Erosion" reprinted by permission of Dacotah Territory Press and the author. "The Names of Central City, Colorado," "Antelopeville, Nebraska," and "When Everything Shall be Known" printed by permission of the author.

LOUIS L'AMOUR: "The Sea, Off Vanua Levu," from *SMOKE FROM THIS ALTAR*. Copyright © 1990 by Louis D. and Katherine E. L'Amour 1983 Trust. Used by permission of Bantam Books, a division of Bantam Doubleday Dell Publishing Group, Inc.

JOHN LITTLE: "Whopper John Fish Tales" printed by permission of the author.

STEPHEN SHU-NING LIU: "My Father's Martial Art" first published in *Antioch Review*, Summer 1981. "On Ch'ing Ming Festival" first published in *American Poetry Review*, Winter 1973. These poems and "Ravens at the Summer Palace" reprinted by permission of the author.

RICHARD LYONS: "The Letter" first published in *Enough to Be a Woman* (Scopcræft Press, 1994). Reprinted by permission of the author.

DEBRA MARQUART: "The Blizzard Rope," "Bronze These Shoes," and "My Father Tells This Story about His Brother Frank and the Wick (Every Time I Ask Him for Money," from *Everything's a Verb*, published by New Rivers Press, 1995, copyright © Debra Marquart, reprinted by permission.

THOMAS MCGRATH: "Invitations" from *Death Song*, published by Copper Canyon Press. Copyright © 1991 by Thomas McGrath. "Love in a Bus," "Against the False Magicians," "Something is Dying Here," and "Praises" from *Selected Poems 1938-1988*. Copyright © 1988 by Thomas McGrath. Reprinted with permission of Copper Canyon Press, P.O. Box 271, Port Townsend, WA 98368. "Poem" from *Movie at the End of the World*, published by Swallow Press. Copyright © 1972 by Thomas McGrath. Reprinted with permission of Sam Hamill, Literary Executor.

JOHN MCKENZIE: "In the Water, Made out of Water" printed by permission of the author.

ANNA MEEK: "Josephine Hopper" and "Heatwave on Boston Common, 1947" first published in *Familiar Places* (New Haven: Jonathan Edwards Press, 1991). Reprinted by permission of the author.

JAY MEEK: "Skylight," "Counting the Birds at Christmas," and "Badlands" printed by permission of the author.

JOHN R. MILTON: "Jamestown" first published in *The Loving Hawk* (North Dakota Institute for Regional Studies, 1962). Reprinted by permission of the author.

HAROLD NELSON: "Rapunzel at the Castle" printed by permission of the author.

KATHLEEN NORRIS: "Gatsby on the Plains: The Small-Town Death Wish," first published in *North Dakota Quarterly*, Autumn 1985. Reprinted by permission of the author.

ANTONY OLDKNOW: "Field" and "Extra Mailman" first published in *North Dakota Quarterly*, Fall 1988. "The Sheep" first published in *Cottonwood #42*. Reprinted by permission of the author.

JANET REX: "Detasseling" and "On the Locked Ward" first appeared in "Revelations," thesis, University of North Dakota, 1994. Reprinted by permission of the author.

CAROLANN RUSSELL: "Silver Dollar" first published in *Poetry Northwest*, 1988, and will be published in *Silver Dollar* (West End Press, 1995). Reprinted by permission of the author.

DAVID SOLHEIM: "Thirtieth Birthday" and "Medicine Hole" first published in *Inheritance* (Dacotah Territory Press, 1987). These poems, "Golden Anniversary" and "Horsemen" printed by permission of the author.

NAOMI STENNES-SPIDAHL: "Walking on Water" printed by permission of the author.

WILLIAM STOBB: "Night at the West Edge of Grand Forks, North Dakota," "With Kari's Family at Lake of the Woods," and "Speculations" printed by permission of the author.

DONNA TURNER: "Blizzard" first published in *Loonfeather* 14, no. 2 (Fall-Winter 1993). "Survivors" first published in *Zone* 3 9, no. 1 (Fall-Winter 1994). Reprinted by permission of the author.

BENET TVEDTEN: "The Healing of Father Albert" first published in *The Seattle Review* 2, no. 1 (Spring 1979). Reprinted by permission of the author.

MARK VINZ: "Country Roads" first published in *South Dakota Review* 28, no. 2 (1990); "Sleepless, Reading Machado" first published in *Thunderbird* 24, no. 1 (1976), reprinted in *Climbing the Stairs*, Spoon River Poetry Press © 1983 by Mark Vinz; "North of North" first published in *South Dakota Review* 21, no. 3 (1983), reprinted in *Mixed Blessings*, Spoon River Poetry Press © 1989 by Mark Vinz, and *Minnesota Gothic*, Milkweed Editions © 1992 by Mark Vinz; "The Last Time" first published in *Abraxas* 37 (1988), reprinted in *Mixed Blessings*, Spoon River Poetry Press © 1989 by Mark Vinz; "The Last Time (for Tom McGrath)" first published as a broadside commisioned by the Rourke Gallery, Moorhead, Minnesota, 1992; "At the Funeral of the Poets" first published in *Minnesota Monthly* 20, no. 9 (1986), reprinted in *Mixed Blessings*, Spoon River Poetry Press © 1989 by Mark Vinz. Reprinted by permission of the author.

RON VOSSLER: "Her Week of the Jew" first published in *Plainswoman* June-July 1987. Reprinted by permission of the author.

LARRY WATSON: "Shoveling Snow" first published in *The Seattle Review*, Summer 1989. "Hot Soup" first published in *Review La Booche*, 1990. "The Population of North Dakota" first published in *South Dakota Review*, Summer 1990. Reprinted by permission of the author.

RAY WHEELER: "The Thirteenth Spring" printed by permission of the author.

LARRY WOIWODE: "Beyond the Bedroom Wall" from *THE NEUMILLER STORIES* by Larry Woiwode. Copyright © 1989 by Larry Woiwode. Reprinted by permission of Farrar, Straus & Giroux, Inc.